The MAILBOX® SUPERBOOK™
GRADE 4

Your complete resource for an entire year of fourth-grade success!

Editors:

Becky S. Andrews, Thad H. McLaurin, Stephanie Willett-Smith

Contributing Editors:

Irving P. Crump, Peggy W. Hambright, Elizabeth H. Lindsay, Debra Liverman

Contributors:

Julia Alarie, Marcia Barton, Chris Christensen, Colleen Dabney, Ann Fisher, Dr. Linda Flynn,
Julie Granchelli, Beth Gress, Joy Kalfas, Beverly Langland, Simone Lepine, Elizabeth Loeser, Lauren Medve,
Cindy Mondello, Cathy Ogg, Bonnie Pettifor, Lori Sammartino, Mary Lou Schlosser, Marsha Schmus,
Judith Shutter, Irene Taylor, Meg Turner, Maureen Winkler

Art Coordinator:

Cathy Spangler Bruce

Artists:

Jennifer Tipton Bennett, Cathy Spangler Bruce, Bill Hobbs, Kim Richard, Rebecca Saunders, Barry Slate

Cover Artist:

Jim Counts

www.themailbox.com

The Education Center, Inc.
Greensboro, North Carolina

ABOUT THIS BOOK

Look through the pages of *The Mailbox® GRADE 4 SUPERBOOK™*, and discover a wealth of ideas and activities specifically designed for the fourth-grade teacher. We've included tips for starting the year, managing your classroom, maintaining parent communication, and motivating your students. In addition, you'll find activities for reinforcing the basic skills in all areas of the fourth-grade curriculum. We've also provided reference materials for every subject, literature lists, arts-and-crafts ideas, holiday and seasonal reproducibles, bulletin-board ideas and patterns, and month-by-month activities. *The Mailbox® GRADE 4 SUPERBOOK™* is your complete resource for an entire year of fourth-grade success!

Library of Congress Cataloging-in-Publication Data

The mailbox superbook : grade 4 : your complete resource for an
   entire year of fourth-grade success! / senior editor, Becky S. Andrews ;
   associate editors, Thad H. McLaurin, Stephanie Willett-Smith ;
   contributing editors, Irving P. Crump, Elizabeth H. Lindsay, Debra
   Liverman ; artists, Jennifer Bennett ... [et al.].
      p.   cm.
   ISBN 1-56234-200-2 (paper)
   1. Fourth grade (Education)—Curricula. 2. Education,
Elementary—Activity programs.   3. Teaching—Aids and devices.
4. Elementary school teaching. I. Andrews, Becky S. II. Mailbox.
LB1571 4th.M35 1997
372.24'2—dc21   97-44710
                                                           CIP

©1998 by THE EDUCATION CENTER, INC.
All rights reserved.
ISBN# 1-56234-200-2

Manufactured in the United States
10 9 8 7 6 5 4

TABLE OF CONTENTS

BACK TO SCHOOL

✓ A Getting-Ready Checklist

Preparing for a new school year can feel like trying to fit a size 9 foot into a size 6 shoe—too much to squeeze into too little time! Besides room preparation and teaching plans, you'll need to give some thought to the "hows" of setting up procedures for everything from communicating with parents to collecting student assignments. Make this task easier with the help of the reproducible checklist on page 12. Duplicate the list; then clip it to the top of your plan book. Once you've planned how to manage an item on the list, check it off and move on to the next one.

"Welcome Back!" Bags

Surprise your new students on the first day of school with a treat they'll see as a treasure! Purchase a supply of large zippered plastic bags. Place a colorful self-sticking label on each bag; then write a student's name on the label. Fill each bag with the following inexpensive items:

- ★ a new pencil
- ★ a bookmark
- ★ an eraser
- ★ a desktag or nameplate
- ★ a sticker
- ★ a teacher-made coupon book (see the idea that follows)
- ★ a small index card—decorated with a sticker—on which you've written a "Welcome to my class!" message
- ★ an initial cookie to match the first letter of the child's first name (see the recipe on page 7)

Make a few extra bags to have on hand for students who join your class later in the year. (Substitute a Hershey's Kiss® for the initial cookie.)

Coupons For Your Kids

Prepare your new students for "one of those days" with this no-cost back-to-school gift. Duplicate the patterns on page 13; then follow the directions at the bottom of the page to make a nifty coupon book for each new student. Place each child's book inside his "Welcome Back!" bag (see the idea above); or save the books and use them as holiday gifts or special incentives throughout the year.

Initial Cookies

For a letter-perfect treat that's just right for back-to-school munching, provide your new students with yummy initial cookies. Begin by gathering a set of small bulletin-board letters to use as templates for cutting out the cookies. Next prepare a basic sugar cookie recipe—or use the delicious one provided below. After rolling out the dough, make each child's cookie by using a sharp knife to cut around the bulletin-board letter that begins his first name. If desired, add colorful sugar sprinkles before baking. What a sweet way to add a personal touch to your back-to-school welcome!

Honey-Lemon Cookies

1/3 c. sugar	1 tsp. lemon extract
1/3 c. shortening	2 3/4 c. all-purpose flour
2/3 c. honey	1 tsp. baking soda
1 egg	1 tsp. salt

Preheat oven to 375°. Mix sugar, honey, shortening, egg, and lemon extract. Stir in remaining ingredients. Roll to 1/4-inch thickness. Cut into desired shapes. Place cookies about one inch apart on lightly greased cookie sheets. Bake until no indentation remains when touched, approximately 7–8 minutes. Cool. Makes about 16 four-inch letter cookies (will vary depending on the specific letters used and their size).

Plenty Of Praise

You know it's true—a little praise goes a long way in the classroom. But it's easy to get caught in the rut of repeating "Great!" and "Super!" over and over again until you're as tired of them as your students. Encourage your students creatively with the help of the reproducible list of praise phrases on page 14. Duplicate the list and tape it in your gradebook or another handy spot that's right at your fingertips. Then put on your sunglasses—the beaming smiles you'll get from your students might be a bit bright!

WOW!

Stupendous!

Hip, hip, hooray!

A Penny For Your Thoughts

Start the first day of school on a positive note with this "cents-ible" idea! Provide each student with a coin minted in the current year. Draw students' attention to the common year minted on each coin. Next have each child examine her coin carefully. Discuss the location of the mint marks, color variations, nicks, scratches, and other characteristics of the coins. Ask students, "Why do you think I gave each of you one of these pennies?" Help students arrive at the conclusion that—like the coins—they are each unique, equal, and valuable. Finally, have each student place her coin in her "Welcome Back!" bag (see the idea on page 6) as a token of good wishes for the new school year.

Teeny-Tiny Time Fillers

As a teacher, you know that procedures need to be taught, modeled, and retaught. With so many new things for students to learn each year, it pays to use every available minute. Fill those brief time slots when students are lining up, waiting for the dismissal bell, or making a transition between activities with this easy technique. On slips of paper, write questions about your classroom procedures (see the list of examples); then place the slips in a container. When you have a few extra minutes between activities, have a student select a slip from the container. Then have him describe or model the answer to the question on the slip.

What does our class do when there is a fire drill?

What should you do with items you have found in our classroom?

Describe how to check out a book from our class library.

What are three activities you can do during free time?

How is lunch count taken?

If you've been absent, how do you find out the assignments you've missed?

What happens if a student turns in an assignment late?

Where do you place your work that has already been graded?

Welcoming Windsocks

For a back-to-school art project that also helps you get to know your new students, here's an idea that's a breeze to do! Provide each student with a colorful 12" x 18" sheet of construction paper, a copy of the pattern on page 15, glue, scissors, colorful crepe-paper streamers, a stapler, a hole puncher, and a 16-inch length of yarn. Begin by discussing the qualities of a responsible student with your new class. After the discussion, have each child write a paragraph describing the qualities he has that can help him be responsible and make school a breeze this year. After editing his paragraph with the help of a partner, have the student copy it onto the pattern duplicated from page 15. Then have him follow these instructions to make a welcome-back-to-school windsock:

1. Cut out the pattern duplicated from page 15.
2. Glue the pattern in the center of the 12" x 18" construction paper; allow the glue to dry.
3. Roll and staple the construction paper into a cylinder shape.
4. Use a hole puncher to make two holes opposite each other about two inches below the top edge of the cylinder. Pull the yarn length through the holes and knot each end to make a hanger.
5. Glue six to eight crepe-paper streamers to the inside bottom of the cylinder.
6. When the glue has dried, hang the windsocks from your ceiling or a bulletin board. (Makes a great Open House display!)

A Classroom Guidebook

The first week is so hectic, how can you be sure your students will even remember all the important information you shared? Here's how! After the first couple of weeks, review with students the important information, routines, and procedures that keep your class running smoothly (such as rules for sharpening pencils and using the classroom computer, and locations of important places in your school). Have the class choose the 10–15 most important items from the list. Write each item at the top of a 12" x 18" sheet of white construction paper. Divide the class into pairs and give each pair one of the labeled papers to illustrate. When students have finished, have them share their work with the class; then bind all the pages together behind a decorated cover to make a class guidebook. Keep the guidebook handy so you can review information when necessary. Also use the guidebook when a new student arrives. Simply have a study buddy go over each page with the newcomer.

Sharpen your pencil first thing in the morning.

Don't forget!

Place found items in Miss Simon's lost-and-found box in the morning.

LOST & FOUND

Time Capsule With A Twist

Start the new year with a different twist on the tried-and-true time capsule. For each student, seal one end of a paper-towel tube with a rubber band and a cupcake liner as shown. Have each student label his tube with his name, and then decorate it with markers, colored paper, and other art materials. Next divide students into pairs. Provide each pair with about ten feet of yarn, a yardstick, tape, scissors, a centimeter ruler, two sheets of notebook paper, and four sheets of construction paper. Then have each pair of students complete the following tasks:

1 ▶ **On a sheet of construction paper, trace your hand, making sure your fingers are spread apart. Cut out the tracing. Now measure diagonally from the tip of your thumb to the tip of your pinkie. Record the number of centimeters on the handprint.**

2 ▶ **With your partner, cut a length of yarn that measures your exact height. Tape a slip of scrap paper that you've labeled with your height to your length of yarn.**

3 ▶ **Remove one of your shoes. Trace your footprint on a sheet of construction paper. Cut out the tracing. Now measure the length of your foot in centimeters. Record this measurement on your footprint.**

4 ▶ **Use the centimeter ruler to divide a sheet of notebook paper into six rectangles. Cut out the rectangles. On each, write one of these starters and finish it:**

—The best thing about me is…
—My favorite subject in school is…
—I'm happiest when…
—One thing that really bugs me is…
—One change I'll make this year is…
—This year I will…

5 ▶ **Fold the rectangles and slip them into your time capsule. Put the handprint, footprint, and yarn length into the capsule, too. Place another cupcake liner over the open end of the capsule; then secure it with a rubber band.**

Place the finished time capsules in a box and store away until the end of the year. At that time, return the tubes to their owners. Students will love measuring how much they've changed over the course of the year!

Back-To-School Bingo

Help students learn each other's names with this fun variation of an old favorite. Duplicate the bingo board on page 16 for each child. Have each student write his name in one space on his board; then let him walk around the room and ask each classmate to sign a blank space on his board. (If you have more spaces than class members, let students duplicate names *after* they've gotten the signature of each classmate.) After the grids have been completed, play a game of bingo. First cut apart a student list and put the names in a container. Next provide each child with a handful of markers (try Froot Loops® cereal for a tasty after-game treat). Select a slip and call out the child's name. Continue until a student covers five spaces in a row. Save the bingo boards to use later as a rainy-day recess game.

Getting To Know You

What kid isn't more than just a little bit curious about her new teacher? Give students a peek into your life while you learn about their reading comprehension, sentence development, and handwriting skills. Begin by reading over the questions on page 18; then write a brief autobiography that includes the answers to these questions. Duplicate a copy of the autobiography for each child or prepare a transparency of it. Or have a local copy facility enlarge the autobiography to poster size. Give each child a copy of page 18. Have students first read your autobiography, then complete the questions on their reproducibles. Now, how's that for an introduction?

A Cool School Tool

Discover your students' writing abilities early on with an activity that gets right to the point—pencil point, that is! Provide each student with a new sharpened pencil and the following directions:

- Examine your pencil carefully.
- On a sheet of paper, list as many words to describe your pencil as possible.
- Describe how your pencil feels right now—while it is new.
- Describe how your pencil might answer this question: "What do you hope to be able to write this year?"

After each student has written his thoughts, give him a cut-out copy of the pencil pattern on page 17. Direct each child to take the information he listed and use it to write a brief biography about his pencil on the pattern. Allow time for students to share their biographies; then display the cutouts on a bulletin board titled "A Cool School Tool!"

Wheel Of Fame

Help your students learn about their classmates with a bulletin board that doubles as a handy review tool. First draw and cut out a large circle from butcher paper. Divide the paper into eight sections as shown. At the edge of each section, write one of the following sentence starters:

- ☆ **A goal I hope to achieve is…**
- ☆ **When I get older, I hope to…**
- ☆ **I love to play…**
- ☆ **I like to read stories about…**
- ☆ **My best talent is…**
- ☆ **I know a lot about…**
- ☆ **Three words to describe me are…**
- ☆ **One of the things I like best about me is…**

After labeling the sections, laminate the circle. Post it on a bulletin board, along with a long strip of laminated paper labeled with two rows of boxes as shown. During the first week of school, have each student copy the sentence starters and finish them on a sheet of paper to turn in to you.

Each Monday choose one student's paper; then use a wipe-off marker to write his endings to the sentences on the large wheel. On Friday, ask students review questions relating to the topics covered during the week. If a student answers a question correctly, let him guess a letter in the name of the mystery student whose answers have been written on the wheel. As in the popular "Wheel Of Fortune" television show, fill in the space(s) in the letter board when a student guesses a letter correctly. If the letter giver can't identify the mystery student, ask another review question and continue the game. Award a small prize to the student who correctly identifies the mystery child. Then wipe the wheel and letter board clean so they will be ready for next week's game.

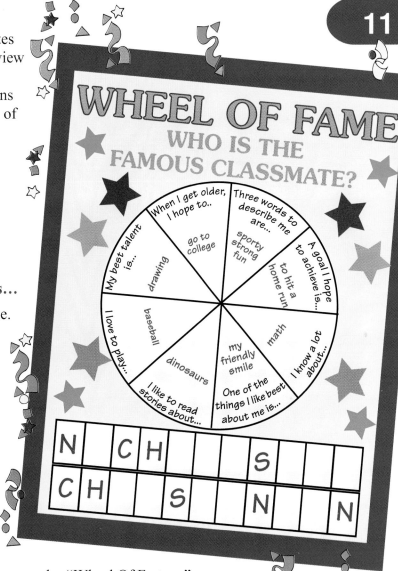

ABCDEFGHIJKLMNOPQRSTUVWXYZ

Letter Collages

As students are munching on their initial cookies (see the idea on page 7), continue the letter theme with this fun getting-to-know-you art activity. Prior to the start of school, cut a large oaktag cutout of the first letter in each student's name. On the first day, provide each child with her letter cutout, old magazines, glue, and scissors. Challenge the student to cut pictures and words that tell something about her from the magazines; then have her glue the cutouts atop her letter. Set aside time for each child to share her completed project with her new classmates.

PREPARATION STATION

It won't be long before your new students arrive—and that means it's time to establish your classroom procedures and policies. Make that task easier with the help of this handy checklist. Check each item after you have planned how you will manage it this year. If an item is not applicable to your class or teaching situation, write "NA" in the blank.

I have planned my procedures/policies for:

CLASSROOM MANAGEMENT:

__taking roll
__dealing with latecomers to class
__taking lunch count
__distributing and keeping up with textbooks
__attending to class first-aid needs
__managing telephone usage
__classroom rules and behavior
__lunchroom rules and behavior
__a discipline plan
__homework
__progress reports
__rewards and incentives
__student-work displays
__student-work folders
__free-time activities
__a computer schedule
__going to the restroom, pencil sharpener, water fountain, etc.
__learning centers
__our class library
__classroom helpers
__being ready for a substitute teacher
__recognizing birthdays

STUDENT ASSIGNMENTS:

__how students will head their papers
__assignments for absent students
__late assignments
__incomplete assignments
__returning work to students
__materials each student will need in his/her desk
__collecting homework
__collecting classwork
__my grading policy
__documenting student progress

WORKING WITH PARENTS:

__first-week communications
__communicating regularly with parents
__using parent volunteers
__sending work home
__sending tests home
__sending notes home
__setting up conferences
__conducting conferences
__following up conferences

Note To The Teacher: Use with "A Getting-Ready Checklist" on page 6.

COUPONS FOR A
_____ KID!

©1997 The Education Center, Inc.

Hot Dog—
No Homework!

Good for one free homework assignment.

Date: _____

Name: _____

Assignment: _____

©1997 The Education Center, Inc.

Bye-Bye, Blues!

Having a bad day? (Everyone does every now and then!) Ask your teacher for a special treat—then say, "Bye-Bye, Blues!"

Bye-Bye   **Adios!**   **So Long!**

©1997 The Education Center, Inc.

It's The "Write" Time...

...to get a brand-new pencil from your teacher!

©1997 The Education Center, Inc.

In Case You Forgot...

...attach this coupon to one assignment and turn it in one day late without penalty.

Name: _____

Date: _____

©1997 The Education Center, Inc.

You're Number 1!

In line, that is! Enjoy being the line leader today.

Name: _____

Date: _____

©1997 The Education Center, Inc.

Three Minutes With Me

Need to talk? Enjoy a three-minute uninterrupted chat with the teacher.

©1997 The Education Center, Inc.

Take Ten!

Take ten minutes of free time to enjoy your favorite classroom activity.

Activity: _____

Teacher approval: _____

©1997 The Education Center, Inc.

Note To The Teacher: Use with "Coupons For Your Kids" on page 6. Before duplicating, write your last name in the blank of the coupon book cover above. Duplicate a copy of this page for each of your new students. Cut apart the cover and seven coupons; then staple the coupons behind the cover to make a booklet.

Pocketful Of Praise

Store this list of encouraging words and phrases in your gradebook or another handy spot that's right at your fingertips. Add more praises in the blanks as you think of them.

Wow!	A+ job!	Sensational!	Hang in there!	You're the best!
Marvelous!	Hot stuff!	What a brain!	What neat work!	You made my day!
Awesome!	Fantastic!	You're great!	You're a winner!	Now you're flying!
Way to go!	Dynamite!	Remarkable!	Great discovery!	A grand slam!
Bingo!	Creative!	Magnificent!	I'm impressed!	Very creative!
Terrific!	How nice!	Bravo!	Cowabunga!	Nice going!
Super-duper!	It's brag time!	Spectacular!	Exactly right!	Superior work!
Clever!	Keep trying!	This is so nice!	Good thinking!	I'm proud of you!
Excellent!	Out of sight!	You're special!	What a treasure!	You're on target!
You did it!	A-OK!	Hurrah for you!	Beautiful work!	Congratulations!
Neat!	Zowie!	Keep it up!	Stupendous!	You tried so hard!
You care!	Well done!	How smart!	Hip, hip, hooray!	Looking good!
Ba-Da-Bing!	Outstanding!	Bingo-bango!	"Elephantastic!"	Incredible!
Olé!	Impressive!	Nicely done!	You figured it out!	A beautiful job!
Sharp!	Much better!	Good for you!	You are too cool!	Blue-ribbon work!

It's a pleasure to work with students who try!
I love the way you're thinking!
OOOOs and XXXXs *(hugs and kisses)*
You really outdid yourself today!
You put a lot of effort into this!
You've discovered the secret!
You made my heart do a happy hop!
You make it look so easy!
That's an excellent observation!
You've got the idea!
This is something to brag about!
You deserve a pat on the back!

Keep up the fantastic work!
You're on your way!
That's using your noodle!
I knew you could do it!
You were really listening!
Nothing can stop you now!
You brightened my day!
What an imagination!
Exceptional performance!
You're on the right track!
What a great sample of your work!
I've discovered another one of your strengths!

Note To The Teacher: Use with "Plenty Of Praise" on page 7.

School's A Breeze When...

Back-To-School-Bingo

Go for five in a row!

Note To The Teacher: Use with "Back-To-School Bingo" on page 10.

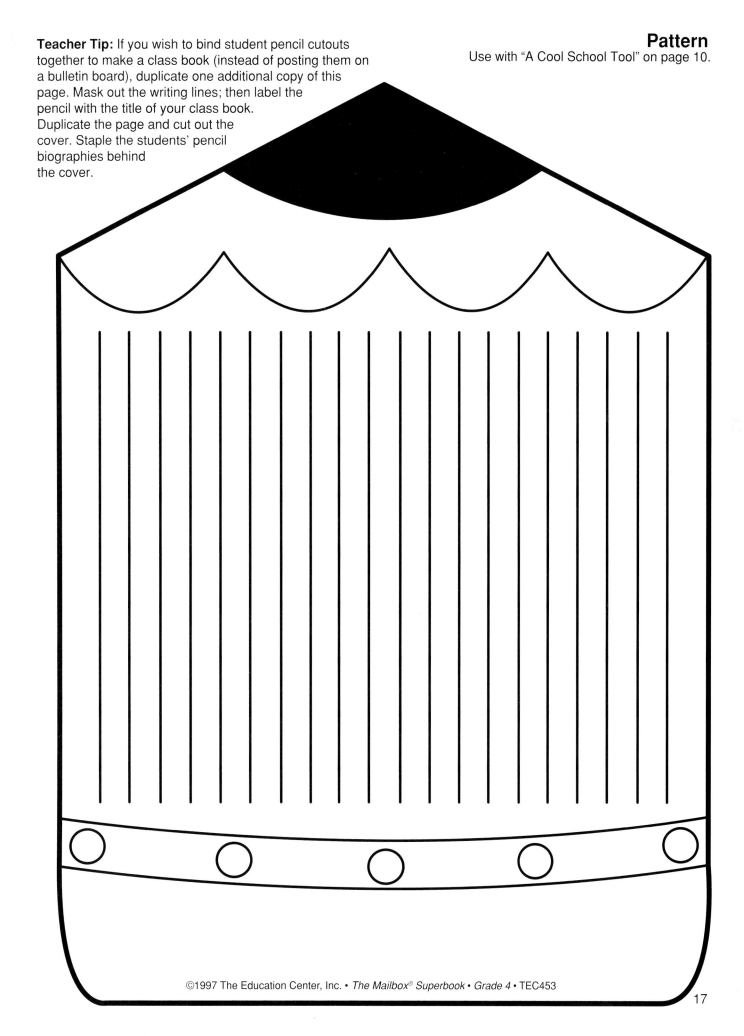

Teacher Tip: If you wish to bind student pencil cutouts together to make a class book (instead of posting them on a bulletin board), duplicate one additional copy of this page. Mask out the writing lines; then label the pencil with the title of your class book. Duplicate the page and cut out the cover. Staple the students' pencil biographies behind the cover.

So You Want To Know About Your Teacher?

Who wouldn't? Everyone is curious about his or her new teacher, and you're probably no exception! Carefully review the questions below. Then read the autobiography your teacher has prepared for you. After you have read all about your teacher, answer each question below in a complete sentence. Use the back of this sheet if you need more space.

1. When and where was your teacher born?_____
   _____

2. What is one thing you learned about your teacher's family?
   _____
   _____

3. What is one thing you learned about your teacher's growing-up
   years?_____
   _____
   _____

4. Why did your teacher decide to become a teacher?_____
   _____
   _____

5. How long has your teacher been teaching?_____
6. What subject does your teacher enjoy teaching the most?_____
   _____

7. What does your teacher like to do for fun?_____
   _____
   _____

8. What is one thing your teacher definitely *doesn't* like to do?
   _____
   _____

9. What kinds of books does your teacher like to read?_____
   _____

10. What would your teacher like to do when he or she retires?
    _____
    _____

Bonus Box: On the back of this sheet, write five more questions you'd like your teacher to answer.

BULLETIN BOARDS

BULLETIN BOARDS

Bulletin-Board Bonanza

Bulletin boards are a vital part of the classroom. In addition to adding a decorative touch, bulletin boards can also be used to exhibit good work, as informative displays, and as interactive teaching tools. Try some of the following suggestions to create distinctive displays in your classroom.

Background Paper With Pizzazz

Let the theme of your bulletin board inspire your choice of background paper. Gift wrap comes in a variety of designs that can enhance a bulletin-board display. Use birthday wrap to cover a board that features students' birthdays, or holiday wrap to add spark to a seasonal display. Wrapping paper also comes in many colors and patterns that are not available in standard background-paper choices.

Create other interesting displays with the following background-paper ideas:

newspaper	wallpaper
road maps	colored cellophane
calendar pages	plastic tablecloths
fabric	bedsheets

Borders That Beautify

If you're looking for just a touch of color to add to a bulletin board, use items from the above list to create a border for a board covered with a solid-colored background. Make your own border by tracing several strips of precut border onto the new material. Laminate the strips before cutting them out for added durability.

Interesting borders can also be made using:

doilies	dried leaves
cupcake liners	die-cut shapes
adding-machine tape that students have decorated	

Distinctive Lettering

The title on a bulletin board can be a work of art in itself! Try cutting letters from these materials:

wallpaper samples	magazine pages
sandpaper	posters
greeting cards	paper bags
foil	

Keep It On File

Take a picture of each bulletin board before you take it down. Store the photos in an album or in an appropriate file. You'll have a wonderful collection of bulletin-board ideas to choose from in the coming years as well as a handy reference showing the completed displays.

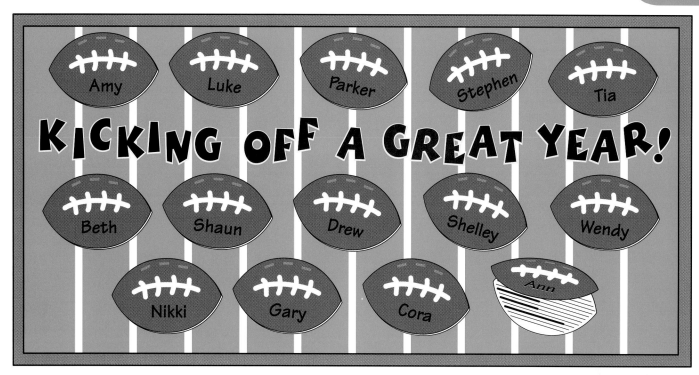

Kick off another year with a gridiron display that's a cinch to tackle! Duplicate a class supply of page 33 on brown paper. After cutting out each pattern, use white chalk to draw stitch lines on the unprinted side; then add a student's name with a black marker. Duplicate another class supply of page 33 on white paper. Give each student a copy to cut out and complete; then have him staple his brown football atop his white copy. Post the projects on a bulletin board covered with green paper and lined with white chalk to resemble a football field.

This entertaining display will have your class cheering " 'Ears' to you!" Have each student cut a piece of lined paper into a rectangle as shown. On the paper, have the student write a paragraph describing his hopes for the new school year. Provide students with various art materials; then challenge each child to create a pair of cut-out ears to staple to the top or sides of his paper. For an alternate title, try " 'Ears' To A New Year!"

Make no bones about it—this reading display is sure to be a hands-down favorite! On a copy of page 35, have each child create a new cover for a book she's read; then have her write a book review and staple it at the top behind the pattern. Mount the projects on a board decorated with an enlarged copy of the skeleton on page 34. Encourage students to visit the board and read each other's reviews.

Introduce a fall bounty of children's periodicals with this colorful display. With your librarian's help, collect six to seven different children's magazines. Give each of several groups a magazine to review. Have each group describe its magazine's highlights on a copy of page 36; then have group members cut out the leaf, staple it to colored paper, and trim around the edges. Store the magazines in tagboard pockets on the board beside their leaves so students can check them out during free time. Brighten the display by having students add colorful cut-out leaves to it.

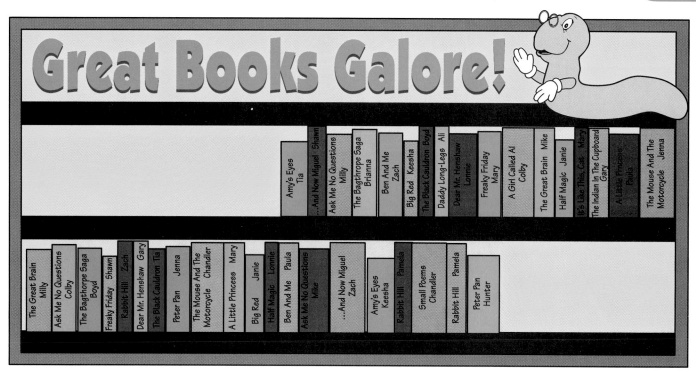

Get ready for National Children's Book Week in November—or encourage reading any time of the year—with this motivating display. Attach three strips of black paper on a board as shown. Add the bookworm character on page 37. Near the display keep a supply of colorful construction-paper strips in a variety of widths and lengths. After a student has read a book, have him write the book's title and his name on a strip, then mount the strip on the board. How long will it take your class to fill the shelves?

Provide fine-feathered punctuation practice with this Thanksgiving board that doubles as a learning center. Enlarge a turkey to mount on the board with a speech bubble as shown. Label cut-out feathers with quotations for students to correct on their papers. Place a folder with an answer key near the display. Change the feathers frequently.

To celebrate Hanukkah, cover a board with aluminum foil or silver foil wrapping paper. After reading about Hanukkah on page 38, have each student mount a copy of the page on blue paper, then trim around the edges to leave a colored border. On the pattern, have the student write about a miraculous event he would like to see happen, focusing on one that would help the largest number of people possible. Mount the dreidels on the board around a copy of the symbols.

Deck the halls with a student-made display that spans the globe! Post the list of international holiday greetings below. Have each child print one greeting on a holiday cutout; then challenge him to research the greeting's country to learn five fascinating facts about it. Have the student trace his cutout on notebook paper, cut out the tracing, and write his facts on the resulting shape. Then have him staple his facts behind his cutout at the top to make a flip-up book. Post the projects on a bulletin board backed with holiday gift wrap.

Belgium—*Zalig Kerstfeest*
China—*Sheng Tan Kuai Loh*
Denmark—*Glaedelig Jul*
England—*Happy Christmas*
Finland—*Hauskaa Joulua*
France—*Joyeux Nöel*
Germany—*Froehliche Weihnachten*
Greece—*Eftihismena Christougenna*
Italy—*Buon Natale*
Mexico—*Feliz Navidad*
Netherlands—*Hartelijke Kerstroeten*
Norway—*Gledelig Jul*
Poland—*Boze Narodzenie*
Portugal—*Boas Festas*
Spain—*Felices Pascuas*
Sweden—*God Jul*
Wales—*Nadolig Llawen*

Warm up even the "humbuggiest" holiday grinch with this cooperative display. Divide the class into four groups. Assign each group one part of the holiday scene shown: fireplace/fire, tree, wreath, and mantel/stockings. Provide groups with a variety of art materials. Let students who finish their portion first make holiday gifts to go under the tree or ornaments to add to it.

Wonderful winter work deserves to be displayed—"snow" fooling! Enlarge the snowman pattern on page 37. Create a large pond for the snowman from aluminum foil. Have students display their favorite papers on the board, along with snowflakes they've made and then decorated with silver glitter.

The time is here for a new year—so get ready to "watch" students show their creativity in this display! Provide each student with a large sheet of paper on which to design a unique wristwatch. Have students cut out their watches and post them as shown. To add to the display, have each student write a paragraph about his goals for the new year titled "Just <u>Watch</u> Me Meet My Goals This Year!"

Keep alive the message of Dr. Martin Luther King, Jr., with a simple, yet dramatic display. Use a marker or colored tape to divide a large square of white paper into nine windowpane sections as shown. Have students cut pictures from magazines and newspapers showing people of different ethnic groups working together; then have them glue the pictures collage-style in the sections. Pin a piece of fabric around the window to resemble curtains.

A kind word is everyone's cup of tea! Post a large red heart as shown. Have each student label a copy of the teacup pattern on page 39 with his name; then have him color the cup, cut it out, and add it to the board. Next have each child draw a classmate's name from a bag. Give each student a piece of string on which you've attached a small paper square. Have the student write a compliment about his chosen classmate on the tea bag, then tape the string to his classmate's cup.

Tip your hat to the contributions of African-Americans this February! Give each student paper and other art materials with which to create a large hat. Next have each student research a famous African-American (see the list on page 292) and write five facts about the person on an index card. Post the hats and cards as shown. When Afro-American History Month is over, change the title to "Hats Off To Role Models"; then have students research other famous people they admire and add facts about them to the board.

For St. Patrick's Day, cut out several shamrocks, along with several gold paper coins. Attach a leprechaun sticker on the back of eight cutouts. Post the shamrocks and coins (so any stickers are hidden) around a large pot. Each day your class meets a goal, remove a cutout. If a sticker is on the back, the class earns a letter—written on the pot with white chalk—in "LUCKY YOU." When all stickers have been found, reward the class with a special treat.

Dig up an enthusiasm for recycling with this display for Earth Day (April 22) or for any time you want to focus on the environment. Have each student list a recycling tip or a way his family recycles on a colorful index card. Post the cards on the board, along with an earthworm (pattern on page 39) peeking from a mound of brown paper dirt.

Summing Up This Year!

Add this eye-catching display to your end-of-the-year plans! Enlarge the character on page 40; then mount it on the board. Duplicate a class supply of the small addition symbols on page 40 onto colorful paper. Have each student use a fine-tipped marker to label a symbol with her favorite memory of the year; then have her cut out the symbol and attach it to the board.

When it comes to displaying good work, here's a display that fits the bill! Enlarge the long-beaked bird on page 41 to mount at the top corner of a board. Duplicate a class supply of the fish on page 41. Have each student color his fish with markers, cut it in half, and display it with a favorite paper as shown. Nothing fishy 'bout that!

Recognize students for improvement in their work with this cute canine display. Enlarge the puppy pattern on page 42 and place it in a doghouse as shown. Duplicate a supply of the bone patterns on page 42. Each time a student improves a grade in spelling, let him write his name on a bone cutout and add it to the display. To adapt the idea, change the subject in the title.

Sharpen math problem-solving skills with this student-made display. Ask each student to bring in one empty, clean food/grocery package. Display each package with a price tag. Add an enlarged copy of the cash-register pattern on page 43. Have each student use the information to write a math word problem on an index card. Place the cards (with an answer key) in a pocket on the board for students to solve during free time.

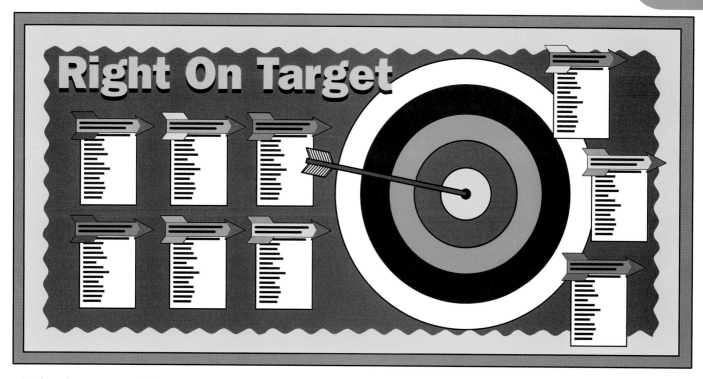

Take aim at recognizing good work with a display that's right on target! Mount an arrow and five large concentric circles on the board as shown. Duplicate the arrow patterns on page 44 so that each child has one arrow. Have each student choose a favorite paper to display, complete the information on his arrow, and then cut out and color the arrow. Post the papers and arrows on the board as shown.

LOOK WHAT WE'VE LEARNED!

FEBRUARY 10–14

Jeepers peepers—you've never seen an easier way to review information your students have learned! Cut out a large pair of glasses from construction paper; then mount the glasses on a board with a piece of chart paper as shown. Each week review new information students have learned, listing their responses on the paper. On Monday staple a new sheet of chart paper atop the old one. At the end of the month, remove the papers and save them. At the end of a quarter, display all the sheets so students can see all they've learned!

Ask each student to bring in the wrapper from a favorite candy bar. (Have a few extras on hand.) Give each child an oaktag rectangle to cover with aluminum foil; then have the student cut a piece of paper to wrap around his foil-covered rectangle. Challenge students to decorate their candy bar wrappers to look like their favorites. Post the bars with your students' favorite papers. Success is sweet!

Hand students their thinking caps with this easy display. In a large cut-out hand, place an open-ended question ("What would you do if a bully were teasing you?", "What would you do if you left your notes at school the day before a big test?", etc.). During free time, a student traces his hand on colorful paper, writes his answer on the tracing, and then cuts out the tracing to pin on the board. Change the question frequently, removing the students' hand cutouts each time you do.

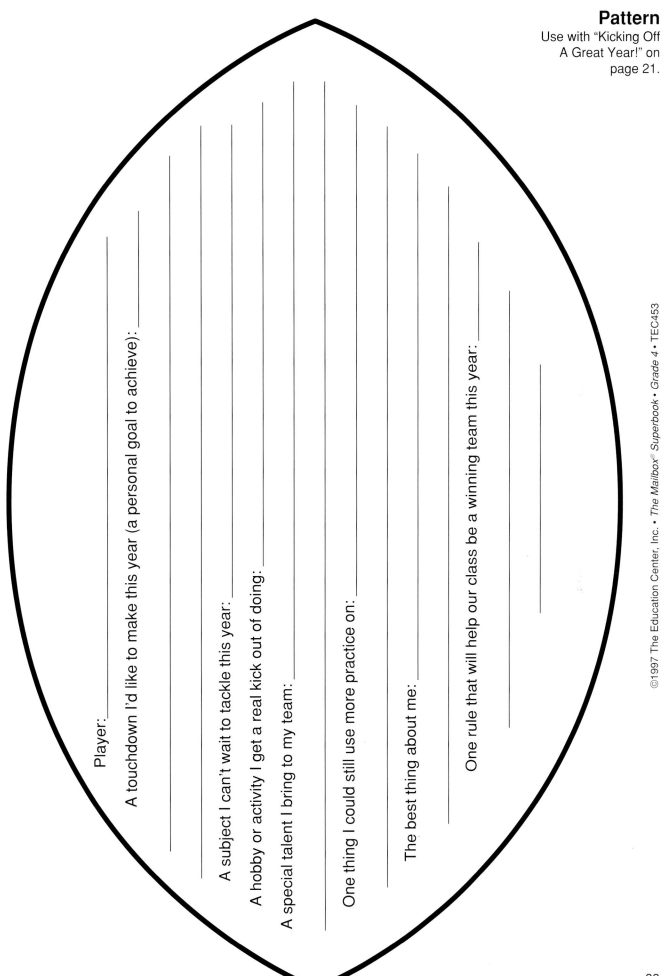

Player: _____

A touchdown I'd like to make this year (a personal goal to achieve): _____

A subject I can't wait to tackle this year: _____

A hobby or activity I get a real kick out of doing: _____

A special talent I bring to my team: _____

One thing I could still use more practice on: _____

The best thing about me: _____

One rule that will help our class be a winning team this year: _____

Pattern

Use with "I feel it in my bones…" on page 22.

Pattern

Use with " 'Leaf' Through A Good Periodical!" on page 22.

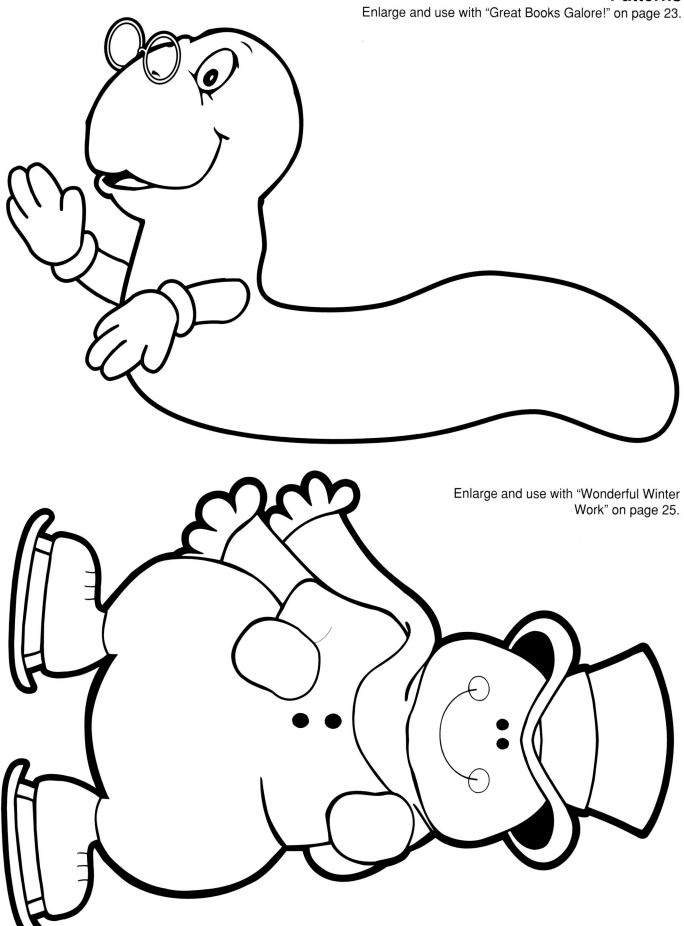

Enlarge and use with "Wonderful Winter Work" on page 25.

Pattern
Use with " 'A Great Miracle Happened There!' " on page 24.

nun

gimel

he

shin

"A Great Miracle Happened There!"

Name: _____

_____

_____

_____

_____

_____

_____

_____

_____

_____

_____

_____

Hanukkah is a Jewish festival that is celebrated in December. It honors the time when the Jews took their temple back from the Syrians. The Syrians had put out the Eternal Light (an oil lamp) in the temple. When the Jews took back the temple, there was enough oil in the Eternal Light for only one day. The Jews lit the lamp anyway. Miraculously, the lamp stayed lit for eight days, not just one.

The eight days of light are symbolized by the eight candles of the *menorah*. The menorah is a special candleholder used during Hanukkah. The dreidel is another symbol of Hanukkah. The four Hebrew letters on it are the first letters of the Hebrew words that mean "A great miracle happened there." Hanukkah remembers the joy that the Jewish people felt when they were able to worship again in their temple.

Enlarge and use with "Unearth Ways To Recycle" on page 28.

Patterns

Use with "Summing Up This Year!" on page 29.

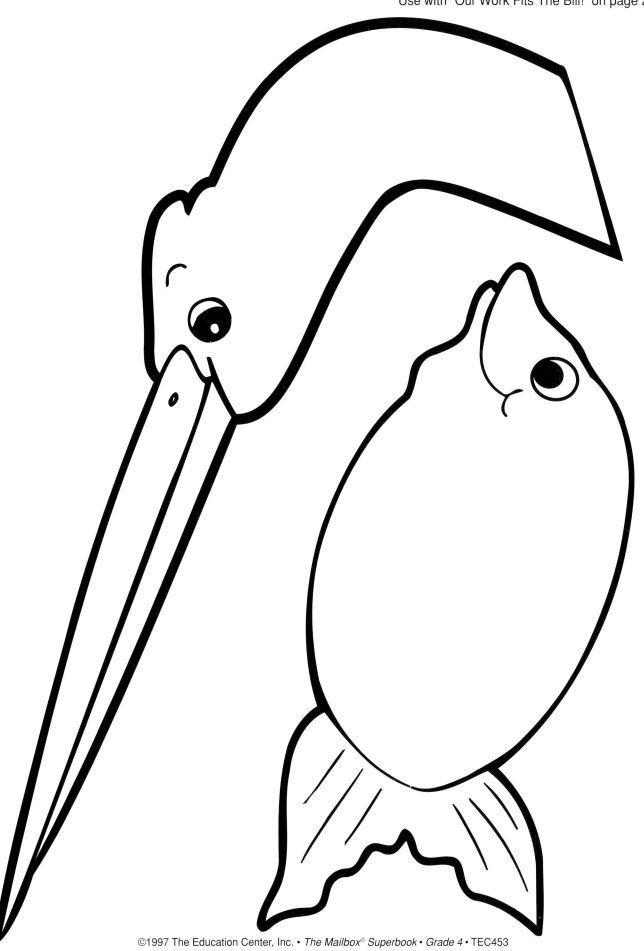

Patterns

Use with "Make No Bones About It…" on page 30.

Patterns

Use with "Right On Target" on page 31.

Name: _____

Reason I selected this paper: _____

Name: _____

Reason I selected this paper: _____

CLASSROOM MANAGEMENT

Name Reminder

Avoid getting a stack of student papers without names written on them with the help of this handy management tip. Provide a collection tray where students can turn in completed assignments. Then write "name" on a 1" x 2" piece of paper. Tape the label to the back left corner of the collection tray as a reminder to each stduent to record his name on his paper before turning it in. This visual clue is a great way to take the guesswork out of grading student assignments!

Grading Made Simple

Looking for a way to make grading papers easier and quicker? Before students begin an assignment that requires them to answer a series of math problems, have each child create an answer column along the right margin of a sheet of notebook paper. Direct the student to work each problem in the remaining space as she normally would. Then have her transfer the answer for each problem into the answer column. You'll quickly see that checking student papers is much easier when all the answers are conveniently located in one place.

Jennifer Willett
October 3, 1997
Math page 42

1. 2,304
2. 2,187
3. 5,005
4. 1,677
5.
6.
7.
8.
9.
10.

Bulletin-Board Captions

Make captioning bulletin boards easier with this timesaving idea. Cut out all the letters you need to create a caption for a specific bulletin board. Then glue the letters for each word to a sentence strip or a 7" x 11" strip of construction paper. Cut off any excess paper from each strip; then laminate the strips and arrange them on the bulletin board. After you take down the bulletin board, store the captions for reuse the following year. No more worrying about keeping up with all those individual letters!

RELAX WITH A GOOD BOOK

Highlighting Corrections

Shed a little light on correcting papers with the help of a highlighter. When correcting a paper, use a highlighter to mark through incorrect answers. Then return the paper to its owner and direct her to make the necessary corrections. Once the student has corrected her errors, you can easily recheck the incorrect answers by looking at the highlighted areas on her paper.

Mary Fogle
3/3/98

Science
Review Questions

1. photosynthesis
2. chlorophyll
3. stamen
4. pistil
5. oxygen
6. leaves
7. flower
8. stem

GET OFF TO A GREAT START!

1. **Unpack backpack.**
2. **Place homework in stacking trays.**
3. **Sharpen pencils.**
4. **Bring notes to the teacher.**
5. **Complete morning work.**
6. **Use any remaining time to read a book, study for a test, or work at a center.**
7. **Have a great day!**

Getting Off To A Great Start

Get your students off to a great start each morning with this helpful organizational idea. On a sheet of tagboard, write a list of morning tasks like those listed in the example for students to complete in preparation for the day. Decorate and laminate the poster; then post the chart. Each morning before school begins, direct students to complete the listed activities. With the help of this poster, your students will have an easier time staying on task and getting ready for the upcoming day.

Instant Storage Space

Looking for a little extra storage space in your classroom? Push a rectangular table flush against a wall in your classroom. Slide materials you wish to store underneath the table. Then hang several laminated posters or instructional charts from the front edge of the table to camouflage your storage stash. Organizing has never been easier!

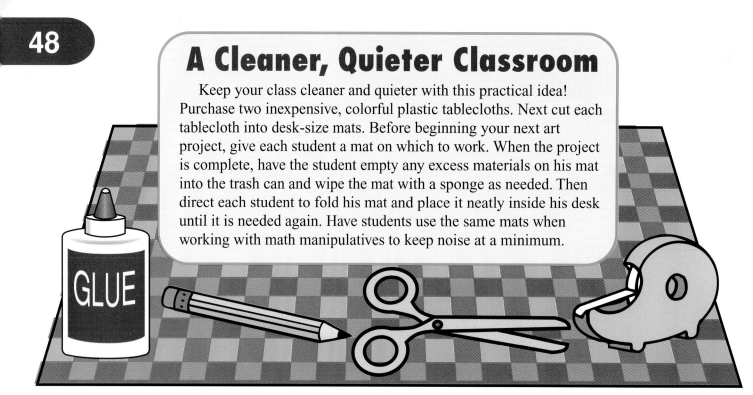

A Cleaner, Quieter Classroom

Keep your class cleaner and quieter with this practical idea! Purchase two inexpensive, colorful plastic tablecloths. Next cut each tablecloth into desk-size mats. Before beginning your next art project, give each student a mat on which to work. When the project is complete, have the student empty any excess materials on his mat into the trash can and wipe the mat with a sponge as needed. Then direct each student to fold his mat and place it neatly inside his desk until it is needed again. Have students use the same mats when working with math manipulatives to keep noise at a minimum.

Storing Poster Projects

Picking a place to store poster projects and other oversize materials is a snap with this convenient storage system! Ask a local bakery or grocery store to donate several stackable bun trays for use in your classroom. Stack the bun trays in a corner of your room or underneath a table. When a student is working on an oversize project, have her store it in one of the trays so that it stays neat. Also store craft paper and other large art supplies in the trays. With this system you won't have to worry about damaging all your delicate, bigger-than-a-breadbox materials!

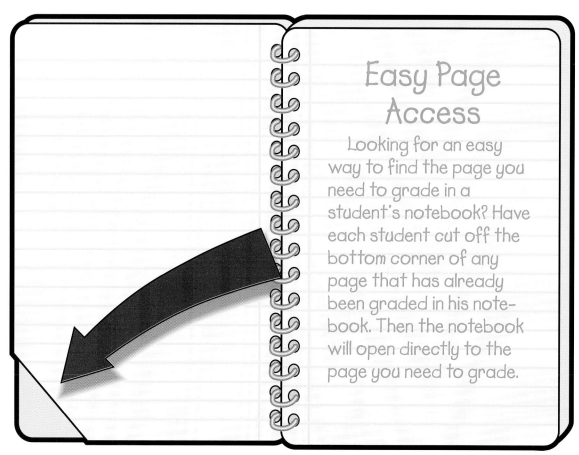

Easy Page Access

Looking for an easy way to find the page you need to grade in a student's notebook? Have each student cut off the bottom corner of any page that has already been graded in his notebook. Then the notebook will open directly to the page you need to grade.

Correspondence Shortcuts

Reduce the amount of time you spend on daily correspondence with the help of some premade, reproducible forms. Duplicate several copies of the absence report, overdue assignment notice, reminder, and incomplete work notice found on page 54. Keep these forms on your desk. Complete a form and give it to a student as needed. Make it a snap to identify the forms by duplicating each type onto a different color of paper.

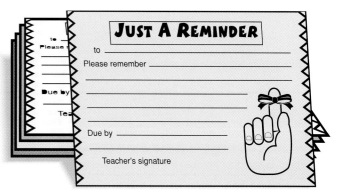

JUST A REMINDER

to _____

Please remember _____

_____

_____

Due by _____

Teacher's signature

The Bottom Line

Looking for an easy way to keep parents informed of what's going on in your classroom? Before duplicating your next worksheet, add a short comment directed to parents at the bottom of the sheet. Tell parents what your class is studying or recommend an extension activity parents might try at home. What a great way to keep parents informed and cut down on unnecessary paper consumption!

Parents: We are studying plants. Encourage your child to plant a seed as an extension of this study.

Ray Newton

It's In The Bag!

Keep absent students right on track with this simple tip. Save handled plastic shopping bags and store them in your classroom. Each time a student is absent, use a permanent marker to write his name on the outside of a bag. Then use the bag to collect necessary books and supplies for that student. At the end of the day, send the bag of supplies to the office for the child's parents to pick up. The bags also come in handy when a student needs to take home an item that will not fit into his backpack.

Conflict-Resolution Action Plan

Do you find yourself spending too much time resolving minor student disputes? Instead of taking valuable time to sort through both sides of a story, have each student involved in the disagreement fill out a copy of the conflict-resolution action plan found on page 55. Once each student has completed his plan, briefly meet with the children involved in the conflict and review the action plans. If necessary send the plans home for parents to read and sign. You'll quickly find that many times the students are able to come up with a workable solution themselves, saving you both time and effort. Also the students soon come to realize that often problems can be worked out without your help.

Fantastic Favorites File

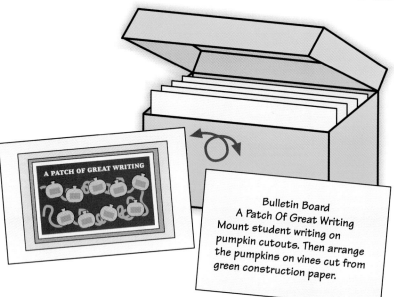

Bulletin Board
A Patch Of Great Writing
Mount student writing on pumpkin cutouts. Then arrange the pumpkins on vines cut from green construction paper.

Do you have a hard time remembering a favorite project or bulletin-board idea from previous years? Keep successful ideas fresh in your mind with the help of a disposable camera. Store the camera in your desk drawer and use it to take photos of your favorite bulletin boards and project ideas. Have the film developed; then write a short summary of the pictured idea on the back of each photo. Store the photos on your desk in a small photo box for future reference. Share a few of the photos at the beginning of the school year to give your new students a sneak peek of the months ahead.

Eye-Catching Classroom

Create an inviting atmosphere for your students with these simple tips designed to brighten your classroom. Ask a local carpet store to donate a supply of discontinued carpet samples. Piece several of the carpet samples together to form patchwork rugs for your classroom centers. Use colored spray paint to paint trash cans, file cabinets, and other similar items. Cover tables and work stations with brightly colored fabric remnants. Use some of the same fabric to make valance curtains for your classroom windows. With this extra effort, your students will be proud to call your classroom their own!

Simple Center Scheduling

Need an easy way to set up a regular schedule for students to visit classroom centers? For each center, divide an 11" x 14" sheet of construction paper into five columns. Label each column with the name of a different day of the week, Monday through Friday. Then record each student's name under a specific day. Explain to each student that he can visit the center during center time only on his assigned day. When it is not center time, allow a student to visit any center once he completes his classwork. To avoid center overcrowding, have students follow the helpful rule "No more than four."

READING CENTER

Monday	Tuesday	Wednesday	Thursday	Friday
			Ed	Alex
Jennifer	Andrew	Carrie		

Color-Coding Genres

Keep your reading center organized and ready to use with this easy color-coding system. Purchase at least six different colors of round stickers. Assign a different-color sticker to each literary genre; then place a sticker on the binding of each book according to the genre into which it is categorized. Mount one sticker of each color on a poster board and write the name of the genre it represents beside it as shown. When a student reshelves a book, instruct her to return it to the shelf with the same-color stickers. Be sure to keep a supply of stickers on hand to label new additions to your classroom library.

REALISTIC FICTION

MYSTERY

HISTORICAL FICTION

ADVENTURE

FANTASY

HUMOR

Know Their Strengths...And Weaknesses

The best way to help each of your students improve is to know his personal strengths and weaknesses. Find out this information by having each child complete the self-evaluation sheet on page 56. Explain to each student that his responses are confidential and are not going to be graded. Finding out this important information will help you better understand where each child is coming from and ways you can help him.

Storage Solutions

Students' desks and lockers always seem to be overflowing with supplies! Create additional storage space with this practical idea. Provide each student with a cardboard magazine box. Direct the child to place the supplies she needs for the morning inside the magazine box. After lunch have each student put away morning supplies and fill the box with the materials she needs for the afternoon. Students will appreciate the added space in their desks or lockers as a result of the organizers. Plus they won't have to go digging around to find necessary materials in the middle of a lesson!

Dear Andrew,
I know you will enjoy reading this book. I hope you have a wonderful birthday!

Mr. Reitz

Shiloh

Birthday Book Bonanza

Recognize student birthdays in a special way with this unique idea. Begin by listing your students' birthdays on a poster. Purchase (or use bonus points from a book club to gather) a supply of inexpensive paperback books appropriate for fourth graders. Then allow each child to select a book from your cache on his birthday. Write a short birthday wish to the child inside the cover of his selected book before giving it to him. You'll create a permanent reminder of the student's special day as well as providing him with a great piece of literature!

Give Students A Little Credit

Cash in on this idea for some great student behavior! For each student cut out a 2" x 3 1/2" credit card from heavy stock paper. Allow each student to decorate one side of his card as shown. Then attach a library pocket to the cover of each student's notebook and have the student place his credit card inside the pocket. Stamp the card's blank side with a small rubber stamp when you see the student exhibiting positive behavior. After a student earns a designated number of stamps, allow him to purchase a treat from your treat box or enjoy a special classroom privilege.

School Express
12345678
Exp. 9/30/01
Alex Lundein

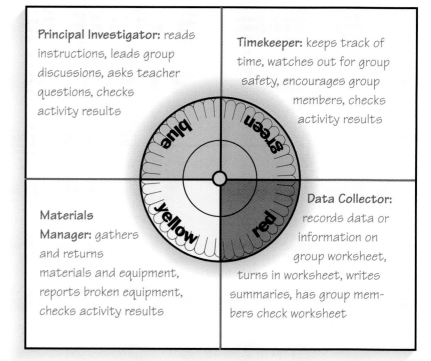

Principal Investigator: reads instructions, leads group discussions, asks teacher questions, checks activity results

Timekeeper: keeps track of time, watches out for group safety, encourages group members, checks activity results

Materials Manager: gathers and returns materials and equipment, reports broken equipment, checks activity results

Data Collector: records data or information on group worksheet, turns in worksheet, writes summaries, has group members check worksheet

Wheel Of Tasks

Set your students on the right track for group work with the help of a task wheel! Divide your class into groups of four students each. Assign each student within a group a different color—red, yellow, blue, or green—and place a correspondingly colored sticker on the student's desk. Then divide a small paper plate into four equal parts. In each section of the paper plate, write the name of one of the four colors. Then draw two lines to divide an 11" x 11" square into four equal squares. Push a brad through the center of the paper plate and attach it to the center of the paper square. Label each of the four squares on the paper as shown; then record the job summary for each task. Each time you have a group activity, rotate the plate one slot to the left so that each color is beside a different group task.

The Art Of Organization

Looking for a way to help your students keep from losing all their arts-and-crafts supplies? Use a permanent marker to write each of your students' names on a separate gallon-size, resealable plastic bag. Give the student the bag and direct her to fill it with all of her art supplies—glue, scissors, colored pencils, crayons, etc. Cover a large cardboard box with brightly colored paper. Then place each student's labeled bag inside the box. Each time a student needs her art supplies, she can retrieve them from the box and return them when she is finished. No more spilled glue and lost materials!

Your Attention, Please!

Capture your students' attention quickly with these simple tips. Purchase a call bell from an office supply store. Ring the bell three times as a sign to students that they need to "stop, look, and listen"—stop what they are doing, look at you, and listen to what you have to say. Or send the same message by clapping your hands in a rhythm. Repeat the rhythm a second time and then have your students copy it. Conclude this attention-getting exercise by clapping your hands twice and placing your index finger on your lips as a sign for quiet.

Positive Perks

Looking for the most effective way to reward students for positive behavior? Find out what incentives your students respond to best by having each child complete a short survey. Use the following questions to gather helpful incentive information from your class:

- Two of my favorite things to do are…
- If I improve in school, I would like my teacher to…
- Something I really want is…
- The best reward I ever received was…

- I do my best work when…
- My favorite place to be in school is…
- The activity in school I most enjoy is…

Dive Into Discipline

Informing students and parents of your expectations right from the start can make your school year run much more smoothly. At the beginning of school, present each student with a classroom discipline plan. Include important information in the plan such as classroom rules, consequences for breaking rules, and rewards for following rules. Review the plan with your class; then have each student sign and date her copy. Make the contract more official by signing it yourself and personally shaking hands with each child. Direct each child to take her signed plan home and have her parent review and sign it. File each student's plan in her portfolio; then refer to it as needed to remind the student of her commitment to follow the established classroom rules.

**Dicipline Plan
for Mrs. Newton's Class**

By signing, I agree that I have read and fully understand the policies outlined in this booklet.

_____
Student Signature   Date

_____
Teacher Signature   Date

_____
Parent Signature   Date

INCOMPLETE WORK

_____
Date

Dear Parent,

_____ needs to complete the following
assignment(s): _____

This work is due by _____ .

_____
Teacher Signature

_____
Parent Signature

Please sign and return.

©1997 The Education Center, Inc. • *The Mailbox® Superbook • Grade 4* • TEC453

JUST A REMINDER

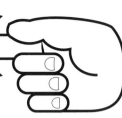

Please remember _____
to _____

Due by _____

_____
Teacher Signature

©1997 The Education Center, Inc. • *The Mailbox® Superbook • Grade 4* • TEC453

ABSENCE REPORT

_____
Date

Dear Parent,

Our records show that _____ was ab-
sent on _____ . Please send in a written excuse for
this absence.

Sincerely,

_____
Teacher Signature

We Missed You!

©1997 The Education Center, Inc. • *The Mailbox® Superbook • Grade 4* • TEC453

NOTICE OF OVERDUE ASSIGNMENTS

_____
Date

Dear Parent,

_____ has the following overdue
assignment(s): _____

If not completed, this missing work may affect your child's grades.
These assignments must be turned in by _____ .

Thank you.

_____
Teacher Signature

_____
Parent Signature

Please sign and return.

©1997 The Education Center, Inc. • *The Mailbox® Superbook • Grade 4* • TEC453

Note To The Teacher: Duplicate several copies of each form to use as described in "Correspondence Shortcuts" on page 49.

Building A Better Solution

Directions: Answer each of the questions below to help solve the problem you are experiencing.

What is the problem?

_____
_____

What caused the problem? (List all causes and any other people involved.)

_____
_____
_____

What can <u>you</u> do to solve this problem?

_____
_____
_____

What could others do to help solve this problem?

_____
_____
_____

In the future, what steps can you take to keep this from happening again?

_____
_____
_____
_____

_____   _____
Student's Signature   Teacher's Signature

_____   _____
Parent's Signature   Date

Note To The Teacher: Use with "Conflict-Resolution Action Plan" on page 49. Duplicate several copies and keep them on hand for future use.

Name_____ *Student self-evaluation*

Celebrate Yourself!

Directions: Read each subject listed in the table below. Then fill in the things you do well in that area and the things that you could improve upon. Remember that everyone has both strengths and weaknesses, so be sure to be honest! Include any of your likes and dislikes, too.

	Things I Do Well	Things I Need To Work On
Reading		
Spelling		
Writing		
Math		
Science		
Social Studies		
Health		
Art		
P.E.		
Music		
Group Work		
Behavior		

BUILDING CHARACTER & SELF-ESTEEM

BUILDING CHARACTER AND SELF-ESTEEM

Popcorn!

Help develop your students' sense of good judgment with this fast-paced activity. Divide your class into groups of five students. Give each group five different-colored cut-out squares to distribute among its members. Then call out a question from the list below. Give each group two minutes to discuss the situation. When time is up, call out the color of one of the squares. Direct each student who has that color square to pop up. The first student to pop up explains his group's answer and wins a point for his group. Declare the team with the most points at the end of the game the winner.

What would you do if...

→ you found a wallet containing $1,000?

→ you saw someone cheating on a test?

→ someone started a fight with you?

→ you had to choose between finishing a homework project and going camping with a friend?

→ you went to a friend's house for dinner and didn't like what was served?

→ you lost a school textbook?

→ you forgot your homework?

→ a stranger offered you a ride?

→ you forgot your parent's birthday?

→ you got a terrible grade on a test that needed to get signed by your parent?

Getting It All Together

Encourage responsibility with this motivating idea. Give each student one copy of the puzzle pattern on page 63, two envelopes, scissors, and crayons. Instruct the student to draw a picture on the puzzle, leaving no piece uncolored. Then direct the student to cut out the puzzle pieces and write his initials on the back of each piece and on both envelopes. Next have the student put the puzzle pieces in one envelope and place the empty envelope in his desk. Collect the envelopes containing puzzle pieces.

Each time a student exhibits responsibility, allow him to draw one puzzle piece from his envelope to place in the envelope in his desk. When the student has collected all nine pieces, have him glue the puzzle together on a sheet of construction paper. Write a congratulatory message on the back of the puzzle and allow the student to take it home; then give him another blank puzzle to start over.

KINDNESS—THE SWEETEST TREAT!

Give students a taste of kindness with this sweet idea! Name several examples of kind acts; then discuss how being the recipient of a kind act makes a person feel. Give each student a copy of page 64. Tell him that he has two weeks to fill his candy jar with examples of kindness. Each time the student shows kindness toward a classmate, he should explain the act on one piece of candy in his jar. When a student completely fills his jar, have him color, cut out, and post it on a bulletin board titled "Kindness—The Sweetest Treat!"

To: David
Deed: Helped Teacher Aide

To: Michelle
Deed: Gave Mike Paper

To: _____
Deed: _____

To: _____
Deed: _____

To: _____
Deed: _____

To: _____
Deed: _____

The ABCs Of Good Citizenship

Work with a primary class in your school to teach students the ABCs of good citizenship. Discuss the meaning of good citizenship with your students. Then explain that they are going to make a book about how to be a good citizen to give to a younger class. Next give each student a sheet of 12" x 18" white construction paper. Assign each student a different letter of the alphabet. Instruct her to write a sentence that begins with her assigned letter and tells how to be a good citizen. Direct the student to neatly print her sentence at the bottom of the paper; then have her draw a character modeling that sentence in the remaining space (see the illustration). Allow a few students who finish early to create a cover, title page, and dedication page for the book. Bind the pages in alphabetical order; then schedule a time to present the book to your buddy class.

Obey the Laws.

Take time to be a friend.

Always be honest.

Friendly-Deeds Scrapbook

Encourage kindness in your classroom with this one-of-a-kind scrapbook. Obtain a large photo album containing transparent sleeves. Decorate the front cover with a class photo and the title "Our Friendly Deeds." Once a week secretly select a student to be the class spy. Instruct this spy to be on the lookout for classmates who are exhibiting kindness. When the spy spots a kind act, have him write down what he observed and report it to you. Then give the spy a sheet of construction paper on which to illustrate and write a sentence explaining the kind act. (Vary the sizes, colors, and shapes of the paper to create an appealing visual effect.) Have the spy date the illustration; then add it to the scrapbook. Let students view the scrapbook in their spare time.

Stepping Stones

Challenge students to change stumbling blocks into stepping stones! Discuss examples of situations that appear to be stumbling blocks, such as moving to a new school or not making the basketball team. Then help students understand that there is more than one way to view a situation. For example, it may be upsetting if you don't make the basketball team, but it may give you more time to practice and get better at baseball. Next have each student think about a time when he met a stumbling block that eventually became a stepping stone. Give each student a gray, oval-shape cutout on which to write a paragraph describing that situation. Allow students to share their paragraphs; then collect the stone cutouts and arrange them in a path on a bulletin board as shown.

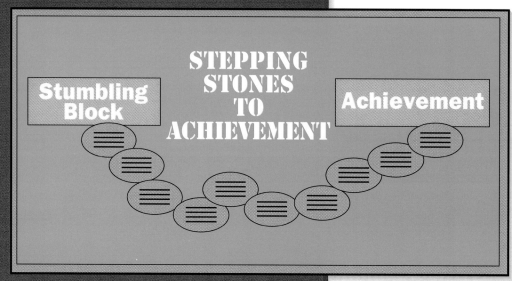

STEPPING STONES TO ACHIEVEMENT

Stumbling Block

Achievement

He is really good at math.

He's a great kickball player.

TOM

He always has a clean desk.

Heads Up!

Target self-esteem with this whole-class game. Write each student's name on a different 1" x 18" construction-paper strip. Place the strips facedown in a pile at the front of the classroom. Select a student volunteer to come to the front of the room and take a strip from the pile. Fasten the strip like a headband across his forehead so that the class can read the name written on it, but the student wearing it cannot. Challenge the student to identify the name on his headband by calling on classmates to give positive statements about the mystery student. Play until the volunteer can correctly identify the student. Direct the child who gave the final clue to choose a strip and become the next guesser.

Provide students with a golden opportunity to boost their self-esteem! Decorate a cigar box or other lidded box to resemble a treasure chest. Then give each student a coin cut from yellow paper. Instruct the student to write a sentence telling one thing she likes about herself on the coin. Have her write her name on the back of the coin and place it in the treasure chest. Each day pull one coin from the chest and read the name on it. Then have classmates take turns guessing what they think the named student wrote on the front of her coin. By the time the statement is identified, that student is sure to be wearing a golden smile!

I won the county championship in spelling.

I'm good at math, especially fractions.

I'm captain of my soccer team.

Logo Designs

Those golden arches, that rainbow-colored apple—today's kids are bombarded with logos that identify major businesses or products. Show students several examples of company logos, such as the Macintosh® apple or the mailbox for The Education Center®. Next challenge each student to design a symbol that represents himself. Give the student two 6" x 6" sheets of construction paper in contrasting colors. Instruct the student to draw and cut out his logo from one sheet, then glue it to the remaining sheet. When the glue is dry, allow each student to share his logo. Post the logos on a bulletin board with students' work displayed underneath.

SMILES ARE CONTAGIOUS!

Spread smiles through your class with this catchy idea! Decorate three plastic cups with smiley-face stickers and staple them together in a row. Label the cup on the left "In," the cup in the center "Smiles," and the cup on the right "Out." Then write each student's name on a different craft stick and place it in the "In" cup. Also label each of several craft sticks with a different sentence starter, such as "Congratulations for…," "Good luck with…," and "Thanks for…." Place these sticks in the "Smiles" cup. Every few weeks have each student draw a stick from the "In" cup and keep the name drawn a secret. Explain that the classmate whose name is drawn is that student's secret smile buddy for the day. The student's job is to deliver a compliment (or "smile") to her buddy during the day. Once the smile has been delivered, have the student place the stick in the "Out" cup. Invite students to pull a stick from the "Smiles" cup if they're having a difficult time deciding what to say to their buddies.

In   Smiles   Out

We Can!

Help students focus less on the "I can't" and more on the "I can!" Draw a soup can on a sheet of poster board and decorate it with a label identifying your class (see the illustration). Cut out and laminate the can; then post it on a classroom wall within students' reach. Position several different-colored overhead marking pens near the display; then invite students to record their "I Can" successes on the can. When writing space becomes limited on the poster, simply wash off the marker and start over. With this "soup-er" display, you <u>can</u> easily remind students of their accomplishments!

Christensen's
I can serve the volleyball over the net in gym class. Sara
I can divide two-digit numbers. Josh
I can remember all my multiplication facts. Joseph

WE CAN SOUP

I'm "Soup-er"!

Extend the "We Can!" idea above with this self-esteem builder. Instruct each student to write a paragraph about what makes her "soup-er." Explain that the paragraph can be about school, sports, hobbies, or special talents. Then give the student a copy of the pattern below on which to write the final copy of her paragraph. Have the student glue a photograph of herself in the blank circle on the can and write her name on the line. Direct the student to mount her completed label onto a sheet of construction paper. Bind all the labels into a booklet titled "[Teacher's Name]'s 'Soup-er' Students."

Pattern
Use with "I'm 'Soup-er!' " above.

I'm Soup·er" Soup

Name: _____

Kindness—The Sweetest Treat!

Being treated with kindness is like biting into your favorite candy! Help your classmates get a taste of this good feeling by delivering some good deeds. Each time you are kind to a classmate, write that student's name and what you did on a piece of candy in the jar. Can you fill the jar with your sweet acts of kindness?

To: _____
Deed: _____
_____

To: _____
Deed: _____
_____

To: _____
Deed: _____
_____

To: _____
Deed: _____
_____

To: _____
Deed: _____
_____

To: _____
Deed: _____
_____

Bonus Box: On another sheet of paper, explain in a paragraph how one or all of your classmates reacted after you treated them with kindness.

WORKING
WITH
PARENTS

Stick It To 'Em

With this Open House project, important information is guaranteed to stick with your students' parents! On brightly colored construction paper, duplicate the cutouts on page 71. Provide each student with the cutout of his choice. Direct the student to use a black marker to write his name, your name, your classroom number, and the school telephone number on the cutout. Laminate the cutouts; then have each student attach a small strip of magnetic tape to the back of his shape. Give each child's parents their special magnet at Open House. Suggest that the parents take their magnet home and put it on the refrigerator for future reference.

Jonah Willett
Mrs. Gilleland
Room 24
356-7488

Piece By Piece

Dazzle parents at Open House with this attractive student-made display! Begin by discussing quilts with your class. Guide students in understanding that a quilt is made up of scraps of material that have been pieced together to create a design. Next provide each student with a copy of page 72. Review the instructions at the top of the sheet with your students; then allow each child to design her own quilt square on the reproducible. Once each student has completed her square, have her share it with the rest of the class. Then have her cut out her square and mount it on a slightly larger square of brightly colored construction paper. Punch one hole in each of the four corners of each square; then use brightly colored yarn to tie the squares together to form a quilt. Tie the completed quilt on a dowel and display it on your classroom wall.

Get Set For A Great Year!

Take advantage of Open House night to supply parents with the information they need to help their child have a successful year. Give each student one copy of the top half of page 78. Have the student fill in all the information on his sheet; then staple or tape it to the back of a large manila envelope. On the envelope's flap, write the student's name. Then have each child decorate his envelope with a self-portrait. Inside the envelope, place work samples you have collected up to that point in the year. Also include handouts on such topics as school policies, classroom rules and procedures, study tips, and other important information. Have each student arrange his envelope on his desk along with the textbooks you use. Invite parents to review the materials at Open House. What a great way to share a ton of information in a short amount of time!

A Hands-On Welcome

Welcome parents to Open House with this handy student-made bulletin board. During the week before Open House, cover a bulletin board with colorful paper and attach a decorative border. Label the bulletin board "We All Have A Hand In Our Success!" Then mix several colors of tempera paint. Direct each student to select one paint color; then pour a small amount of that paint onto a paper plate. Have the student place her hand in the paint and make a handprint on the covered bulletin board. Once the paint has dried, have each student write, below her print, her name and a short message welcoming parents to Open House.

Veronica Boons
I hope you enjoy our Open House presentation!

Homework Notebooks

Get your students organized right from the start with the help of homework notebooks. Each week make one copy of the homework notebook pages found on pages 73 and 14 for each student. Have each student keep the forms in a special homework folder. On Monday, have the student fill out the dates in his forms. At the end of each day, have him copy the day's homework assignments in the appropriate boxes. Ask parents to sign the form when the home-work assignments have been completed. Include notes to parents in the homework folder too. This is a great way to open up communication about school between students and their parents. Plus it turns over homework responsibility to students!

Randy's Homework Notebook
4th Grade
Mrs. Nilson's Class
Room 32

Parent Signature
Mrs. Kwarta

Parent Signature
Mr. Comte

Testing 1-2-3!

Keep your parents informed of their child's academic progress with this easy tip. Using a computer, type a page of assorted parent signature lines. Add cute clip art or graphics for a special touch. Then simply cut out the signature lines and paste one onto each test before making individual student copies. After you grade each student's test, direct him to have it reviewed and signed by a parent. Make sure that parents receive other materials sent home by adding parent signature lines to any correspondence or other important assignments or notices.

Reminder Stamps

Keep the reminders you send home with students from getting lost with this practical suggestion. Instead of sending home small slips of paper with individual announcements on them, use message stamps to stamp the reminders in students' homework notebooks. Look for sets of these message stamps in your teacher supply store or order them from a company that creates made-to-order rubber stamps. Collect stamps with messages such as "Study For Test," "P.T.A. Meeting," "Project Due," etc. Or use your computer to print out sheets of labels featuring the important messages. Just stick a message onto the correct page in each student's homework notebook.

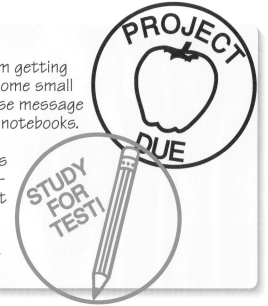

Positive Postcards

This idea is sure to get the stamp of approval from parents and students alike! Purchase some inexpensive decorated postcards, or decorate some index cards with colorful stickers. Then, each week, put one card in your lesson plan book. During the week, select one student who deserves a special pat on the back for an accomplishment at school or a kind deed. Write a quick note of praise to the student and his or her parents; then place a postage stamp on the card and add the student's address. (Your principal will probably be glad to provide the stamps for this positive project.) Sending these praise postcards will really brighten up a student's day and make her parents proud!

Dear Mr. and Mrs. Hladke,

Liz is doing a great job with her multiplication tables. Please encourage her to keep up the good work!

Sincerely,
Mrs. Ringo

Mr. and Mrs. Hladke
1408 Beachside Road
Virginia Beach, VA 23456

File-A-Conference

Documenting conferences and conversations with parents is a snap with the help of this handy organizational system. Write the last name and first initial of each child on an individual index card. Then place the cards in alphabetical order in a card file box. Each time you speak to a child's parents, record the date, with whom you spoke, what was discussed, and the conference format (phone call or personal visit) on the card. After the conference, add additional notes on the conference outcome to the card. Also use the file to store copies of notes you have sent home or notes you have received from parents. The card file instantly places a wealth of important information right at your fingertips!

The BUG Club

Rather than reward just those students who achieved high grades for a grading period, reward those who demonstrated academic improvement or exemplary behavior, too. Organize a special BUG Club for students who were caught "Bringing Up Grades" or "Being Unusually Good." Reward each child who earns membership in the BUG Club with his own special membership card (patterns on page 75) and extra bonus points. Then send home a BUG telegram (also on page 75) to parents, praising the student's behavior or academic improvement.

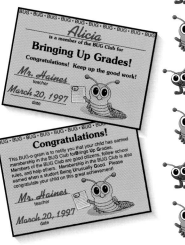

Monthly Newsletter

Keep your students' parents in-the-know with the help of a student-written monthly newsletter. Duplicate one copy of the monthly newsletter template on page 77. Group students; then have them write short summaries about units of study or special events that have occurred in your classroom over the past month. Record these summaries—along with student birthdays and important announcements—on the newsletter template. Then duplicate one copy for each student, being sure to make several extra copies for other interested parties. Repeat this procedure monthly to keep everyone informed!

Student Self-Evaluation

Students are often the best judges of their behavior, effort, and academic success. On a regular basis, give each student a copy of the self-evaluation form on page 76 and have him answer the questions. Add specific comments of your own to the forms of those students who need additional reinforcement. Spot-check student forms for fairness and accuracy. Then attach each student's graded work for the week to the sheet and send the evaluation home. Have each student return his evaluation form to school after getting a parent's signature.

How did I do this week?

Conference Scheduling Made Easy

Scheduling conferences at convenient times is a challenge for even the most experienced teacher! Make the task more manageable—and communicate openness to your parents—with the help of the conference request form on page 78. At the beginning of the school year or just prior to parent-teacher conferences, send home a copy of the form on the bottom of page 78. After each parent completes the form and suggests several workable conference times, select one of the suggested times to hold the conference. Then send a confirmation letter to the parent. Allowing parents to choose the conference times most suitable to them is just one more way you can demonstrate the value you place on frequent home-school communication.

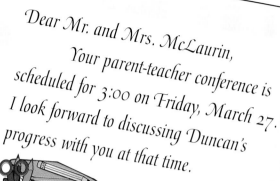

Dear Mr. and Mrs. McLaurin,
Your parent-teacher conference is scheduled for 3:00 on Friday, March 27. I look forward to discussing Duncan's progress with you at that time.

Sincerely,
Mrs. Smith

Summing It All Up

Provide closure to your next parent-teacher conference by summarizing the main points covered. Duplicate one copy of the conference summary form on page 80 for use during each scheduled parent-teacher conference. During each conference, take notes on what is being discussed under each area outlined on the form. At the conclusion of the conference, review the notes; then have each participant sign the summary to indicate that the information recorded is understood and agreed upon.

Conference Action Plan

Take advantage of your next parent-teacher conference to develop an individual action plan for each student. Prior to scheduled conferences, make a copy of page 79 to use during each of your meetings. As you and a child's parents discuss areas of concern and goals, record that information in the corresponding section of the action plan. Then discuss and list steps to be taken by you, the student, and the parents to reach the outlined goals. Review the action plan at the end of the conference; then provide the child and his parents with a copy for future reference. At your next conference, pull out your copy of the plan so you can discuss progress on meeting the goals.

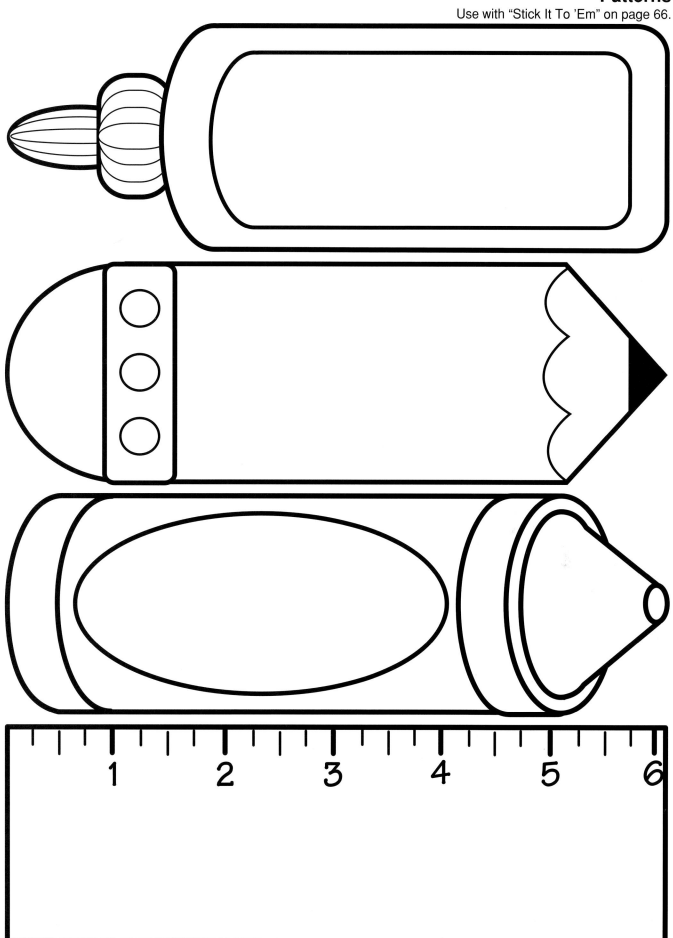

Piece By Piece

Materials: crayons, glue, scissors, one wallet-size photo of yourself

Instructions for filling in the quilt-square sections:

1. Color this space your favorite color. Then glue your photo in it.
2. Write your first name using creative lettering.
3. Write your date of birth.
4. Write your last name using creative lettering.
5. Write the names of the city and state where you were born.
6. & 7. Draw pictures to represent two of your hobbies.
8. & 9. Draw pictures to represent two skills you possess.
10. & 11. Illustrate two goals you hope to achieve.
12. Draw the animal you consider to be most like yourself.
13. Draw a picture that illustrates a personal achievement that makes you proud of yourself.

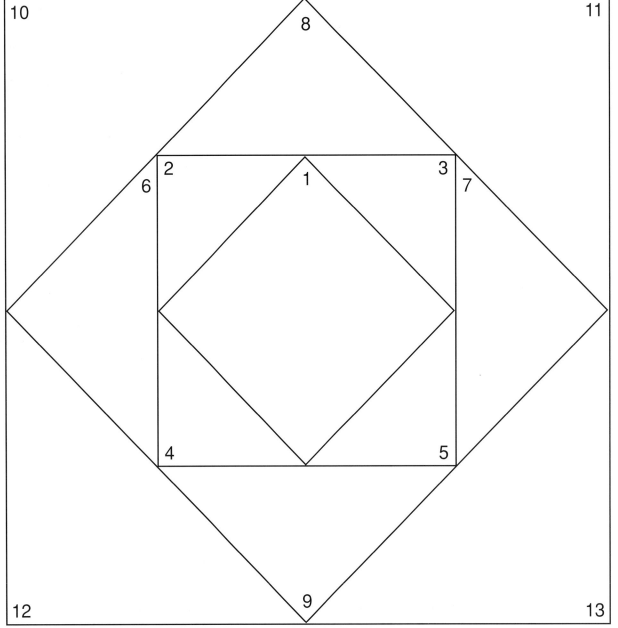

©1997 The Education Center, Inc. • *The Mailbox® Superbook • Grade 4* • TEC453

72   **Note To The Teacher:** Use with "Piece By Piece" on page 66.

 # Homework Assignments

Name _____	Week Of _____

MONDAY

Date _____	Assignment	Due Date	Complete
Math			
Reading			
English			
Spelling			
Health/Science			
Social Studies			
Other			

Parent Signature _____

TUESDAY

Date _____	Assignment	Due Date	Complete
Math			
Reading			
English			
Spelling			
Health/Science			
Social Studies			
Other			

Parent Signature _____

WEDNESDAY

Date _____	Assignment	Due Date	Complete
Math			
Reading			
English			
Spelling			
Health/Science			
Social Studies			
Other			

Parent Signature _____

Note To The Teacher: Make one copy of this sheet and page 74 weekly for each student. Use as described in "Homework Notebooks" on page 67.

Homework Assignments

Name _____	Week Of _____

THURSDAY

Date _____	Assignment	Due Date	Complete
Math			
Reading			
English			
Spelling			
Health/Science			
Social Studies			
Other			

Parent Signature _____

FRIDAY

Date _____	Assignment	Due Date	Complete
Math			
Reading			
English			
Spelling			
Health/Science			
Social Studies			
Other			

Parent Signature _____

NOTES

Note To The Teacher: Make one copy of this sheet and page 73 weekly for each student. Use as described in "Homework Notebooks" on page 67.

BUG • BUG • BUG • BUG • BUG • BUG • BUG • BUG • BUG • BUG • BUG • BUG

_____

is a member of the BUG Club for

Bringing Up Grades!

Congratulations! Keep up the good work!

_____
teacher

_____
date

BUG • BUG • BUG • BUG • BUG • BUG • BUG • BUG • BUG • BUG • BUG • BUG

Congratulations!

This BUG-o-gram is to notify you that your child has earned membership in the BUG Club for **B**ringing **U**p **G**rades. The BUG Club encourages students to do their best and always strive for improvement. Membership in the BUG Club is also earned when a student is **B**eing **U**nusually **G**ood. Please congratulate your child on this great achievement!

_____
teacher

_____
date

BUG • BUG • BUG • BUG • BUG • BUG • BUG • BUG • BUG • BUG • BUG • BUG

_____

is a member of the BUG Club for

Being Unusually Good!

Congratulations! Keep up the good work!

_____
teacher

_____
date

BUG • BUG • BUG • BUG • BUG • BUG • BUG • BUG • BUG • BUG • BUG • BUG

Congratulations!

This BUG-o-gram is to notify you that your child has earned membership in the BUG Club for **B**eing **U**nusually **G**ood. Members of the BUG Club are good citizens, follow school rules, and help others. Membership in the BUG Club is also earned when a student **B**rings **U**p **G**rades. Please congratulate your child on this great achievement!

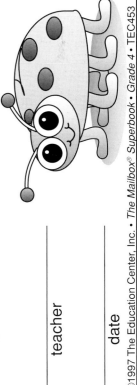

_____
teacher

_____
date

Note To The Teacher: Use with "The BUG Club" on page 69.

 # Student Self-Evaluation

Name _____ Week Of _____

Subject	Grades Received	Missing Assignments
Math		
Reading		
English		
Spelling		
Writing		
Science		
Health		
Social Studies		
Other		

Directions: Circle the word or phrase that best describes your performance in each area.

My behavior this week was…

       excellent   good   fair   poor

I did my work carefully and accurately.

       always   most of the time   sometimes   never

I turned in my assignments on time.

       always   most of the time   sometimes   never

I paid attention in class and followed directions carefully.

       always   most of the time   sometimes   never

I was courteous and helpful in class, in the lunchroom, on the playground, and on the school bus.

       always   most of the time   sometimes   never

Teacher Comments _____

_____

_____

Parent Signature _____

Parent Comments _____

_____

_____

Note To The Teacher: Duplicate one copy for each student and use with "Student Self-Evaluation" on page 69.

In The News

Teacher_____   **Date**_____

Subject Summaries

Don't Forget!

Special Events

Birthday Bashes

Help Wanted!

Note To The Teacher: Use as described in "Monthly Newsletter" on page 69.

GET SET FOR A GREAT YEAR!

Student _____ Room Number _____

Teacher _____ School Phone Number _____

Weekly Schedule

Time	Subject	Special Classes		
		Class	Day	Time

Other Important Information:

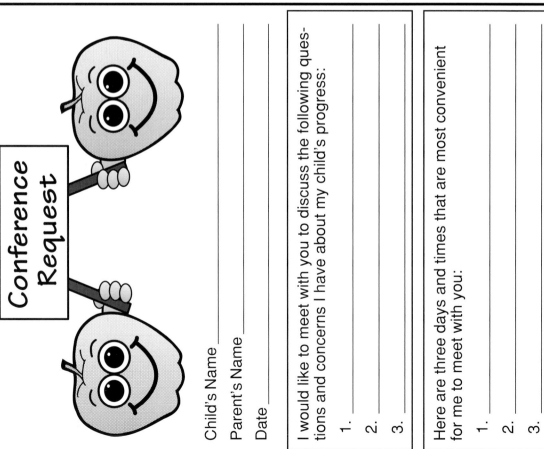

Conference Request

Child's Name _____

Parent's Name _____

Date _____

I would like to meet with you to discuss the following questions and concerns I have about my child's progress:

1. _____
2. _____
3. _____

Here are three days and times that are most convenient for me to meet with you:

1. _____
2. _____
3. _____

Evening phone number: _____

Daytime phone number: _____

PLEASE RETURN TO YOUR CHILD'S TEACHER.

Note To The Teacher: Use the top form as described in "Get Set For A Great Year!" on page 66. Use the bottom form with "Conference Scheduling Made Easy" on page 70.

Conference Action Plan

Conference Date _____

Parent(s) _____

Student _____

Teacher _____

Area Of Concern	Goal	Plan Of Action		
		Teacher	Parent	Student

Follow-Up Phone Call Scheduled For _____

Next Scheduled Conference Date _____

Note To The Teacher: Use as described in "Conference Action Plan" on page 70.

Conference Summary

Date _____   Student _____

Parent(s) _____   Teacher _____

This conference included a discussion of the following:

Issue/Area Of Concern	Outcome/Solution

We have read over the information and agree that it is accurate.

Teacher signature _____

Parent signature _____

Note To The Teacher: Use as described in "Summing It All Up" on page 70.

ARTS & CRAFTS

ARTS & CRAFTS

Back-To-School Bookmarks

Start your students off to a year of good reading habits with this easy art project. Provide each student with a paint-color sample card like those found near paint displays in home-supply stores. Then give him scissors, glue, and a supply of gift wrap, paper scraps, and stickers. Direct him to use the materials to decorate his paint card—covering the paint-color names—to make a bookmark. Suggest that he add a positive reading message, such as "Take Time For A Good Book," to his bookmark. To increase durability, laminate each completed bookmark or cover each one with clear Con-Tact® paper.

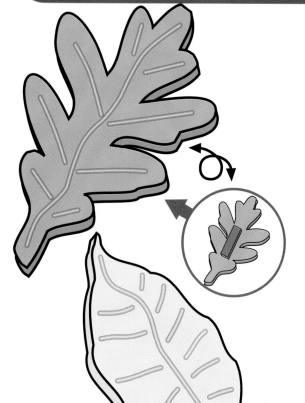

Fall-Foliage Magnets

These leaf magnets will add a spectacular display of fall foliage to any refrigerator!

Materials for each magnet:
thin piece of craft foam in a fall color
dimensional craft paint (available at craft stores)
1 leaf pattern from page 98
scissors
one 1 1/2" strip of magnetic tape
glue
pencil

Directions:
1. Cut out the leaf pattern and place it on top of the craft foam.
2. Use a pencil to trace around the leaf outline.
3. Cut out the foam leaf.
4. Glue the strip of magnetic tape to the back of the leaf cutout.
5. Use dimensional craft paint to add veins and other markings to the leaf.
6. Allow the paint to dry for 24 hours.

This cute little Halloween pin will add pizzazz to an outfit or make a great gift for a faculty member or nursing-home resident!

Materials for each pin:
metal soda-bottle cap
sandpaper
orange acrylic paint
paintbrush
plastic cup for paint
acrylic sealant
felt, green and black
scissors
glue
pin back

Directions:
1. Lightly sand the top of the bottle cap.
2. Paint the cap orange.
3. Let the paint dry; then apply a second coat and let it dry.
4. Spray the orange cap with acrylic sealant and let it dry.
5. Cut a jack-o'-lantern's facial features from the black felt. Cut a stem from the green felt. Then glue the cutouts to the orange cap.
6. Cut a felt circle to fit inside the bottle cap; then glue it in place.
7. Glue the pin back to the felt circle and let it dry.

The Great Pumpkin Doorstop

Give your room's decor a festive Halloween flair with this seasonal doorstop that's straight from the pumpkin patch!

Materials for each doorstop:
newspaper
1 brick
black and orange acrylic paint
paintbrush
black felt scrap
glue
pencil
scissors
12" length of 1 1/2" green craft ribbon

Directions:
1. Cover your workspace with newspaper.
2. Stand the brick upright and paint its two large rectangular faces orange. Let the paint dry.
3. Paint the four remaining sides of the brick black. Let the paint dry.
4. Trace one of the brick's small black sides onto the felt. Cut out the resulting rectangle and glue it to the matching side.
5. Cut out pieces of black felt to make two jack-o'-lantern faces. Glue the cutouts to the orange sides of the brick.
6. Tie the green craft ribbon into a bow and glue it to the top of the brick to complete the jack-o'-lantern doorstop.

GOBBLIN'-GREAT
Turkey Magnets

Your students will gobble at the chance to make this seasonal project that can decorate the front of their desks or help display their work!

Materials for each turkey magnet:
half of a tongue depressor
one 1 1/2" strip of magnetic tape
1 large black button (about 1" in diameter), or a
  same-sized black cardboard circle
2 wiggle eyes
glue
scissors
brightly colored craft feathers
felt scraps, orange and red
fine-tipped black marker

Directions:
1. Glue several feathers to the front and back of the rounded end of the tongue depressor as shown.
2. Glue the black button near the bottom of the cut end of the tongue depressor.
3. Glue two wiggle eyes to the center of the button.
4. Cut a beak from orange felt and glue it below the wiggle eyes.
5. Cut a wattle from red felt; then glue the wattle to the button just below the eyes.
6. Use a marker to draw two feet on the turkey.
7. Glue the strip of magnetic tape to the back of the tongue depressor to complete the turkey magnet.

Thanksgiving Cards

Here's the vehicle your students need for sending holiday greetings to the people for whom they're most thankful. You could even have students make extra cards and bundle them together in fours to sell at a school bazaar!

Materials for each card:
1 sheet of 8" x 12" construction paper, folded
  greeting-card style
paper scraps—wallpaper samples, gift-wrap
  scraps, corrugated cardboard, brown paper
  bags, construction paper
glue
scissors
fine-tipped marker

Directions:
1. Cut an assortment of triangles from different types of scrap paper.
2. Arrange the triangle cutouts on the front of the card to create a pleasing design.
3. Glue the shapes in place.
4. On the front of the card, write a message, such as, "I Couldn't Find A Better [Friend] Even If I 'Tri-ed!' " Change "Friend" in the suggested message to "Teacher," "Mom," "Dad," or whomever you choose.
5. Write a special note to that person inside the card.

I couldn't Find A Better Friend Even If J "Tri-ed!"

Gingerbread-People Ornaments

Spice up your holiday tree or bulletin board with these easy-to-make gingerbread-people ornaments!

Materials for each ornament: 1 sheet of sandpaper, gingerbread-person pattern on page 98, raisins, hard candy, scissors, glue, white yarn, hole puncher, pencil

Directions:
1. Trace the gingerbread-person pattern on page 98 onto the back of a sheet of sandpaper; then cut out the tracing.
2. Glue white yarn to the figure to represent frosting.
3. Glue on candy and raisins to decorate the gingerbread person.
4. Punch a hole in the top of the figure and hang the gingerbread person with a length of yarn.

Festival Of Lights

Involve your students in a cooperative project to help them learn more about Hanukkah. Explain that Hanukkah, the Festival of Lights, is an eight-day Jewish holiday celebrated every year in December. Point out that one symbol of Hanukkah is a *menorah*—a special type of candelabra with eight candleholders and a central helper candle, or *shammash* used to light one candle the first night, two candles the second night, and so on during the celebration. Divide your class into nine groups and have them follow the directions below to construct a class menorah.

Materials for each group: 1 empty paper-towel tube, yellow and orange construction paper, magazines, scissors, glue

To make each candle:
1. Cut out magazine pictures that show images of light.
2. Glue the pictures collage-style to the paper-towel tube, covering it completely.
3. Cut out a yellow candle flame and a smaller orange candle flame.
4. Layer the cutouts and glue them together as shown; then glue the flame to the inner front of the tube's opening.

Materials for the menorah's base: one 2-foot length of 2" x 4" board, one 4-inch section of 2" x 4" board, white paint, paintbrush, hot glue gun, glue sticks, 9 empty standard-size thread spools

Directions for constructing the menorah:
1. Glue the four-inch section of board to the center of the two-foot length; then paint them white.
2. Glue one spool to the center of the four-inch section of board; then evenly space and glue four spools on each side of the centered spool.
3. Position a candle on the center spool (to represent the shammash) and glue it in place. Then position and glue the remaining candles in place.

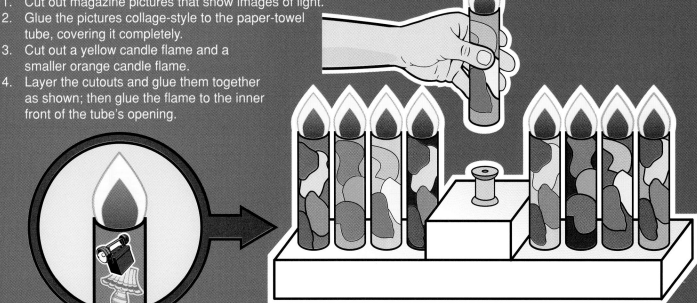

Gingerbread-House Bank

Have your students make this cute gingerbread-house bank to save up dough for their holiday shopping!

Materials for each house: 1 empty 1/2-pint milk carton, 3 graham crackers, heavy-duty packaging tape, dimensional craft paint in assorted colors, art knife, glue

Directions:
1. Rinse and thoroughly dry the milk carton.
2. Tape the top of the carton closed.
3. Using an art knife, cut one 3/4" slit for inserting money on one of the slanted carton sides.
4. Cut a 1" x 1" hole in the carton bottom and cover it with packaging tape.
5. Glue graham crackers to cover the carton's surface, making sure not to cover the money slit.
6. Decorate the gingerbread house using dimensional craft paint.
7. Allow the gingerbread house to dry before using it to save money for holiday gifts.

'Twas The Night Before Christmas

Not a creature was stirring, not even a mouse.

Bring to life the classic Christmas poem " 'Twas The Night Before Christmas" by personalizing the illustrations. Have each student bring in a small photo of himself. Then read the classic poem aloud, and have your students list all the characters mentioned in the text—the mouse, St. Nicholas, the children, Mom, Dad, Dasher, Dancer, Prancer, Vixen, Comet, Cupid, Donner, and Blitzen. Assign each student a different character from the poem. Then give each student a sheet of construction paper, and have him cut a small circle from the paper's center. Direct the student to tape his school photo on the back of the paper so that his face shows through the circle's opening. Next have him draw the body of his assigned character, using his photo as the character's face.

Meanwhile make a big book by punching holes in several sheets of poster board and fastening them together with yarn. Write a section from the poem on each poster-board page. Glue the completed characters to the appropriate pages in the book and share it with other classes. Or use the characters to decorate a wall space.

MAKING A MKEKA

Introduce your students to one of the seven principles of Kwanzaa—*kuumba* (creativity)—with this fun project. Explain that a *mkeka* is a woven mat that symbolizes African-American tradition and history. Then have students make their own variation of a mkeka to give as *zawadi* (gifts) by following the directions below.

Materials for each mkeka:
1 sheet of 11" x 14" black construction paper
3 sheets of 8 1/2" x 11" construction paper—1 red, 1 green, and 1 white
crayons or markers
scissors
glue
ruler

Directions:

1. On the white construction paper, draw a colorful picture of an important event in your family's history that covers the whole paper.
2. Fold the black construction paper in half lengthwise.
3. Starting at the fold, measure and cut strips one inch in width, stopping your cuts one inch from the end. Unfold the paper.
4. Use a ruler to measure one-inch-wide strips on the red and the green construction paper. Cut out the strips.
5. Weave the strips over and under the slats of the black paper, alternating red and green.
6. Use small dabs of glue to secure the strips to the black paper.
7. Mount your drawing on the mkeka.

Frosty's Fresh Fashions

Frosty will dazzle everyone in the new clothes your students create for him in this fashionable activity. Explain that Frosty is getting tired of his old silk hat, button nose, and two eyes made out of coal. Explain further that for health reasons, Frosty has given up his corncob pipe. Then challenge each student to create a new image of Frosty—complete with an updated wardrobe. Give each student a circular object, such as a butter-tub lid. Direct him to trace the lid on white paper to make a snowman's body. Also provide him with scissors, glue, and scraps of wallpaper, gift wrap, and fabric for designing Frosty's fresh new wardrobe. Display each completed model of Frosty on a bulletin board titled "Fresh And Fabulous Fashions For Frosty."

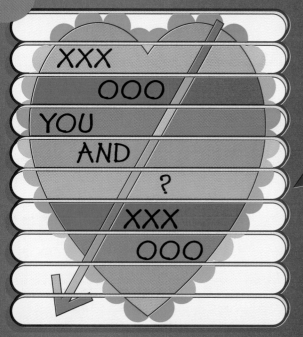

XXX
OOO
YOU
AND
?
XXX
OOO

Be Mine!
Believe it or not,
It will mean a lot
If you will be my valentine.
If you say, "OK, it's fine,"
I'll jump for joy all day.
But if "No" is what you say,
I'll just ask you again
Sometime now and then.
X?XOXOXOX?O?X?

A Puzzling Valentine Message

Your students will have a great time piecing together this Valentine's Day activity.

Materials for each puzzle:
10 craft sticks
two 5" lengths of masking tape
colored markers
1 envelope

Directions:
1. On your desk, position the pieces of masking tape sticky side up so that they are parallel to each other and about four inches apart.
2. Line up ten craft sticks side by side on the tape.
3. Use markers to draw a valentine design on the sticks.
4. Flip the sticks over, tape and all.
5. Carefully remove the tape and write a special valentine message on the sticks as shown.
6. Shuffle the pieces and seal them in an envelope.
7. Exchange your valentine puzzle with a friend and challenge him to solve it.

My Family

It Makes My Heart Sing

Give a musical lift to a blank bulletin board this Valentine's Day with this thought-provoking art activity. Provide each student with a one-inch square of white construction paper, a two-inch square of red construction paper, black construction paper, a ruler, scissors, glue, and construction-paper scraps in a variety of colors. Have him cut a heart from his white square and mount it on the two-inch square of red paper, trimming it to make a red heart slightly larger than the white one. Direct the student to continue mounting each subsequent heart on a different-colored paper square and cutting a border around it until he has a heart that is about six inches wide. Next have him think of the one thing in life that makes him happiest, and write it on the white heart. Instruct him to cut the tail of a musical note from black construction paper and glue it to the back of the heart. Meanwhile draw a free-flowing musical staff on a classroom bulletin board under the heading "It Makes Our Hearts Sing." Then mount each student's heart-shaped note on the staff to create an attractive display.

Prints O' Green

Your little leprechauns will be leaping with joy when you set up this fun art center in your classroom! Cut a supply of nine-inch, white construction-paper squares. Write the directions below on an index card. Place the paper squares and student directions at a designated table in your classroom along with pencils, black markers, scissors, glue, rulers, black construction paper, and a green-ink stamp pad.

Student directions:

1. Select a construction-paper square.
2. Use a ruler and pencil to draw grid lines that divide the square into nine equal boxes.
3. Trace over the grid lines with a black marker.
4. Press your thumb or fingertip on the ink pad; then make one fingerprint in each of the nine boxes.
5. Use a black marker to turn each fingerprint into a leprechaun or a St. Patrick's Day symbol.
6. Mount your completed designs on a ten-inch square of black construction paper.

Springtime Art

Colorful blooms will be opening up all over your classroom with this seasonal art project. Give each student scissors and glue along with one green and one light blue sheet of 4 1/2" x 12" construction paper. Also provide him with construction-paper scraps in a variety of colors. Have the student cut four 12-inch flowing vines from the green construction paper and glue them to the light-blue paper. Next direct him to cut four flowers from the colored-paper scraps, curl the flowers' tips by wrapping them around a pencil, and glue the flowers in an attractive arrangement on the vines. Then have him cut a center for each flower from contrasting paper and glue it to the center of each flower. For a finishing touch, have each student add a construction-paper cutout of a butterfly or a hummingbird to his springtime arrangement. Display the completed scenes on a bulletin board featuring student-written poems.

Spectacular Spring Suncatchers

Catch some of the spring sunshine you've been pining for all winter with the help of a spring suncatcher. Take your class outside; then direct each student to collect interesting leaves (or blossoms) from plants and flowers. After returning to the classroom, set up a pressing station in a safe location, complete with an iron, a towel, and a supply of newsprint. Give each student two 4 1/2-inch squares of waxed paper, and have him arrange the leaves he collected on the waxy side of one waxed-paper square. Next direct him to gently lay the remaining square—waxy side down—on top of the leaves. Ask one student at a time to bring his arrangement to you. Place the arrangement on a towel and lay a sheet of newsprint over it. Then, using a warm iron, press gently until the waxed-paper sheets melt together.

After the waxed paper cools, give each student 16 craft sticks for making two frames, constructing each frame from four pairs of sticks as shown. Direct the student to glue the print so that it's sandwiched between the two frames. Then supply paint pens, glitter, and other art materials so each student can personalize his frame. Use a hot glue gun to glue a length of fishing line to the back of each suncatcher. Then hang the completed suncatchers in a classroom window, or have students give them as gifts.

A Gift Worth "Weight-ing" For!

This decorative paperweight will become a Mother's Day gift that each mom can't "weight" to use! Mix a batch of plaster of paris as directed on the package. Fill plastic candy molds with the mixture and allow it to dry. When the plaster is dry, have each student cover her desk with newspaper and pop each form out of its plastic mold. Give each student a paintbrush and an egg carton that has different colors of tempera paint in its sections. Direct her to decorate the paperweight with the paint. After it dries, have her wrap the paperweight and give it to her mother as a special Mother's Day gift.

Perfumed Pillow Sachet

This fragrant sachet makes a great Mother's Day gift!

Materials for each pillow:

two 4" fabric squares
1/2 cup of scented potpourri
polyester filling
1 needle

thread
scissors
fabric paint
3 1/2" paper square

Directions:

1. Layer the two fabric squares so that the decorated sides are facing each other.
2. Sew a simple basting stitch—a stitch woven in and out of the fabric—around three edges of the fabric.
3. Turn the fabric right side out so that the printed side of the material is showing.
4. Slide the paper square between the fabric squares; then decorate the fabric with fabric paint.
5. Allow the paint to dry. Then remove the paper square.
6. Stuff the fabric with a mixture of polyester filling and scented potpourri.
7. Stitch the open edge closed to complete the pillow.

A PICTURE-PERFECT YEAR!

End-Of-The-Year Frames

Use this end-of-the-year project to frame memories of a great year!

Materials for each frame:

several old puzzle pieces, spray-painted different colors
three 3 1/2" x 5" tagboard cards
glue
scissors
ruler

hot glue gun
black permanent marker
class photo

Directions:

1. Cut away the interior of a tagboard card to make a frame with a one-inch border.
2. Glue the puzzle pieces around the border's perimeter.
3. After the glue has dried, have an adult hot-glue a second tagboard card to the back of the frame at the bottom and sides only, leaving the top open for inserting the photo.
4. Use the permanent marker to write the date or other words on the frame, such as "A Picture-Perfect Year!"
5. Make a stand for the frame by cutting away one corner from the remaining tagboard card. Fold the card in half; then glue the uncut half to the back of the frame.
6. Insert your class photograph, cutting it to fit if necessary.

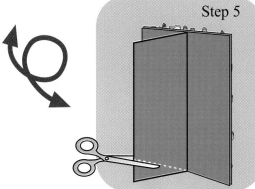

Step 5

PACKED AND READY TO GO!

Capture the excitement of summer vacation with this fun art project.

Materials for each suitcase:

1 shoebox
sandpaper
newspaper
brown tempera paint
paintbrush
scissors
colored construction paper

yarn
1 copy of the suitcase handle on page 99, duplicated on brown
 construction paper
glue
crayons
copies of puzzles, brainteasers, and travel games

Directions:

1. Spread newspaper over your work surface. If your shoebox has a glossy surface, rub it with sandpaper to prepare it for painting. Then paint the outside of your shoebox and its lid brown.
2. Allow the box to dry; then cut out and glue the suitcase-handle pattern to one of the long sides of the box.
3. From colored construction paper, design stickers to decorate the outside of your box. Include on each sticker the name and symbol of a different country or state.
4. Fill the completed box with copies of summer-enrichment activities—puzzles, games, and brainteasers—provided by your teacher. Then tie the box closed with yarn.
5. Take your suitcase along with you on your summer travels and enjoy the activities inside.

Take A Closer Look

Strengthen your students' observation skills with this art activity. Provide each student with scissors, colored pencils, and a copy of the magnifying-glass pattern on page 100. Ask each student to select an object in your classroom to examine closely. Next direct the student to cut out her magnifying-glass pattern, draw an enlarged section of the object she's studied directly on the pattern, and color it. Assign each drawing a different number; then list each number on paper along with a description of what it depicts. Post the drawings on a bulletin board titled "Take A Closer Look At Your World." Challenge students to study the drawings and guess what each drawing is. Once students have written their guesses on paper, refer to the list you compiled to reveal what each drawing represents. As a natural follow-up activity, have students examine and draw objects found outdoors!

Decidedly Different Dwellings

Combine your next art lesson with an award-winning children's book. Read aloud *Smoky Night* by Eve Bunting (Harcourt Brace & Company, 1994). Discuss with students how the people in that community, which is plagued by race riots, sought to get along despite their race differences. Next discuss how the background of each page in the book represents materials of different textures. Challenge students to identify the materials used by the story's illustrator to create such a textured effect. List students' responses on chart paper. Then have each student save a clean milk or juice carton from lunch and bring in different pieces of fabric, cardboard, gift wrap, or other supplies that represent textured materials. Instruct him to use the materials he collected to decorate his carton, making it resemble a building. Arrange the completed buildings as a community; then have students brainstorm a name for the community. If desired, extend the activity by having students work together in teams to create a set of laws for the newly established community and to design its seal and flag as well.

STRIKING SILHOUETTES

Re-create the beauty of a multicolored sky at dusk with this creative art project.

Materials for each silhouette:
one 8 1/2" x 11" sheet of white construction paper, one 8 1/2" x 11" sheet of black construction paper, colored tissue paper, glue, 1 small Dixie® cup, water, 1 paintbrush, 1 white crayon or chalk, scissors

Directions:
1. Cut and glue an uneven strip of black paper to the bottom edge of the white paper.
2. Mix equal amounts of glue and water in the Dixie® cup.
3. Tear a variety of colored tissue paper into small pieces.
4. Use a paintbrush to spread the glue mixture on a small area of the white paper.
5. Overlap the tissue-paper pieces on the glued area.
6. Repeat Steps 4 and 5 until the white paper is covered.
7. Allow the glue to dry.
8. Think of an object or a living thing that's often silhouetted against the evening sky; then use a white crayon or chalk to draw that object's outline on the remaining black paper.
9. Cut out the shape and glue it to the tissue-paper background.

Extend the activity by having students create underwater scenes with cutouts of different-colored fish glued against a background of blue and green tissue paper.

Personalized Name Plaques

Students will love making these personalized name plaques to hang on their doors at home!

Materials for each plaque:
tile square, 4" or smaller
picture from a greeting card or comic strip
Mod Podge®
12" length of 2"-wide craft ribbon
1 1/4" metal ring
scissors
glue
paintbrush
permanent black marker

Directions:
1. Cut out a picture from a greeting card or comic strip.
2. Paint Mod Podge® onto the back of your cutout and position it on the tile front.
3. Press down on the picture to make sure it is firmly attached; then let it dry.
4. Use a permanent black marker to write "[Your Name]'s Room" on the tile next to or below the picture.
5. Apply additional coats of Mod Podge®, letting each coat dry between applications until you achieve the desired finish.
6. Slide the metal ring onto the ribbon and fold the ribbon in half.
7. Glue the ribbon ends together and let the glue dry.
8. Glue the ribbon to the back of the tile to make a hanger.

FIELD-TRIP NAME BADGES

Liven up your next field trip with these easy and fun-to-make animal name badges.

Materials for each badge:
heavy white cardboard
tempera paint
paintbrushes
scissors
1 safety pin

masking tape
dimensional craft paint
animal pattern from page 99
pencil

Directions:
1. Cut out an animal pattern from page 99 or draw your own pattern.
2. Trace the animal pattern onto white cardboard.
3. Cut out the cardboard animal.
4. Paint the animal using tempera paints; then allow the paint to dry.
5. Use dimensional craft paint to write your name on the animal's body.
6. After the paint dries, flip the animal over and use masking tape to attach a safety pin to the back of the badge.

Your students will go wild over these groovy pencil cases. Just prepare the fabric dye according to package directions, place it at a work station in your room, and have each student follow the directions below!

Materials for each case:
one 18" x 3" strip of white cotton fabric, cut along the edges with pinking shears
rubber bands
fabric dye (prepared according to package directions)
hard plastic cup to hold dye
needle
thread
1 safety pin
one 12-inch length of 3/8"-wide craft ribbon
scissors

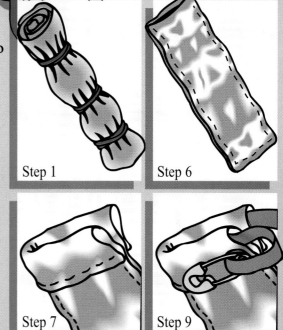

Directions:
1. Fold and roll the fabric into a newspaper shape. Fasten rubber bands around the rolled fabric at different intervals to create a unique design.
2. With adult help, dye the fabric according to the package's instructions.
3. Rinse the fabric and remove the rubber bands.
4. Hang up the fabric and let it dry.
5. Fold the fabric in half, right sides together.
6. Use a needle and thread to sew narrow seams up both sides of the bag as shown, stopping 1/2-inch from the top on one side.
7. Turn down the top one-inch of the bag's fabric and sew just above the raw edge to make a channel for the ribbon.
8. Turn the bag right side out.
9. Attach a safety pin to the craft ribbon and thread it through the channel.
10. Tie the ends of the ribbon together in a knot; then pull the ribbon to close the bag.

Step 1

Step 6

Step 7

Step 9

Can It!

Discover more about your students' interests—and help them get organized—with this collage-style pencil can.

Materials for each pencil can:
1 empty frozen-juice can
magazines
glue
scissors
Mod Podge® (optional)
paintbrush (optional)
decorative craft trim

Directions:
1. From magazines, cut pictures and words that describe your personality and your likes and dislikes.
2. Glue the cut-out items to the outside of your juice can, covering the whole can.
3. Apply a coat of Mod Podge® to the can.
4. Glue craft trim around the top and bottom of the can's edges for decoration.

ART ESSENTIALS

Easy-To-Do Recipes For A Variety Of Art Supplies

These easy-to-make arts-and-crafts recipes are just what your students need to create their own masterpieces.

Homemade Play Dough

Use homemade play dough in place of expensive store brands for your next class project.

1 cup flour
1/2 cup salt
2 teaspoons cream of tartar
1 cup water
1 teaspoon vegetable oil
food coloring

Mix the dry ingredients. Then add the remaining ingredients and stir. In a heavy skillet, cook the mixture for two to three minutes, stirring frequently. Knead the dough until it becomes soft and smooth. Stir up several colors and store them in icing tubs.

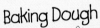

No-Cook Modeling Dough

Begin your next modeling project with a batch of this no-cook dough that's a snap to make!

2 cups flour
1 cup salt
water
food coloring or tempera paint
2 tablespoons vegetable oil (optional)

Mix the ingredients together. Add oil if you do not want the dough to harden.

Baking Dough

Bake this dough in the oven after your students use it to create their art projects.

2 cups flour
1 cup salt
water

Mix enough water with the dry ingredients to make a dough. Give each student a portion of the dough with which to work. After students create their master-pieces, bake the dough at 300° for about an hour—longer for thicker objects.

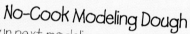

To-Die-For Dye

Use this simple method of dyeing to yield an abundance of bright and colorful art materials.

1/3 cup rubbing alcohol
food coloring
items to be dyed (beans, rice, macaroni, seeds, etc.)
waxed paper

Pour the rubbing alcohol into a container; then add food coloring to obtain the desired color. Drop the materials to be dyed into the liquid and let them soak for a few minutes. Finally spoon the mixture onto waxed paper to dry. The alcohol evaporates quickly, leaving the dyed objects ready for art.

Papier-Mâché

Stir up a quick-and-easy batch of papier-mâché to fan your students' 3-D creativity!

1 part liquid starch
1 part cold water
newspaper strips

Mix equal parts of liquid starch and cold water. Tear strips of newspaper, and dip each strip into the mixture before applying it to a form of chicken wire, rolled newspaper, or an inflated balloon.

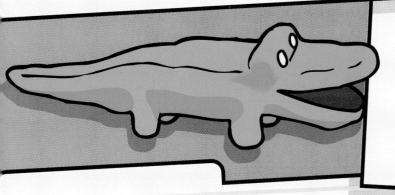

Salt Paint

Add an icy touch to winter pictures with salt paint.

2 teaspoons salt
1 teaspoon liquid starch
several drops of tempera paint

Mix the ingredients together and apply with a paintbrush. Then allow the painting to dry.

Shiny Paint

Give your next painting project a wet look with this easy recipe.

1 part white liquid glue
1 part tempera paint

Mix equal parts of liquid glue and tempera paint; then apply with a brush. Shiny paint provides a wet look even when its surface is dry.

Patterns

Use with "Fall-Foliage Magnets" on page 82.

Use with "Gingerbread-People Ornaments" on page 85.

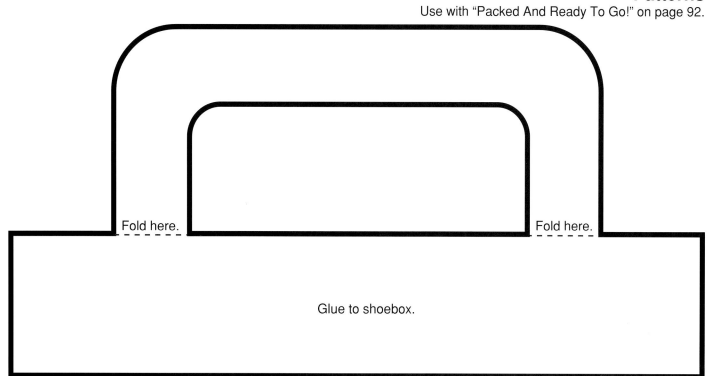

Fold here.

Fold here.

Glue to shoebox.

Use with "Field-Trip Name Badges" on page 94.

LEARNING CENTERS

LEARNING CENTERS

Stick To It!

Little space for centers? Then try this simple cure for the no-room blues:

1 Gather a file folder for each of your center ideas. Label each folder with a center's name.

2 Staple together each folder's sides to create a pocket.

3 Apply a strip of Velcro® to the back of each folder pocket; then attach its corresponding strip to an empty student desk.

4 Place the center's instructions, an answer key, and any needed materials inside each folder.

For a variation, attach a corresponding piece of Velcro® to each student's desk. When it's a student's turn to complete a center, attach the center's folder to his desk. After he finishes the center, move it to the next child's desk.

Four-In-One Center

Need a little space for a lot of fun and learning? Obtain a large appliance box from a local appliance store. Cut out one side of the box; then place three desks against the other three sides. Post a different learning center idea on the box in the area above each desk. Place materials for each center in or on each desk. Make the inside of the box a quiet-time reading center by placing a pillow in the center for a student to use while he's reading.

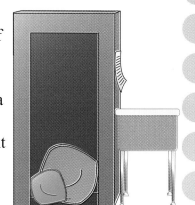

Learning Center Library

Think keeping track of your centers and student work is an impossible task? Follow these simple steps and you'll be organized in no time:

 1. Label a laminated chart with student names and center titles as shown on a wall.

 2. Position a desk below the chart. Put a hanging-file box and wipe-off marker on the desk.

 3. Label a folder with the name of each center activity. Store each activity in its folder; then place each folder in a separate hanging file in the box.

 4. When a student is ready to use a center, have him write a √ in the appropriate box next to his name.

 5. After the student finishes the activity and returns the folder to its file, have him draw an X over his original check.

Centers			
Student Name	Math Mania	Reading Roundup	Science Sources
John	✓		
Leslie		✓	
Anne	✗		
Joe			✓

Science Sources
Reading Roundup
Math Mania

Soda-Bottle Centers

Use this idea for a center that's bubbling with activity! Collect several empty, two-liter soda bottles and a matching number of index cards. Write an activity—such as those suggested below—on each card; then tape each card onto a bottle. Place the bottles and any materials at a center. Have each student visiting the center choose one of the bottles and complete its activity. After each student has completed one activity, have him share his work with the class; then reprogram each bottle with a new activity card.

▶ Pretend you are stranded on a deserted island and want to send a message in a bottle to someone. Draw an illustration of your island. Include labeled pictures of your shelter, food sources, and the island's features. Then write a paragraph describing what a typical day is like for you.

▶ Estimate the number of beans that could be placed in this bottle. Then make a list of other items the same size that could be placed in the bottle.

▶ Your favorite wild animal is nearing extinction! Research the animal; then make a list of the things your animal must have to survive. Write these items on a bottle cutout labeled "Bubble, Bubble, The (name of animal) Is In Trouble!"

▶ What issue is really bothering you? It can be a situation that concerns the world, your country, your state, your community, your home, or your school. Write a paragraph that begins "I'm tired of bottling up my opinion about…"

Great Greeting Cards

Descriptive sentences are in the cards with this fun center idea! Collect a supply of used greeting cards from various holidays. Cut off the front of each card. On the back of each card, draw a blank for a student's name and the numbers 1–5 with blanks as shown. Laminate the cards; then place them in a decorated box or folder. Place the box and several wipe-off markers at a center.

Direct each student visiting the center to use a marker to label any five cards with her name. Then have her fill in each blank with a different adjective describing the scene in the card's picture. Finally direct the student to use four of the adjectives on one card to write a brief paragraph about the card's picture.

Name: Liz
1. colorful
2. festive
3. warm
4. fun
5. bright

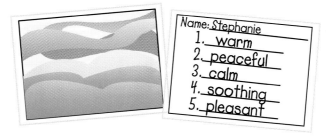

Name: Stephanie
1. warm
2. peaceful
3. calm
4. soothing
5. pleasant

Name: Debra
1. snowy
2. happy
3. cold
4. cheerful
5. jolly

Gift Bag Centers

Sharpening critical-thinking skills is in the bag with this fun idea! Gather several decorative gift bags. Duplicate a copy of the gift tags on page 107 onto construction paper. Then cut out each tag and punch a hole at the top of each one. Next label each tag with an intangible gift and a critical-thinking question such as one of those below. Use colorful ribbon to tie each labeled tag to a bag; then place the bags at a center.

Instruct a student visiting the center to choose one of the gift bags, then write a paragraph or story that answers the question on the bag's tag. After the student finishes her story, have her place it in the bag for her classmates to read.

Gift: Love
If you were to give this gift to someone close to you, how would you do it?

Gift: Kindness
Who do you think needs this gift most and why?

Gift: Laughter
Who most recently gave this gift to you, and what will you do with it?

Gift: Knowledge and Wisdom
Who would you give this gift to and why?

Movie Mania

Has your filmstrip projector become a dinosaur during this age of the VCR? If so, blow the dust off it! First place a project board or piece of cardboard (to use as a screen) at a desk as shown. Place the projector, a cassette player, and a set of headphones on the desk. Then choose a filmstrip and an accompanying activity, such as taking notes, writing an evaluative paragraph, or creating original frame captions. Write the activity directions on a large index card; then place the card, and the filmstrip and its cassette at the center. Finally have each student visit the center and experience a little bit of movie mania for himself!

☼ ☼ ☼ Easy As ABC ☼ ☼ ☼

Helping your students practice their spelling words has never been so easy! Place a set of small plastic letters or one-inch letter patterns at a center. Also supply the center with the week's spelling list, brightly colored sheets of construction paper, markers, scissors, and masking tape. Have each student visiting the center use the plastic letters or patterns and a pencil to trace each of his spelling words onto a sheet of construction paper. Next have the student use the markers to decorate each spelling word; then have him cut out each word. Finally have the student use tape to post his words on the wall near the center.

Picturing Mystery Stories

Put excitement into your students' stories with the following mystery-filled center:

1. Label each of five different-colored pocket folders with one of these titles: *Suspect, Victim, Detective, Setting,* and *Clues.*

2. Cut out 10–15 magazine pictures for each folder. Select pictures of real or imaginary people, places, and objects.

3. Glue each picture to a different sheet of construction paper; then put each picture in its appropriate folder. Place the folders at a center.

4. Have each student visiting the center take one picture from each folder. (If desired, have him take more than one clue picture.) Then have the student write a nonviolent mystery story that incorporates the pictures.

5. After each student has written his story, have him share it with the class.

Big Words

Increase your students' vocabularies in a BIG way with this "dino-mite" activity! Duplicate the pattern on page 108. Color the pattern, cut it out, and glue it on a sheet of poster board. Label the poster as shown; then laminate it. Next place the poster and several wipe-off markers at a center. Divide students into groups of five. Instruct each group to research the word for information about each topic listed on the poster. Have the first group to find all of the information use the wipe-off markers to write its findings on the poster. At the beginning of the next week, erase the board and write a new big word for students to research.

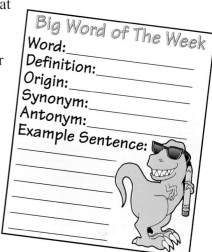

Big Word of The Week
Word:_____
Definition:_____
Origin:_____
Synonym:_____
Antonym:_____
Example Sentence:_____

4x6=   8x8=   9x7=   5x3=

Shovelful Of Math

Want to dig up some math fun? It's as easy as A, B, "Sea"! Duplicate the shell patterns on the bottom of page 107 onto construction paper. Laminate the paper and cut out each shell. Use a wipe-off marker to write a math problem on the front of each shell and its answer on the back. Place the shells in a bucket; then put the bucket, a shovel, and a timer at a center. Direct each student visiting the center to scoop some shells out of the bucket; then, on a sheet of paper, have her complete as many of the problems as she can in one minute. After the student completes the problems, have her turn over each shell and check her answer. When everyone has finished the activity, simply wipe off the shells and reprogram them with new problems.

Paper-Clip Math

For a hands-on center that combines math and science, look no farther than the paper clips inside your desk drawer! First duplicate page 109 for each student. Place the reproducibles and an answer key (see page 316) at a center along with jumbo and regular-size paper clips, a ruler, and a balancing scale. Instruct each student to follow the directions on the reproducible to complete the activities. Finally have the student use the answer key to correct her sheet.

Measuring Up

How do your students' measuring skills measure up? For an easy-to-do center that sharpens measurement skills, duplicate the reproducible on page 110 for each student. Place the reproducibles and a standard measuring tape at a center. Direct one pair of students to the center. Instruct each student, in turn, to measure her body parts and record her measurements on the reproducible. Then direct the student to use these measurements to answer the questions on the sheet. Finally have the pair check each other's work, then set up the center for the next pair of students.

Tape Measure

Spin And Spell

Invite students to sit, spin, and spell with this fun center! Divide a large tagboard circle into 24 sections. Color each section; then laminate the wheel. Use a wipe-off marker to label each section with a spelling word. Next create a spinner by attaching a brad fastener and a large paper clip at the center of the circle as shown.

Place the wheel at a center; then invite two students at a time to play. In turn, have each student spin the wheel while his partner closes his eyes. Have the student who spins the wheel read aloud the word on which the spinner lands, then direct his partner to spell the word. If the partner spells the word correctly, he earns two points. Direct students to continue until one player earns 20 points. After each student has played the game, wipe the wheel clean and reprogram it with the new week's spelling words.

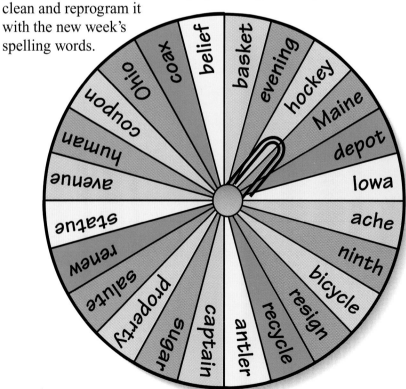

Patterns
Use with "Shovelful Of Math" on page 105.

Pattern
Use with "Big Words" on page 105.

Paper-Clip Math

Here's a fun activity that uses those small, shiny, metallic objects found in schools, offices, and homes around the world—paper clips! Use a supply of small and large paper clips, a metric and customary ruler, and a balancing scale to complete each of the activities below. Record the answers to each activity in the blanks provided.

1. Measure and record the number of small paper clips it takes to equal two grams. _____
   Measure and record the number of large paper clips it takes to equal two grams. _____
   About how many small paper clips equal the weight of one large paper clip? _____

2. Put ten small paper clips on one side of a balancing scale.
   About how many large paper clips do you have to put on the other side of the scale to make it balance? _____

3. Measure the length in inches of one small paper clip. _____
   Measure the length in inches of one large paper clip. _____
   About how much longer is the larger paper clip? _____

4. Arrange the small paper clips end-to-end in a line that measures about six inches in length.
   About how many paper clips are in the line? _____
   About how many large paper clips would it take to make this line? _____

5. Line up six large and six small paper clips end-to-end.
   About how long is this line in inches? _____
   About how long is this line in centimeters? _____

6. Arrange the large paper clips in a circle so that the diameter of the circle is six inches.
   (Diameter is the measurement of an imaginary line that passes through a circle's center.)
   About how many paper clips are in the circle? _____
   About how many paper clips do you have to remove from the circle for the diameter to equal three inches? _____

7. Make a circle with 20 small paper clips.
   About how many inches in diameter is this circle? _____

8. Make a square that has three small paper clips and three large paper clips on each of its sides. Measure one side to the nearest inch.
   About how long is each side of the square in inches?_____
   What is the perimeter *(4 x the length of one side)* of the square in inches? _____
   What is the area *(length x width)* of the square in square inches? _____

Note To The Teacher: Use this with "Paper-Clip Math" on page 106. Provide each student (or small group of students) with a supply of small and large paper clips, a metric and customary ruler, a balancing scale, a copy of this page, and a pencil.

How Do You Measure Up?

Find out just how you measure up with the following measurement activities. Following the diagram below, use a measuring tape to measure each of the body parts named. Then record each measurement on the blank beside its picture. Use this information to answer the questions on the right.

1. If you meet a basketball player who is 7 feet tall, how much taller will he (or she) be than you? _____ ft. _____ in.

2. How long would a shin guard have to be to cover the length from your knee to your ankle? _____ in.

3. Imagine that your waist doubles in size in the next 10 years. How big will it be? _____ in.

4. How tall would you like to be when you are 20 years old? _____ ft. _____ in.
   How much taller will you have to grow to reach that height? _____ ft. _____ in.

5. Imagine that the Statue of Liberty's nose is 4 feet 6 inches in length. How much longer is it than your nose? _____ ft. _____ in.

6. Add the length of your arm and the length of your shin. What is the total? _____ ft. _____ in.

7. About how many of your feet would you have to line up end-to-end to equal 36 inches?

8. How much bigger is your waist than your neck? _____ in.

9. If 2 1/2 centimeters is equal to 1 inch, how many centimeters long is your hand? _____ cm

10. If two other students' heads measure the same as yours, what will be the total circumference? _____ in.

Height from the top of head to the bottom of feet:
_____ ft. _____ in.

Circumference (distance around a circle) of head: _____ in.

Length of nose: _____ in.

Length from shoulder to wrist: _____ in.

Circumference of neck: _____ in.

Length from wrist to tip of index finger: _____ in.

Circumference of waist: _____ in.

Length from knee to ankle: _____ in.

Length of foot: _____ in.

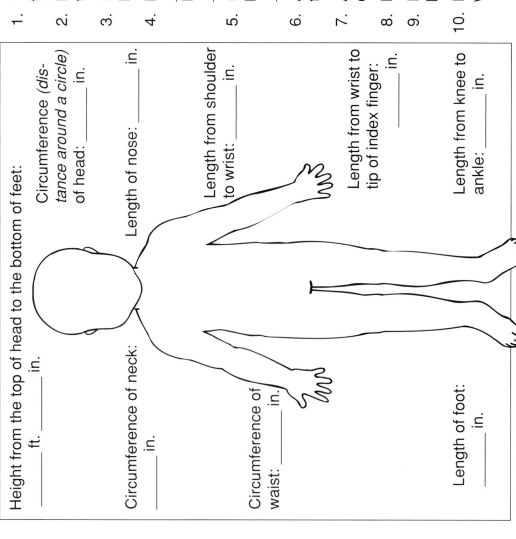

Note To The Teacher: Use with "Measuring Up" on page 106.

GAMES

Gold Diggers

Get your students diggin' up answers with this subject-centered scavenger hunt. Create a list of 10–15 review questions that cover a variety of subjects. Divide students into pairs. Duplicate and distribute to each pair a copy of the questions. Challenge the pair to go for the gold and answer 100 percent (or another percentage) of the questions correctly. Direct the pair to search its textbooks and other resources for the answer to each question. Have the pair record an answer, name of reference, and answer-page number for each question on the back of its sheet. After 20 minutes, discuss students' findings. Award students who answer the appropriate percentage of questions correctly with pieces of candy wrapped in gold-colored paper.

Think Tank

Provide your students the opportunity for daily critical thinking with this yearlong contest. Turn a small bulletin board into a think tank by covering it with blue background paper and mounting a large fish pattern in the center as shown. Next duplicate multiple copies of the hooks and small fish patterns (page 119) onto different-colored sheets of paper. Cut out the fish and hook patterns. Place the fish in a small bowl near your desk along with some pushpins or tape. Post the hooks at the top of the think tank with pushpins.

Each morning post a critical-thinking problem or question—such as a math word problem, a logic puzzle, or an analogy—on the bulletin board. Instruct each student to solve the problem during his free time. Then, at the end of the day, have several student volunteers share their answers and the strategies used to solve the problem. Have each student who answered correctly pull a fish out of the bowl, write his name on the fish, and attach it to the think-tank display.

At the end of the month, give a student volunteer a hook from the display. Stand the student in front of the display, blindfold him, and turn him around in a circle. Then have the student pin or tape the hook onto the display. Reward the student whose fish is "caught" with a small prize. Finally clear the names from the display and start the contest over.

Jeopardy® Game Sheet

Categories	$10	$20	$30	$40	$50
Plant Parts	A: Q:	A: Q:	A: Q:	A: Q:	A: Q:
How Plants Reproduce	A: Q:	A: Q:	A: Q:	A: Q:	A: Q:
Seeds	A: Q:	A: Q:	A: Q:	A: Q:	A: Q:
Photosynthesis	A: Q:	A: Q:	A: Q:	A: Q:	A: Q:
Parts Of A Flower	A: Q:	A: Q:	A: Q:	A: Q:	A: Q:
Plant Uses	A: Q:	A: Q:	A: Q:	A: Q:	A: Q:

Jeopardy® Is The Name Of The Game!

If the answer is "a fun way to review information learned in school," then the question is, "What is Jeopardy®?"! Utilize this fun, educational game to reinforce facts and concepts throughout the year. First duplicate multiple copies of the "Jeopardy® Game Sheet" on page 120, and make a transparency of the sheet. If desired record the TV show's theme music. Place these items in a file folder for easy access throughout the year. Then, during any unit of study, pull out a copy of the game sheet to label with categories, questions, and answers. Label the game-sheet transparency with the same categories; then display the transparency on an overhead projector. Next divide your students into three teams. Begin the game by playing the theme music and reading aloud the category names. Instruct a student on Team 1 to select a category and dollar value. Read the corresponding answer from your game sheet, and give the student one minute to respond. If the student responds correctly, mark an *X* in the dollar-amount square; then record the dollar amount earned under his team's name on the chalkboard. If the student responds incorrectly, deduct that dollar amount from his team's score. (Do not give the correct response; the category may be chosen later.) Then move to a player on Team 2 and continue the game. The game is over when all categories have been chosen and correctly answered. The team with the highest dollar amount wins the game.

Lotto Review

It's not just the luck of the draw when it comes to this review game! First label a container "Lotto Review." Then have each student cut a sheet of paper into eight to ten strips. Direct each student to write his name on each strip and store the strips in a notebook or folder. Then, any time you have a review, ask students several lotto questions about the topic they are currently studying. Give each student time to record each answer in a complete sentence on one of his strips; then have him put his strips in the container. At the end of the day or review, pull several strips from the container. Reward each student whose name is pulled and who answered a question correctly with a small prize. Leave the remaining strips in the jar for later rounds of Lotto Review. Students will be more motivated to review when they realize that the more questions they answer, the better their chances for rewards.

Arthropods are insects that have exoskeletons and jointed legs.

Double Or Nothing

Review recently studied material with a game that encourages teamwork. Have each student write a question that pertains to a recent unit of study (and its answer) on a slip of paper. Collect the slips; then determine which questions you will use and the amount of points the winning team must earn. Next divide students into two teams and have each team stand in a line on one side of the classroom. Place a bell on a desk in the center of the classroom. Then read one of the questions aloud. Direct the first student on each team to quickly confer with her teammates about the answer, then go to the desk and ring the bell. If the first student to ring the bell answers correctly, award her team five points. If she answers incorrectly, allow the first student from the other team to answer. If the student on the opposing team answers correctly, award her team double the amount of points (ten). Continue to play the game until a team earns the winning number of points. Reward the team with a double-time treat such as double minutes of free-reading time or recess.

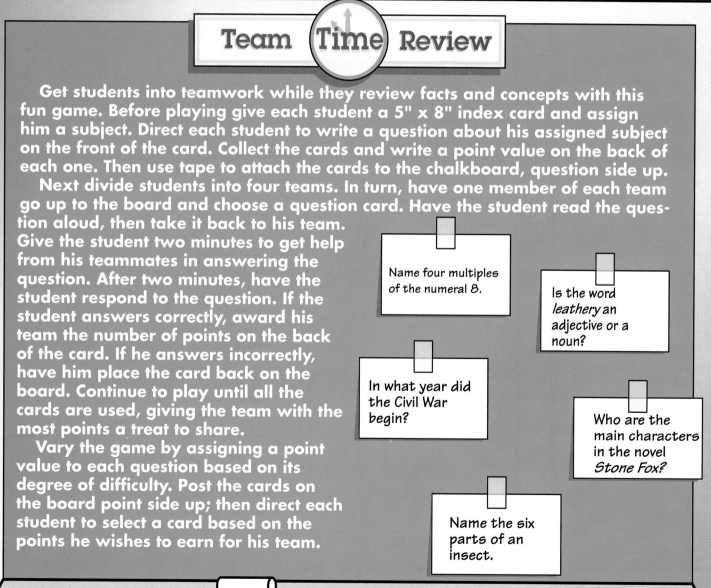

Team Time Review

Get students into teamwork while they review facts and concepts with this fun game. Before playing give each student a 5" x 8" index card and assign him a subject. Direct each student to write a question about his assigned subject on the front of the card. Collect the cards and write a point value on the back of each one. Then use tape to attach the cards to the chalkboard, question side up.

Next divide students into four teams. In turn, have one member of each team go up to the board and choose a question card. Have the student read the question aloud, then take it back to his team. Give the student two minutes to get help from his teammates in answering the question. After two minutes, have the student respond to the question. If the student answers correctly, award his team the number of points on the back of the card. If he answers incorrectly, have him place the card back on the board. Continue to play until all the cards are used, giving the team with the most points a treat to share.

Vary the game by assigning a point value to each question based on its degree of difficulty. Post the cards on the board point side up; then direct each student to select a card based on the points he wishes to earn for his team.

Name four multiples of the numeral 8.

Is the word *leathery* an adjective or a noun?

In what year did the Civil War begin?

Who are the main characters in the novel *Stone Fox?*

Name the six parts of an insect.

Buzzing About A Spelling Bee

Is your average spelling bee just that—*average?* Add this twist to the game and get your students buzzing! Obtain a supply of clothespins (one for each spelling word) and several gallon jugs. Divide your students into teams of four or five, and have each team stand in a row. In turn, give each team a spelling word. Direct the team to spell the word together, with each member saying a consecutive letter of the word until it is spelled. If the team spells the word correctly, award it with a clothespin and give the next team a new word. If the team spells the word incorrectly, give that word to the next team. After all the words have been spelled correctly, have each team place its jug on the floor and, one member at a time, try to drop its clothespins into the jug from a standing position. The team that drops the most clothespins into its jug wins.

Secret Words

Help your students build a strong vocabulary with this easy, spur-of-the-moment game. Compile a list of vocabulary words from various subjects. Write each word on a different index card. Shuffle the cards and stack them on a desk or table. Next divide students into teams of five. Have one person from the team go into the hallway while his teammates choose a word from the stack. Give each team member time to think of a clue about the selected word. Then have the student return to his team. In turn, have each teammate give a clue about the secret word, allowing the student to guess the word after each clue. If the student correctly guesses the word, award the team points based on the number of clues it took to guess it. If the student cannot guess the word in four clues or less, add five points to his team's score; then have his team return the card to the bottom of the stack and move on to the next team. Play until all cards have been used and/or each team has had an equal number of turns. The team with the lowest score wins.

POWER WORDS

Expanding your students' vocabularies will be in the bag with this fun, yearlong game. Attach a picture of a Power Ranger® or other superhero to a colorful gift bag. Label the bag "Power Words!" When you find your students overusing a weak word—such as *said*, *good*, or *walk*—label a slip of paper with the word and place it in the bag. Keep the bag in an accessible location, filling it with slips throughout the year. Then, whenever you have a few spare minutes, play the "Power Words" game with your students.

To play the game, divide students into teams of five. Direct a member from one team to pull a slip from the bag and read aloud the slip's word. In turn, have each team member give a more descriptive synonym for the word (see the examples below). Award the team one point for each powerful response; then have the next team take a slip from the bag. Play the game for as long as desired, giving each team an equal number of turns. The team with the most points wins. Have students return the slips to the bag for future games.

stated, expressed, grunted, shouted, whispered

said

POWER WORDS

Mental-Math Basketball Shoot

Keep your students' bodies *and* minds in shape with a math and basketball shoot-out! Take your class to your school's basketball court; then divide your students into two teams. Direct the teams to stand in two different lines at the baseline on one end of the court. Have one student from each team stand on his team's side of the opposite net to retrieve balls. Then use masking tape to mark team stopping points at various places on the court. (See the diagram.)

In turn, challenge one player on each team to a mental-math problem. If the player answers correctly, direct him to move to the first stopping point. If he answers incorrectly, direct him to go to the end of his team's line. As each team's player gives a correct response, have players progress to succeeding stopping points. Once a team's player reaches the free-throw line, have him shoot a basket. If he makes the basket, award his team two points and have him stand in for his ball retriever, who then goes to the end of his team's line. Play the game until each player has had a chance to answer a math question. Reward the team that has the most points with a special treat.

Four Heads Are Better Than One!

Challenge your students to put their heads together in this problem-solving extravaganza! Prepare a list of about ten math word problems. Next divide your students into teams of four; then give each team a sheet of paper, a pencil, and a signaling device such as a bell. Next write a math word problem on the chalkboard. Instruct members on each team to work together to solve the problem. As soon as a team completes the problem, have it sound its signaler, then give its answer. If the answer is correct, have the team explain how it arrived at the answer; then give it a point marker such as a game chip. If the team responds incorrectly, have the other teams continue solving the problem. After all the word problems have been solved, reward the team that has the most point markers with a special treat.

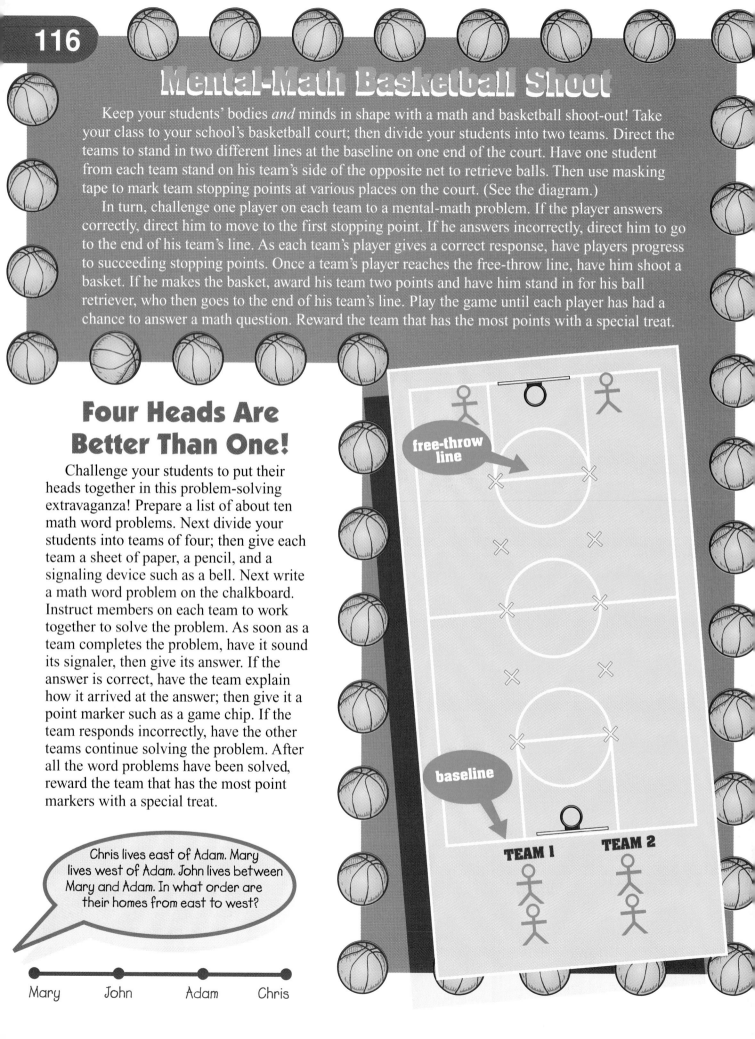

free-throw line

baseline

TEAM 1   TEAM 2

Chris lives east of Adam. Mary lives west of Adam. John lives between Mary and Adam. In what order are their homes from east to west?

●————●————●————●
Mary   John   Adam   Chris

Now You See It!

Give your students a chance to show you what they know about geography with this simple activity. Make a transparency of a blank outline map of a state, region, or country that your students are currently studying. Then label each of several index cards with the name of a state, capital city, landform, body of water, or other feature within that area. Place these cards facedown in a pile by the overhead projector. Next divide students into teams of four and give each team a different-colored wipe-off marker. In turn, have one student from each team select a card and mark the place or feature on the transparency map. If the student locates the place or feature correctly, have him keep the card. If he does not locate the place or feature correctly, have him wipe off his answer and return the card to the bottom of the pile. Continue the game until all of the places or features have been identified correctly; then reward the team that has the most cards with a special treat or homework passes.

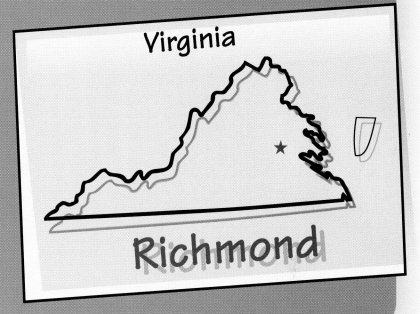

Is it a person?
Is this person alive today?
Was this person born before or after George Washington?

Abraham Lincoln

Your students will surely give this social-studies review game a thumbs-up for fun! Before beginning the game, write the name of a person, place, or event that is related to a current social-studies unit on a 4" x 6" index card. Make one card for each student in your class. Next cut different-colored sheets of construction paper into 2" x 18" strips. Create a headband by stapling the ends of each strip together; then staple each index card to the center of a different headband as shown.

Next divide students into groups of four or five. Distribute a headband to each student so that she does not see the front of her card. Then instruct each team member to take turns asking her teammates yes/no questions in order to gather clues about the person, place, or event listed on her headband. Direct each student to respond *yes* with a thumbs-up and *no* with a thumbs-down. Challenge each student to try to guess the person, place, or event in fewer than ten clues. Reward each student who does this with ten minutes of free time or ten bonus points on a social-studies assignment.

Five-Up Kick Ball

Your students are sure to get a kick out of this variation of a favorite outdoor game! Gather together five different-colored or patterned kick balls (or label each ball differently); five large jump ropes; and a base marker. Take your students and equipment out to a field area. Use the ropes to make five large circles at one end of the field. Space the circles about three feet apart and place one of the balls in each circle. Then designate a base about 40 feet away from the circles at the opposite end of the field.

Next choose five players to be up, and have each player stand in a circle while the other students stand in the outfield. At your signal, direct each of the five players to kick his ball into the outfield, run to the designated base, and run back again to his circle. At the same time, have the students in the outfield try to field one of the balls and return it to its appropriate circle before the kicker returns. If the kicker returns to her circle first, she gets to remain in the circle and kick again. If a fielder returns to the circle first, he remains in the circle to kick the next ball, and the kicker then becomes an outfielder. Continue to play the game until all students have been up to kick a ball.

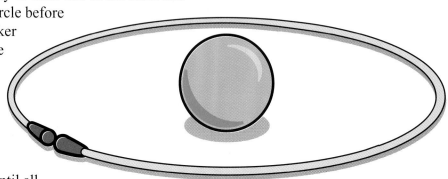

Zany, Crazy Relays

For a recess time that is sure to generate loads of laughter, organize a series of zany, crazy relays! Take your students out to a playground area. Mark a Start/Finish line and a halfway line. Next divide your class into teams of four or five, and have each team stand in a straight line behind the Start/Finish line. Before the race announce a zany direction for students to perform during the relay (see the examples listed below). Direct each student to perform the task from the Start line to the halfway line, then back again to the Finish line. As in any relay, have one team member at a time perform the task, then return to tag the next team member to go. Recognize the first team to finish the race; then give a new direction for the next relay.

- pirouette
- tango
- soldier walk
- duck waddle
- "walk like an Egyptian"
- hop on one foot
- play an imaginary instrument
- walk like a zombie
- crab walk
- use an imaginary Hula Hoop®

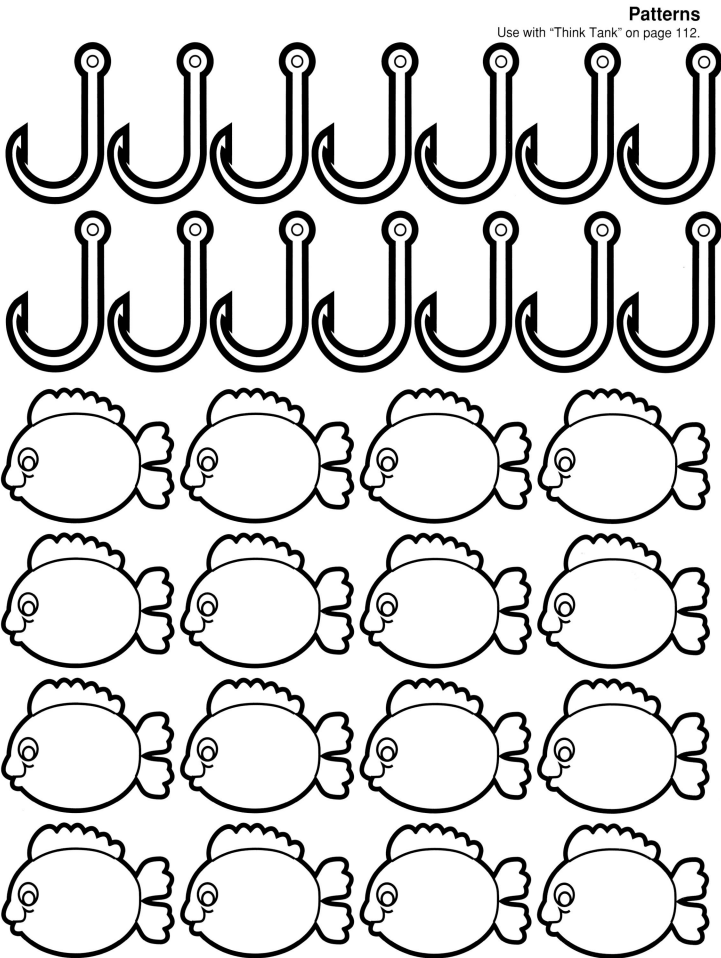

Jeopardy® Game Sheet

Categories	$10	$20	$30	$40	$50

Note To The Teacher: Use with "Jeopardy® Is The Name Of The Game!" on page 113. Fill in a category name in each space in the first column. Then write a corresponding answer and question in each dollar-value space. Make the answers/questions increasingly difficult as the dollar value increases.

SUBSTITUTE TEACHER TIPS

SUBSTITUTE TEACHER TIPS

Substitute Buddies

Team up with another teacher on your grade level to become substitute buddies. Learn each other's routines and organizational systems. When you are out for the day, have your buddy help your substitute by finding materials and answering any questions that arise. What an easy way to ensure things run smoothly in your absence!

Dear Substitute,
        Mrs. Newton in Room 25 will be more than happy to answer any questions you have. Have a great day.

Mrs. Kreger

Job Cards

Guarantee that your room will be in the same order as when you left with this simple suggestion. Write a different classroom job on each of several index cards. Number and laminate the cards. When you are absent, have the substitute pass out one card to each student at the end of the day for a trouble-free cleanup. Direct the sub to collect the cards by calling out the numbers once each job has been completed.

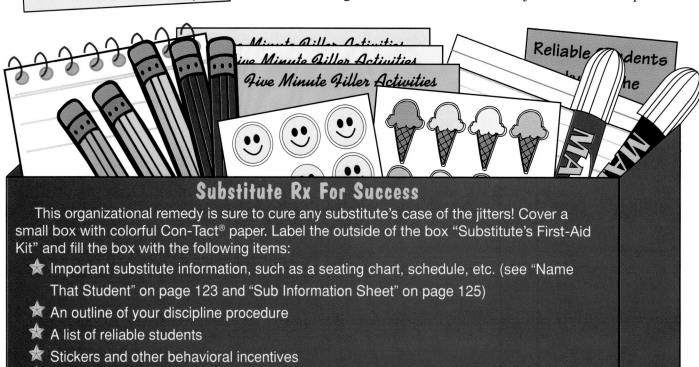

Substitute Rx For Success

This organizational remedy is sure to cure any substitute's case of the jitters! Cover a small box with colorful Con-Tact® paper. Label the outside of the box "Substitute's First-Aid Kit" and fill the box with the following items:

⭐ Important substitute information, such as a seating chart, schedule, etc. (see "Name That Student" on page 123 and "Sub Information Sheet" on page 125)

⭐ An outline of your discipline procedure

⭐ A list of reliable students

⭐ Stickers and other behavioral incentives

⭐ A list of several favorite class games

⭐ Pens and pencils

⭐ Index cards labeled with quick, five-minute filler activities

⭐ Nonperishable munchies, such as granola bars, crackers, candy, etc.

⭐ Change for the soda or coffee machine

⭐ An evaluation form to fill out at the end of the day

Place the kit on your desk beside your lesson plans when you are going to be absent.

Name That Student

Help your substitute familiarize himself with your students' names with the aid of easy-to-make name cards. Have each student fold a large index card in half lengthwise and label it with her name. Collect students' cards and rubber band them together. Keep the name cards with your other substitute materials. Direct your substitute to have each student stand her name card on her desk when you are absent. These cards are much easier to read than a seating chart!

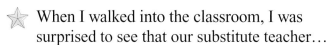

Emily   Jake

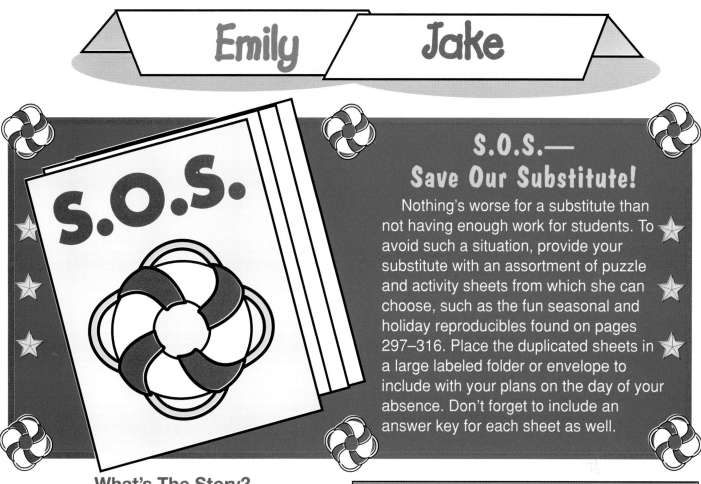

S.O.S.— Save Our Substitute!

Nothing's worse for a substitute than not having enough work for students. To avoid such a situation, provide your substitute with an assortment of puzzle and activity sheets from which she can choose, such as the fun seasonal and holiday reproducibles found on pages 297–316. Place the duplicated sheets in a large labeled folder or envelope to include with your plans on the day of your absence. Don't forget to include an answer key for each sheet as well.

What's The Story?

Get your substitute off to a great start with a list of creative story starters. Direct her to use any extra class time to have each student write a creative story using one of the following writing topics:

- ☆ When I walked into the classroom, I was surprised to see that our substitute teacher…

- ☆ Our substitute teacher screamed when…

- ☆ If I could have any person in the world as my substitute teacher…

- ☆ I couldn't believe it when our substitute said…

- ☆ If I were asked to be the substitute teacher…

- ☆ I knew our substitute was no ordinary teacher when…

- ☆ Our substitute teacher laughed out loud when…

I couldn't believe it when our substitute said...

Our substitute teacher laughed out loud when...

If I were asked to be the substitute teacher...

Emergency Plans

Unfortunately not all absences can be predicted. Prepare in advance for an unplanned absence by writing up a set of emergency lesson plans. Place a copy of your schedule, a seating chart, and a collection of activities from which the substitute can choose in a labeled folder. Leave these lesson plans in an easily accessible location or give them to a co-worker. If an emergency situation occurs, you'll have one less thing to worry about because your plans will be ready.

Emergency Plans

Planning Time-Saver

Make preparing sub plans a snap with the help of a pre-made outline. At the beginning of the year, make a skeleton outline of your daily schedule. Keep several copies of the outline at school and at home. When you need to make sub plans, simply fill in the outline with specific plans for the date of your absence. The outline saves you from having to rewrite the same information each time you need a substitute and gives you more time to concentrate on feeling better!

8:30–9:00 Arrival/Morning Work
9:00–9:30 Spelling
9:30 Reading
10:30 Social Studies
11:30 Lunch   12:30 Math
1:00 P.E.   1:30 Art   2:00 Science
3:00 Line up for bus

Student Accountability

Foster responsible student behavior in your absence by directing your substitute to provide each student with a copy of the "Student Behavior And Assignment Checklist" on page 126. Have the substitute give each student a sheet as he arrives in the morning; then have her direct the child to fill out his assignments and rate his behavior for the day. Ask the substitute to collect each student's form for you and record any additional information she would like you to know. When you return, you will have a written record of each child's performance while you were out.

✔ Student Behavior And Assignment Checklist ✔
(To be filled out by the student)

Name Andrew Johnson   Date March 26, 1998
Substitute Teacher Mrs. Gleason
Fill in your assignments for each subject as they are assigned today.

Subject	Assignment
Reading	Read pg. 140–148
Spelling	Study List Number 37
Math	Read pg. 156–162 Prob. *6, 8, 10, 12
Social Studies	Fill out worksheet
Science	Bring in a plastic container

Behavior rating (circle one):   Excellent   (Good)   Fair   Poor
How did your day go? I like Mrs. Gleason. She is very nice. I would like her to come back again.
Student signature: Andrew Johnson
Teacher's comments: Andrew was a good helper. He completed all his classwork for the day.

Teacher signature: Mrs. Gleason

Early Finishers

Prepare your substitute for students who finish their work early with this idea. In a labeled box near your desk, place instructions and materials for completing a simple art project such as those suggested below. Your students will love sharing their masterpieces with you when you return! Simple Art Activities:

Let students use ink pads, paper, and fine-tipped markers to make pictures populated with thumbprint animals and creatures.

Provide each child with art paper and crayons to use to draw and color a portrait of you.

Have each child trace his hand on art paper and cut out the tracing. Next have the student label the cutout with the title and author of a favorite book, then decorate it. Have students glue their cutouts to a large piece of poster board that's been labeled "Our Hands-Down Favorite Books!" Mount the poster near the classroom library.

Our Hands-Down Favorite Books!

SUB INFORMATION SHEET

General Information

Teacher _____

Room Number _____

Principal _____

Assistant Principal _____

Secretary _____

Nurse _____

Guidance Counselor _____

Custodian _____

Grade-Level Teachers _____

Aide(s) _____

Special Teachers (name, day of week, time)

Music _____

Art _____

P.E. _____

Media Specialist _____

Resource _____

Other _____

Children With Special Needs

Health _____

Supervision _____

Learning _____

Schedule

Recess _____ Lunch _____

Bathroom Break _____

Other _____

Procedures

Attendance _____

Lunch/Milk Count _____

Before School _____

Beginning Class _____

Assignment Collection _____

Free Time _____

Behavior/Discipline _____

Fire Drill/Severe Weather _____

Ending Class _____

✔ Student Behavior And Assignment Checklist ✔

(To be filled out by the student)

Name_____ Date_____

Substitute Teacher_____

Fill in your assignments for each subject as they are assigned today.

Subject	Assignment

Behavior rating (circle one):   Excellent   Good   Fair   Poor

How did your day go?_____

_____

Student signature:_____

Teacher's comments:_____

_____

Teacher signature:_____

A NOTE FROM THE SUB...

Today we were able to accomplish _____

_____

_____

_____

I thought the lesson plans were _____

_____

Additional comments: _____

_____

_____

_____

_____

_____

Signed: _____   Date: _____

Note To The Teacher: See "Student Accountability" on page 124 for how to use "Student Behavior And Assignment Checklist."
Duplicate "A Note From The Sub…" and include a copy in your substitute folder.

LANGUAGE ARTS

GRAMMAR

A CAPITAL IDEA

Looking for a fun way to teach students the basic rules of capitalization? Give each student a copy of page 145 and have him complete its activity. Once all students have finished, divide them into groups of three or four. Direct each group's members to review the answers on page 145; then have them create a series of capitalization rules based on those answers. Next give each group a copy of the reference sheet on page 140. Instruct the group to compare its list of capitalization rules to those on the reference sheet. Conclude by discussing with students the different situations in which capitalization is needed.

OUR CAPITALIZATION RULES

1. Capitalize proper nouns.
2. Capitalize state abbreviations.
3. Capitalize the title of a book.
4. Capitalize the title of a magazine.
5. Capitalize months of the year.
6. Capitalize days of the week.

PICTURING COMMAS

Give students practice using commas with this hands-on activity. Begin by having each child cut out ten pictures of nouns from magazines. Have the student mount each picture on a separate sheet of 4" x 4" paper, then spread the pictures facedown on his desk. Next direct each student to walk around the classroom and collect a total of ten pictures from classmates' desks. A student cannot take more than one picture from a desk, look at a picture before he selects it, or put a picture back once it's been chosen.

Once each student has collected ten pictures, have him return to his desk and look them over. On the chalkboard post the rules for comma usage found on page 142. Have each student write a story about his ten nouns, using at least four different comma-usage rules. Have each student share his story and pictures; then have him point out the four comma rules he followed as he wrote.

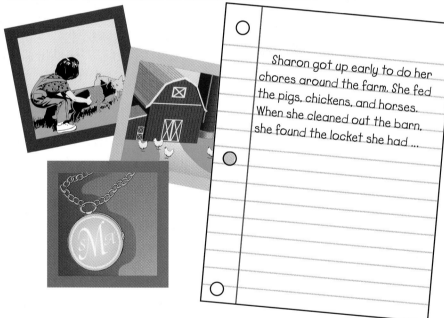

Sharon got up early to do her chores around the farm. She fed the pigs, chickens, and horses. When she cleaned out the barn, she found the locket she had ...

COMMA SCAVENGER HUNT

Send students on a hunt for that pesky punctuation mark, the often confusing comma! Divide your class into groups of five. Review the comma rules found on page 142. Then challenge each group to use textbooks, novels, or other written material to find sentences that illustrate each of the rules. Set a time limit of 15 minutes for the search. Then direct each group to copy each sentence it finds to demonstrate a rule, along with the book's title and the page number. Award one point for each correct example; then declare the team with the most points the winner.

COMICAL CONVERSATIONS

Look no further than the funny papers the next time you want to teach punctuation of direct quotations! Have each student cut one of her favorite comic strips from the newspaper (one that features at least two characters talking with each other). Then challenge each student to take the dialogue in the conversation bubbles and rewrite it as a conversation using quotation marks. Direct the student to write the dialogue so that a person reading it could understand what was happening in the comic without viewing it. Title a bulletin board "Comical Conversations"; then post each student's conversation and its comic strip on the board.

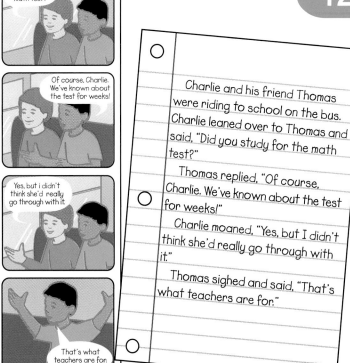

Did you study for the math test?

Of course, Charlie. We've known about the test for weeks!

Yes, but i didn't think she'd really go through with it.

That's what teachers are for.

Charlie and his friend Thomas were riding to school on the bus. Charlie leaned over to Thomas and said, "Did you study for the math test?"

Thomas replied, "Of course, Charlie. We've known about the test for weeks!"

Charlie moaned, "Yes, but I didn't think she'd really go through with it."

Thomas sighed and said, "That's what teachers are for."

BUILDING GREAT SENTENCES

Add a new dimension to your study of punctuation with this fun activity! Collect and thoroughly wash 50–60 small milk cartons from your school's cafeteria. Then divide your class into groups of four. Give each group ten milk cartons, scissors, tape, markers, paper, and glue. Have each group follow these directions:

1. Make a box from each carton by taping the spout down; then cover each box with paper.
2. Write beginning quotation marks on each side of one box. Write ending quotation marks on each side of another box.
3. On each side of a third box, write a different word for *said*, such as *yelled, moaned,* or *shouted.*
4. On each side of a fourth box, write a different person's name.
5. Label each side of a fifth box with a comma.
6. Label two sides of a sixth box with a question mark, two sides with an exclamation mark, and two sides with a period.
7. Give each group member one of the remaining four boxes. Each group member should write a sentence on each side of his box, making sure there is at least one declarative, one imperative, one exclamatory, and one interrogative sentence on his box. Do NOT put any ending punctuation marks on these sentences.
8. Use all of your group's boxes to build sentences that are direct quotations. Write at least ten of the sentences on a sheet of paper.

NAMING COMMON NOUNS

Use this uncommonly good activity to teach students the ins and outs of common nouns. Cut out 26 paper squares; then write one letter of the alphabet on each square and place the squares in a bag. Divide students into groups of three or four. In turn, draw a letter from the bag for each group. Challenge each group to think of four common nouns—one person, one place, one thing, and one idea— that begin with that letter. Award a group one point for each common noun it correctly names. Continue pulling letters from the bag until each group has had several turns. Conclude by totaling each group's points and declaring the team with the most points the winner.

GETTING PROPER WITH NOUNS

Help your students better understand the concept of proper nouns with this exciting lesson. Divide students into groups of three or four. Call out a category from the following list: candy bars, countries, actors, teachers, buildings, restaurants, continents, cereals, holidays, cars, and state capitals. Then direct the group to write down as many proper nouns that fit into the category as possible. For example, if you said "cereals," each group would list as many specific names of cereals as it could. After one minute, direct each group to share its proper nouns. Award one point to the group with the longest list. Continue play by calling out a new category.

PRONOUN POUNCE

Watch students pounce right on this fun pronoun lesson! Instruct each child to bring in a newspaper article. Then review the definitions of subject and object pronouns:

SUBJECT PRONOUN
used as the subject of a sentence
singular—**I, you, he, she, it**
plural—**we, you, they**

OBJECT PRONOUN
used after an action verb or in a prepositional phrase
singular—**me, you, him, her, it**
plural—**us, you, them**

Provide each student with a highlighter. Then have him "pounce" on any subject pronoun he sees in his newspaper article by highlighting it. Remind students to look for pronouns included in contractions. Have each student use a different colored highlighter to find the object pronouns in the text. Ask student volunteers to share examples of each of the pronouns they found in their articles.

Boy Rescues Dog From Drainage Pipe

Staff writer J.J. Johnson

New York—Late yesterday evening a young boy from the Bronx rescued a stray dog from certain death. The dog had fallen into a drainage pipe and gotten its leg caught. The boy used a rope to get down to the dog. He then freed the dog's leg, lifted him from the water, and helped him back to safety. This isn't the first time the boy has been a hero. He once rescued a cat that had climbed too high in a tree.

ACTION-PACKED VERBS

Get students excited about verbs with this action-packed activity! Have each student bring in a magazine picture or a photo showing someone doing a specific action, such as running, biking, or gardening. Direct the student to write a sentence using the action verb depicted in her photograph on a sentence strip. Next have the student write the same sentence on the back of the strip, replacing the action verb with the actual picture. Post each sentence strip on a bulletin board titled "Action-Packed Verbs!" Challenge students to identify the missing action verb on each strip.

My brother Timmy the final ball to win the baseball game.

My friend Denise loves to 🪢 rope.

A WORLD OF PROPER NOUNS

Discover more about the world of proper nouns with an activity that combines grammar and map skills. Give each pair of students a world map, a dictionary, and a copy of page 146. When each pair is finished with the reproducible, review the countries listed by students as well as the proper nouns that name the inhabitants of those nations. Extend the activity by playing a trivia game. Give the name of a nationality such as *Swedish;* then have a student volunteer find the country of origin on a world map.

S.O.S!

Give students a heaping helping of helping verbs with this game!

1 Write each of these helping verbs on a separate index card: **is, are, am, was, were, been, shall, could, will, should, would, must, may, can, might, have, had, has, do, did.** Place the cards in an empty S.O.S.® steel wool soap pads box.

2 Divide your class into two teams, lined up opposite each other.

3 Have the first person on Team One pull a card from the box without showing it to Team Two.

4 Have the first person on Team Two name an action verb. Give Team One's player one minute to correctly use his helping verb in a sentence with that action verb. He must keep the root word of the action verb but can change the tense to agree with the helping verb. Let the student call out "S.O.S!" if he wants help from the teammate standing directly behind him.

5 At the end of the minute, award a point to Team One if its player is able to give a correct sentence. Award the point to Team Two if the sentence is incorrect.

6 Return the card to the box; then have both players go to the ends of their lines. Begin the next round by having the teams switch roles.

PAPER FIGHT!

Get students out of their seats and into learning
with this kid-pleasin' activity!

✳ Label each of the four corners of your room with a sentence type—declarative, imperative, interrogative, or exclamatory.

✳ On one sheet of paper for each student, write one of the four sentence types.

✳ Crumple each paper into a ball; then distribute the balls to students.

✳ At your command, have students throw the paper balls at one another (reminding students not to throw at anyone's head).

✳ Say, "Stop!" Then have each student pick up a paper ball, read what is written on it, and go to the corner labeled with that sentence type.

✳ Once each student has gone to his corner, name a general topic such as "homework," "school," or "vacation." Direct the students in each corner to work together to make up a sentence on the topic that is also of the same type as the corner's label. For example, if the topic is "homework," the students in the interrogative corner might make up the sentence "What is our science homework?"

✳ Have each corner group share its sentence; then direct each student to recrumple his paper and play the game again.

imperative

declarative

interrogative

exclamatory

SUBJECT AND PREDICATE DICE

With a simple roll of the dice, your students will be writing some terrific sentences—and learning about subjects and predicates, too! Give each student two copies of page 147, scissors, glue, and markers or colored pencils. Have each student follow the directions on the page to make two dice. Then direct her to roll her dice and write a sentence on her paper using the two words rolled. The noun she rolls will be the sentence's subject and the verb will begin the sentence's predicate. Allow the student to add as many words as needed to her two core words to make a complete sentence. Also remind her to make the subject and predicate agree. Invite each student to share her sentence; then have her swap her dice with a classmate and come up with a new sentence!

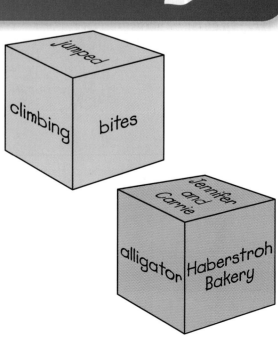

SENTENCE SURGEONS

This lesson on sentence formation is just what the doctor ordered! Explain to students that a sentence fragment is a group of words that does not express a complete thought because it is missing important information such as a subject or verb. Give each student three index cards. Have the student write "subject" on the first card, "predicate" on the second, and "complete" on the third card. Next tell students that you have some sentences that are in need of an examination. Explain that each student must make a diagnosis by telling what a sentence needs in order to be complete. Display one sentence at a time, alternating sentence fragments with complete sentences. Direct each student to hold up the "predicate" card if the sentence is missing a predicate, "subject" if it is missing a subject, and "complete" if it is a complete sentence.

SUBJECT-VERB CARD GAME

Sharpen subject-verb agreement skills with this fun card game. Duplicate one copy of page 148 on sturdy paper for each student pair. Have each pair cut out its cards and place them in two facedown stacks—a subject stack and a verb stack. Direct the first student to take a card from each stack and decide if the pair demonstrates subject-verb agreement. If the subject-verb pair is in agreement, the student keeps the cards. If the pair is not in agreement, he must put the cards into a discard pile. Direct each pair to take turns until the original decks are gone; then have each student count the number of pairs he has earned. The player with the most pairs wins the round.

Vary the game by having students play it like the popular card game Slap Jack. Have one student draw the top card in the subject pile and lay it down while the other player draws the top verb card and lays it down. If the pair matches, the first person to slap the card he did not draw wins the card pair. Have the students discard the card pairs that are not in agreement. At the end of the game, have each player count his card pairs to determine the winner.

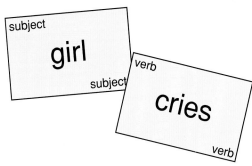

READING

THE CASE FOR CAUSE AND EFFECT

Teach students to recognize cause and effect with this easy idea. Make a two-column chart on your board, labeling one column "cause" and the other "effect." Then list the examples shown below in the chart. Encourage students to suggest additional examples, adding each to the chart.

After completing the chart, have each student look through the novel your class is currently reading, textbooks, or other printed material to find five examples of cause-and-effect relationships. Direct the student to write the five examples on a sheet of paper; then have her share with the class. Finally give each student a sheet of construction paper. Have her fold the paper in half, reopen it, and write "cause" on the top left side and "effect" on the top right side. Then instruct the student to illustrate her favorite cause-and-effect example on the paper.

cause	effect
Andrew jumped in the puddle.	Andrew splashed water on his new pants.
The dog wanted to come inside.	The dog barked loudly until his owner let him in.
Leslie was hungry.	Leslie bought a sandwich from the deli.

Just The Facts…And Opinions, Please!

Here's a nifty activity that "ads" up to great facts-and-opinions practice! Ask students to describe the ways advertisers try to persuade consumers to buy their products. Ask, "Do advertisements contain facts or opinions?" Then explain that most advertising contains both facts and opinions. Challenge each student to look in a magazine or newspaper and cut out ads featuring examples of facts and/or opinions. Have each student divide a sheet of construction paper into two columns, gluing the examples of facts under a "fact" column and the examples of opinions under an "opinion" column. Display the completed projects on a bulletin board titled "Just The Facts…And Opinions, Please!"

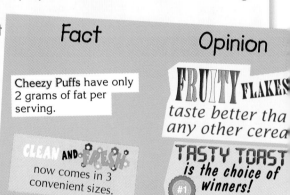

Fact

Cheezy Puffs have only 2 grams of fat per serving.

CLEAN AND FRESH now comes in 3 convenient sizes.

Opinion

FRUITY FLAKES taste better tha any other cerea

TASTY TOAST is the choice of #1 winners!

Drawing Conclusions

Help students jump to all the right conclusions with this activity! Ask students to describe times when they have been able to figure out the ending of a story or television show by drawing conclusions. Explain that people are able to draw conclusions about the ending based on what they learned in the story's beginning and middle. Next challenge each student to write a beginning and middle for a short original story (each in a separate paragraph) on a sheet of paper. On another sheet of paper, have the student write the story's ending. Have each student exchange his story's beginning and middle with a classmate. Then have him read the beginning and middle he receives and write his own ending for the story. Have the student also write several sentences identifying the information in the story's beginning and middle that led him to his conclusion. When he has finished, have the student compare his ending with the author's original ending.

ORDER UP!

Serve up some main-idea practice with this easy activity. Cut a construction-paper sheet into one-inch strips. Select a paragraph from a textbook or novel your class is reading; then copy each sentence from the paragraph onto a separate paper strip. Shuffle the strips and place them in a numbered envelope. Repeat the procedure with several additional paragraphs. Then make an answer key, giving the correct order for each paragraph. Place the envelopes and the answer key in a classroom center. Challenge each student who visits the center to select an envelope and find the sentence that tells about all of the other sentences—the main idea. Have the student put the remaining sentences in the correct order after the main idea and check her work with the answer key.

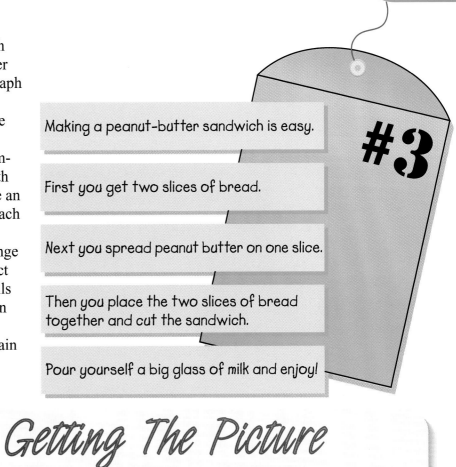

Making a peanut-butter sandwich is easy.

First you get two slices of bread.

Next you spread peanut butter on one slice.

Then you place the two slices of bread together and cut the sandwich.

Pour yourself a big glass of milk and enjoy!

#3

Angela Miller

1. The girl in the picture is at the beach.
Clues: She is wearing a bathing suit and sandals. She is carrying a sand bucket and the waves are crashing on the sand.

Getting The Picture

Help students develop inferencing skills with this picture-perfect activity! Cut out several magazine or catalog pictures that show people dressed for different events such as a beach party, sporting event, or church. One at a time, show each picture to students. As you share each picture, ask a question about it such as, "Where is the person in this picture going?" Have each student write the answer to your question on a sheet of paper, recording the clues in the picture that helped him infer his answer. After showing all of the pictures, have each student share his responses. Explain to students that many of their responses were similar because of what they inferred from the picture clues and their own experiences. Just like pictures, many of the stories we read contain information that is not directly stated. A reader often has to use sentence clues and his own personal experience to understand what he is reading. For additional inferencing practice, give each student a copy of "Collecting Clues" on page 149 to complete.

SPELLING and VOCABULARY

GET FLASHY WITH SPELLING!

Liven up your weekly spelling lessons with the help of flash cards. On Monday have each student make a set of spelling flash cards on colored cards. Then have students use the flash cards throughout the week in the following ways:

Independently:

- Look at a word card; then lay it facedown. Without looking at the card, write the word on a sheet of paper. After you've written all the words, check your spelling using the flash cards.

In Pairs:

- Combine your flash-card set with a friend's set. Shuffle the cards and place them facedown. Take turns selecting two cards to find a match. Turn mismatched cards back over; keep the matched pairs. When all cards have been matched, the player with the most matches is the winner.

- Combine your flash-card set with a friend's set and play Go Fish!

Whole Class:

- Place your cards faceup in a square to make a bingo board. As your teacher calls a word, turn over that word card. Call "bingo" when you have turned over a horizonal, vertical, or diagonal row of cards. Award yourself a point if you spell all the words correctly.

- As your teacher calls out a definition, hold up the card of the matching word.

BUILDING BETTER VOCABULARIES

Build better vocabularies with easy-to-make word booklets. Give each student 20–25 copies of the bottom half of page 144. (Save paper by making two-sided copies.) Then have him fold a 9" x 12" sheet of construction paper in half to make a cover for his booklet. Instruct the student to place the vocabulary pages inside the cover and staple the booklet along the fold. Then have him decorate the cover. Each day write one or two words from a current unit of study on the chalkboard. Direct each student to write each word on a new page in his booklet, then complete the information requested on the page. Encourage students to use the new words in their writing pieces and other assignments whenever possible.

SYNONYM AND ANTONYM SEARCH

They can spell it, but do they know what it means? After giving your spelling test, give each student five minutes to list as many synonyms and antonyms as she can for each spelling word. When time is up, collect the papers for grading. Award one bonus point for each correct antonym or synonym.

Carissa's Vocabulary Booklet

HOMOPHONES HUNT

Take students on a hunt for homophones with this nifty activity! On the chalkboard write a list of homophones—such as *male, flour, I, knows, see, bored, too, sale,* and *fare.* Next have each student draw a dividing line in the center of a sheet of construction paper. Have the student write the homophones in the left column as shown. Then challenge her to cut out a picture or spelling of each word's homophone and glue it in the right column directly across from the word. Have each student share her work; then display it on a bulletin board.

Alex Ludein

I	
flour	
son	
aunt	
knight	
dear	

PERFECTLY PLURALS

Check students' understanding of plural spellings with this fun testing tool. Cut out 10 pictures showing singular nouns from magazines. Glue the pictures onto a large sheet of poster board; then number the pictures. Have each student number a sheet of paper from 1 to 10. Direct the student to look at each picture on the poster and write the singular noun it depicts on his paper. Then have him write the plural form of each noun beside its singular form. Encourage students to make other, similar posters to test their classmates' plural prowess (and earn extra-credit points too!).

Austin Jessup

1. man—men
2. bus—buses
3. bluilding—buildings
4. goose—geese
5. deer—deer
6. woman—women
7. penny—pennies
8. watch—watches
9. cactus—cactuses or cacti
10. foot—feet

BUILDING ON BASE WORDS

Use this small-group game to give students practice using prefixes and suffixes. On a set of index cards, write several base words from the following list: **wind, cheer, open, read, enjoy, agree, done, skill, fix, call, happy, joy, fill,** and **peace**. To begin the activity, show students one of the base-word cards. Give each student one minute to list as many words as possible that include prefixes or suffixes added to the base word. When time expires, award one point for each correct word a student lists. If a student thinks of a word that no other classmate has named, award him a bonus point. Repeat until all the base-word cards have been used; then declare the student with the most points the winner.

RESEARCH SKILLS

TIRED-WORD THESAURUS

Help students avoid overusing words by creating a "Tired-Word Thesaurus." Explain that some writers use the same words over and over again. Discuss the disadvantages that lack of word and sentence variety creates in writing. Provide the example of the word said, listing less-used synonyms for the word, such as whispered, responded, hollered, and moaned. Then have students brainstorm additional overused words and synonyms for each one. (If students have difficulty starting, suggest words such as nice, pretty, small, sad, happy, or walk.) Write each word and its synonyms on an individual sheet of paper. Put the pages in alphabetical order in a binder notebook to create a "Tired-Word Thesaurus." Encourage students to add words and synonyms to the thesaurus during their free time.

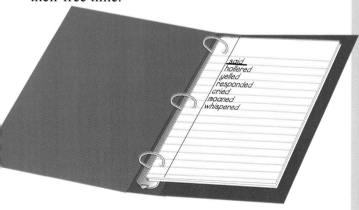

GOING FOR THE GUIDE WORDS

Sharpen dictionary skills with this fun guide-word drill. List ten words selected randomly from the dictionary on the board. Number the words 1–10. Pair students and give each pair a dictionary. Then challenge each pair to find and record the pair of guide words that appear on the same page as each of the listed words. Instruct the partners to raise their hands when they have completed the assignment. Award each student pair that correctly names the ten guide-word pairs with two "Guide-Word Gold Medals"—gold, foil-wrapped chocolate coins.

RESEARCH-REPORT ROUNDUP

Round up your students for this exercise in writing a simple research report. Gather reference materials and resources on a variety of animals. Then post a list of animals on the board (see the list to the right) and direct each student to select an animal to research. Provide each student with a copy of the report outline on page 151 and the bibliography outline on page 152. Have each student research his animal and fill in both outlines. Once the student has completed his outlines, direct him to use the information he collected to write a report and a bibliography. Instruct the student to mount the report, his bibliography, and an illustration of his animal on a large sheet of poster board. Then display the research reports for others to read.

Animals To Research
- African elephant
- armadillo
- bat
- beaver
- blue whale
- boa constrictor
- buffalo
- bullfrog
- camel
- coyote
- deer
- dolphin
- eagle
- gorilla
- hummingbird
- jellyfish
- moose
- octopus
- ostrich
- otter
- peacock
- polar bear
- porcupine
- python
- raccoon
- rhinoceros
- salmon
- seal
- shark
- spider
- starfish
- tarantula
- termite
- toad
- walrus
- woodpecker

The Art Of Alliteration

Challenge students to put their knowledge of figurative language to work with this alliteration activity. Provide each child with a section of the newspaper. Have the student read through his section and find stories or news items of interest. Then direct him to cut out one article and write a summary sentence about it using the literary technique of alliteration. To provide an example for students, write the phrase "Retired Representative Rescues Relative From Raging Rapids" on the board. Suggest it as a possible alliterative summary of an article about a former congressman who saved his nephew from drowning while on a rafting trip. Have each student read his sentence aloud to the class as if he were a reporter on the scene. Then have him copy it onto a colorful sentence strip. Post the strips and articles on a newspaper-covered bulletin board titled "Extra! Extra! Read All About Alliteration!"

Congressman Saves Nephew From Drowning
Staff writer Ben Hamilton

Kenny AZ—Early yesterday afternoon former Congressman Darren Maccaw saved his nephew Seth Maccaw from drowning. Maccaw and his nephew were rafting down the Angelo River when the raft overturned. Maccaw called upon his expert swimming skills to rescue his young nephew. Maccaw, a fo...

Retired Representative

Rescues Relative From

Raging Rapids

IDIOMS HALL OF FAME

Familiarize students with commonly used idioms by creating an Idioms Hall Of Fame. Invite each student to select her favorite idiom or one of those listed on page 144. Provide each student with a sheet of construction paper on which to copy her selected idiom. Challenge the student to illustrate the literal meaning of the idiom on the paper. Then have her write the idiom's actual meaning below the illustration. Label a classroom wall section "Idioms Hall Of Fame." Attach a cut-out loving cup below the title; then surround it with your students' idiom illustrations.

I'm on top of the world.

Don't cry over spilt milk.

THE POWER OF PERSUASION

Get creative juices flowing with this exciting persuasive writing and public-speaking activity. Instruct each student to decide on a new product he would like to market to consumers. Then direct the student to bring in an empty container and decorate it to create a model of that product's packaging. Next challenge each student to write a 30-second commercial promoting his new product. Remind the student of his goal—persuading the audience to buy the product. Give each student time to practice delivering his commercial; then have him present his commercial to the class.

Capitalization Rules

To *capitalize* means to begin a word with a capital letter.
The following items should always be capitalized:

- **the first word in a sentence**
  We went to the store yesterday.

- **proper nouns**
  names of people
  Beverly Cleary

  geographic names
  New Jersey
  Jupiter
  Europe
  Hillside Street
  Mississippi River

  historic events
  Stamp Act
  Civil War

  names of days or months
  Wednesday
  December

  national and local holidays
  Easter

- **proper adjectives**
  Spanish
  American

- **the pronoun *I***
  When I heard the news, I shouted
  for joy.

- **titles and initials**
  Captain Kirk
  Mrs. Krolikowski
  R. J. Hayes

- **words used as names**
  Will you ask Dad if we can go to the
  movies?
  We saw Aunt Ellie at the park.

- **first word in the greeting and closing of a letter**
  Dear Julie,
  My dear friend,

- **titles of written works (first word, last word, all main words)**
  Sports Illustrated for Kids
  The Wizard of Oz

- **abbreviations**
  P.T.A.
  USA
  Dr.

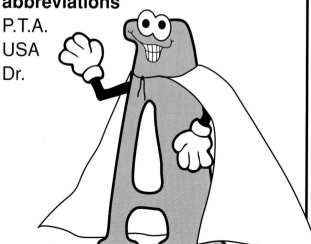

Punctuation Rules

Use a period:
- **at the end of a declarative sentence—a sentence that makes a statement**
  I enjoy playing basketball.
- **at the end of an imperative sentence—a sentence that makes a request**
  Please bring me that measuring cup.
- **after a person's initials**
  A. J. Wydeil
- **after an abbreviation**
  Mrs. Jones
  Dr. McIntosh

Use a question mark:
- **at the end of an interrogative sentence—a sentence that asks a question**
  What number does Mike Smith wear?

Use an exclamation point:
- **to express strong feeling or emotion**
  Ouch!
  Leave me alone!
  Wow!

Use quotation marks:
- **to show a direct quotation**
  Jennifer said, "I am going to the movies with Carrie."
- **to show the titles of written works—poems, plays, stories, or songs**
  "West Side Story"
  "America the Beautiful"

Use an apostrophe:
- **to show that one or more letters have been left out to form a contraction**
  can't—can not
  won't—will not
  don't—do not
- **to show possession**
  Carolyn's keys are in the car.
  The boys' game was over an hour ago.

Use a hyphen:
- **to divide a word between syllables at the end of a line**
  The automobile sales-
  man is named Mr. Sears.
- **to join parts of some compound words**
  drive-in, father-in-law
- **to write number words from 21 through 99**
  twenty-one

(Continued on the next page)

Punctuation Rules

Use a comma:

- **to separate items in a date or address**
  August 22, 1970
  Bardstown, Kentucky 40051

- **after the greeting and closing of a letter**
  Dear Andrew,
  Yours truly,

- **to separate words or phrases in a series**
  Sharon bought eggs, bread, and milk at the store.

- **with quotations to set off the exact words of the speaker from the rest of the sentence**
  Jimmy said, "I want to visit my niece in North Carolina."

- **to separate a noun of direct address from the rest of the sentence**
  Rob, did your team win the hockey game last night?

- **to separate a long clause or phrase from the independent clause following it**
  As I was walking on the beach, I found several conch shells.
  When Jeff bought his new car, he sold his old one.

- **to join two simple sentences into a compound sentence**
  Madeline went to sleep, but Mackenzie stayed up to watch television.

- **to set off an *appositive*** (a word or phrase that renames the noun or pronoun before it)
  Adrienne, a great gymnast, won first place at the meet.

- **with an *interrupter*** (a word, phrase, or clause that interrupts the main thought of a sentence) Swimming, I feel, is the best exercise.
  In the end, however, Carlin couldn't come to the party.

- **when writing the last name first**
  Lundein, Gregory

Use a colon:

- **after the salutation of a business letter**
  Dear Mr. Metcalf:

- **in writing times**
  3:45

- **before a list or series**
  There were three contestants: Angela, Sarah, and Jackie.

- **after the speaker in a play or dialogue**
  Nicholas: When are we leaving?
  Alex: We leave in about 20 minutes.

Use a semicolon:

- **between the independent clauses of a compound sentence when a conjunction is not used**
  Martin washed the car; John waxed it.
  Beverly and Michael went to Hawaii; they stayed there for two weeks.

Common Verb Tenses

Past Tense

indicates an action that happened at a specific time in the past.

Mike *liked* to go to the beach.

He *went* almost every day.

Present Tense

indicates an action that is happening now, or that happens regularly.

Liz *likes* walking in the park.

Stephanie *walks* with her each afternoon.

Future Tense

indicates an action that is going to take place. Future tense is formed by adding *shall* or *will* before the main verb.

Debra *will go* to lunch with us tomorrow.

Don and Cory *will meet* us at the restaurant.

Special Verb Tenses

Past Perfect Tense

indicates an action that began and was completed in the past. Past perfect tense is formed by adding *had* before the main verb.

Becky *had worked* for over three hours without a break.

Present Perfect Tense

indicates an action that is still going on. Present perfect tense is formed by using *has* or *have* before the main verb.

Thad *has slept* for eight hours.

Future Perfect Tense

indicates an action that will start in the future and end at a specific time in the future. Future perfect tense is formed by adding *will have* or *shall have* before the main verb.

Peggy *will have walked* on the treadmill for 30 minutes.

I think I will go for a walk today.

erb

Idioms

An *idiom* is a phrase which means something different than what each of its words taken one-by-one means. For example, "Hold your horses" does not mean "restrain your horses." Instead, the phrase means "wait, or slow down."

Examples:

My brother is driving me up the wall.
Barry always has a trick up his sleeve.
My friend and I don't always see eye to eye.
Ray has a frog in his throat.
Michelle cried her eyes out during the movie.
My little sister can be a pain in the neck sometimes.
I have a bone to pick with my sister.
My mother said my brother was skating on thin ice.
It is raining cats and dogs outside, so be sure to take an umbrella.
My father asked me to lend him a hand.
Jake almost bit my head off when I asked him to help me do the dishes.

I think John has lost his marbles!
I am going to be in hot water if I don't finish this assignment.
Andrew's advice to him went in one ear and out the other.
You just hit the nail right on the head!
Ben is in the doghouse.
Does this ring a bell with you?
Carrie got cold feet and wouldn't go to the haunted house with us.
I held my tongue even though I disagreed with his opinion.
I was shaking in my boots after I watched that horror show.

Word: _____

Definition: _____

_____

_____

_____

_____

Part Of Speech: _____

Word Origin: _____

Sample Sentence: _____

_____

Illustration:

Note To The Teacher: Use the top half of this page with "Idioms Hall Of Fame" on page 139. Make approximately 10–15 two-sided copies of the bottom half of this sheet for each student. Use them with "Building Better Vocabularies" on page 136.

Capital Ideas

Fill in the information requested below. Use encyclopedias and other reference materials if you need extra help. All of the answers will begin with a capital letter.

1. Write your full name. _____

2. Name one of the 50 states in the United States of America. _____

3. What is the title of your favorite book? _____

4. Write the names of your two favorite months of the year. _____

5. Name the five Great Lakes. _____

6. What is the abbreviation for the Central Intelligence Agency?_____

7. Name two streets that are in your neighborhood. _____

8. What war began in the United States in 1775? _____

9. What holiday is celebrated on December 25? _____

10. Name the seven days of the week. _____
    _____

11. Who is the current president of the United States of America? _____

12. What day comes after Tuesday? _____

13. What is your favorite holiday? _____

14. What state is north of Oregon? _____

15. What is the title of your favorite magazine? _____

16. Name the capital of Virginia. _____

17. What month comes after June on the calendar? _____

18. Name a famous war in United States history. _____

19. What is the name of your school? _____

20. Who wrote the book *Charlotte's Web*? _____

21. Name a mountain range. _____

22. What war began in the United States in 1861? _____

23. Name the planet that is closest to the sun. _____

24. What are two of the world's oceans? _____

Bonus Box: Write a short story using as many of the words above as you can.

Note To The Teacher: Use with "A Capital Idea" on page 128.

146

Proper nouns

Proper Places And People

Geography is filled with proper nouns. The names of countries are proper nouns, so they are always capitalized. We also capitalize the names of nationalities and languages. For example, _Somalia_ is a country in Africa. A person from Somalia is called a _Somali._

Directions: Use a map and a dictionary to find countries in each continent listed below. Write the name of each country in the left-hand column. Record the name of the individuals who come from that country in the right-hand column. Remember to capitalize all the words you use since they are proper nouns.

North America

United States of America _____   Americans _____

_____   _____

_____   _____

_____   _____

South America

_____   _____

_____   _____

_____   _____

_____   _____

Europe

_____   _____

_____   _____

_____   _____

_____   _____

Africa

_____   _____

_____   _____

_____   _____

_____   _____

Asia

_____   _____

_____   _____

_____   _____

_____   _____

Australia

_____   _____

_____   _____

Bonus Box: Why does the continent of Antarctica not have a country name? Write your answer on the back of this page.

Note To The Teacher: Use with "A World Of Proper Nouns" on page 131.

A ROLL OF THE DICE

Materials: two copies of this page; scissors; glue; crayons, markers, or colored pencils

Directions:

1. Write a noun in each blank square on one copy of the pattern.
2. Write an action verb in each blank square on the second copy.
3. Cut very carefully along each pattern's solid lines.
4. Fold along the dotted lines to form a cube. (The writing should be on the outside of the cube.)
5. Glue the tabs to the inside of each cube.

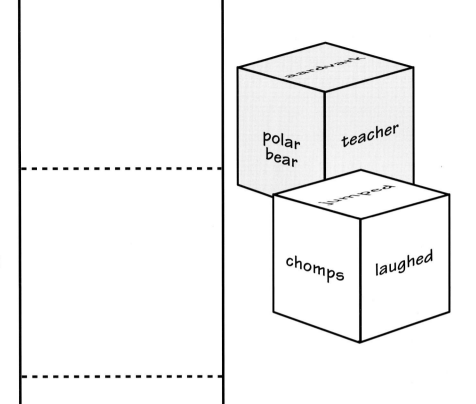

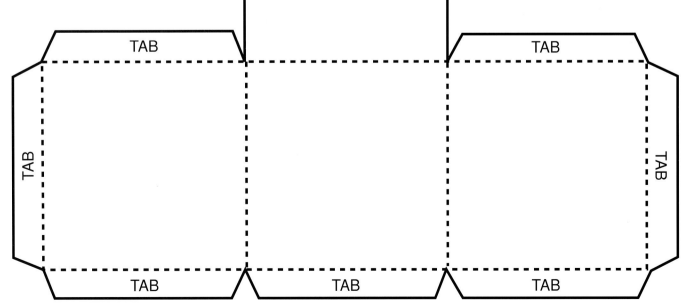

Note To The Teacher: Use this pattern with "Subject And Predicate Dice" on page 132, "Crystal-Clear Explanations" on page 158, and "Rolling Review" on page 198.

Patterns

subject **girl** subject	subject **dog** subject	subject **cat** subject	subject **animal** subject
subject **ostrich** subject	subject **antelope** subject	subject **chicken** subject	subject **frog** subject
subject **pelicans** subject	subject **kittens** subject	subject **roosters** subject	subject **children** subject
subject **bears** subject	subject **pigs** subject	subject **polar bears** subject	subject **geese** subject
verb **run** verb	verb **leap** verb	verb **fly** verb	verb **yawn** verb
verb **growl** verb	verb **drink** verb	verb **eat** verb	verb **talk** verb
verb **cries** verb	verb **sleeps** verb	verb **yells** verb	verb **laughs** verb
verb **croaks** verb	verb **jumps** verb	verb **smells** verb	verb **drives** verb

Note To The Teacher: Duplicate one copy of this sheet on sturdy paper for each pair of students. Use with "Subject-Verb Card Game" on page 133.

Collecting Clues

Authors do not always directly state every detail about a character or situation in a story. Sometimes a reader must make an *inference*—use clues in the story and personal experience to figure out certain details.

Directions: Read each selection below. Then use the clues provided and your own experience to answer each question.

1. The school auditorium was filled with people. The holiday play was about to begin. Andrew was sweating and his knees were shaking as the curtain opened.

   What was wrong with Andrew?

   _____
   _____
   _____
   _____

2. Jennifer arrived at the beach around 12:00. After looking through her tote bag, she realized she had forgotten several things. When Jennifer left the beach several hours later, she had a bad sunburn.

   What is one of the things Jennifer forgot to bring?

   _____
   _____
   _____
   _____

3. There were flies everywhere during the July 4th picnic. When Ray picked up his lemonade, he noticed something floating near the top. Ray decided he really wasn't that thirsty after all.

   What was floating in Ray's lemonade?

   _____
   _____
   _____

4. The girls took down their tents, packed up their gear, and headed toward the car. Their leader said she was proud of them for earning the camping badge.

   What type of group or club might the girls belong to?

   _____
   _____
   _____
   _____

5. The night before an important job interview, Carrie asked her sister Stephanie to call and wake her at 6:30 the following morning. When Stephanie called Carrie's number, she got a busy signal. Carrie slept right through her interview.

   Why was there a busy signal when Stephanie called?

   _____
   _____
   _____
   _____

6. Martin had forgotten to do his science homework. When he woke up, he looked out the window and smiled. A thick, white blanket of snow covered the ground.

   Why was Martin smiling?

   _____
   _____
   _____
   _____

Bonus Box: On the back of this sheet, write a paragraph and question like the ones above. Be sure to leave something out of your paragraph, and don't forget to provide clues. Challenge a classmate to answer the question.

Note To The Teacher: For another inferencing activity, see "Getting The Picture" on page 135.

Name _____

Spelling contract

SPELLING SPEEDWAY

Start your engines and get ready for some fun adventures on the Spelling Speedway! Complete _____ of the activities listed below. Be sure to color in the racetrack segment each time you complete its activity.

START

FINISH

Find as many of your spelling words as possible in the book you are currently reading. Then copy the sentences that contain the words.

Write your spelling words using the hand you normally don't write with.

Write sentences using the letters in each word. Example: *tree* = Tom really enjoys eggs.

Divide each spelling word according to its syllables.

Make a word search with your spelling words on graph paper. Then trade papers with a friend and solve each other's puzzles.

Write a creative story using as many of your spelling words as possible. Be sure to underline each spelling word in the story.

Find out how much each spelling word is worth if A = 1 point, B = 2 points, C = 3 points, and so on.

Make flash cards of your spelling words.

Write your words in reverse alphabetical order.

Use your spelling words to make a word scramble. Then trade papers with a friend and solve each other's puzzles.

Write several silly sentences, each using three of your spelling words.

Write a song or rap using as many of your spelling words as possible.

Write a poem using as many of your spelling words as possible.

Make a crossword puzzle with your spelling words. Be sure to make an answer key.

Classify your spelling words into categories based on each word's part of speech.

Bonus Box: On the back of this sheet, list three other fun ways to practice your spelling words.

Note To The Teacher: Before duplicating the contract, fill in the number of activities you want each student to complete. Give one copy to each student. Instruct students to color in the racetrack segment for each activity they complete.

RESEARCH REPORT ROUNDUP

Select an animal to research. Find information on the animal in reference materials; then write the information in the outline below. Use another copy of this page if you need more space. Use the information you gather to write a report on your animal.

Topic: _____

I. Appearance

A. _____

B. _____

C. _____

II. Habits

A. _____

B. _____

C. _____

III. Habitat

A. _____

B. _____

C. _____

IV. Other Interesting Facts

A. _____

B. _____

C. _____

Note To The Teacher: Use with "Research Report Roundup" on page 138. Duplicate additional copies for those students who need them.

ROUNDING UP THE SOURCES

A *bibliography* lists the materials a writer used to write a research report. Bibliographies are organized alphabetically by the author's last name or by the title of the source if there is no author listed. Bibliography entries vary slightly, depending on the source. As you collect information for your research report, be sure to write information on the different sources you use on the lines below. After you have completed your research report, recopy this information onto another sheet of paper to create your own bibliography. Use the format of this page as your guide.

Books
Author (last name, first name). Title of book. City of publication: Publisher, copyright
    date.

_____

_____

_____

Encyclopedias
"Article title." Title of reference book. Edition. Date published.

_____

_____

_____

_____

Magazines
Author (last name, first name). "Title of article." Title of magazine. Date: Page numbers of
    the article.

_____

_____

Pamphlets
Author (last name, first name). Title of pamphlet. City of pamphlet publication: Publisher,
    copyright date.

_____

_____

Interviews
Author (last name, first name). Type of interview (personal or phone).
    Date.

_____

_____

WRITING

Writing-Process Ideas

Rising Stars

Keeping track of which stage of the writing process each student is in will be a cinch with this colorful bulletin board. Label curved bands of red, yellow, green, blue, and purple bulletin-board paper as shown; then staple the bands to a board titled "Where Are You On Our Writing Rainbow?" Cut out a class supply of white stars; then write each child's name on a different star. If desired, laminate the stars for durability. Then pin the stars to one side of the board. During Writing Workshop each day, have each student move his star to the place on the rainbow that indicates his progress. A quick glance at the board will tell you what you need to know about each student!

Thomas

Chad   Brittany

Leah   Luke

Sharing
Proofreading
Revising
Drafting
Prewriting

Ben   Carrie   Li

Raul   Juan   Mary

Hot-Hot-Hot Writing Topics

With this idea you'll never hear a student ask, "What should I write about?" again! Give each student a sheet of lined paper and have her fold it in half lengthwise. Direct her to write the heading "What's Hot?" at the left side of the paper and "What's Not?" at the right side. Allow each student time to list topics she absolutely would not want to write about under the heading at the right. Expect her to list topics such as "What I Did During My Summer Vacation," "My Favorite Food," and "My Best Friend." As she completes that column, have her also list ideas that she would like to write about in the left-side column as they come to mind. If desired, allow students to share ideas aloud so they can add to their lists any topics mentioned by others that appeal to them. Collect and duplicate the lists to protect against loss before returning them to students. Suggest that each student keep her list in a writing folder so she can refer to the list each time she needs a new writing topic.

What's Hot?	What's Not?
My Favorite TV Show	What I Did During My Summer Vacation
Current Fads	My Favorite Food
Cool Sayings	My Best Friend

Input

Outside Input

It's important for authors to obtain feedback from many different sources as they write. Involve people other than students' classmates in this process. After proofreading each new writing assignment, give each student one copy of the "Tell Me What You Think!" reproducible on page 170 to attach to his work. Suggest that he have a faculty member, a student in another classroom, a parent, a sibling, or an older relative read his work and complete the accompanying form. Positive comments and suggestions coming from other people will very likely guarantee improvement in your students' writings!

Output

Write-O

Use a fun game format to track the different types of writing your students practice. Duplicate a copy of the card at the top of page 175 for each student. Each time he completes one of the types of writing designated on the card, direct him to color that square. Whenever he completes a horizontal or vertical row on the card, reward him with a small treat. Then, when he's colored in the entire card, present him with a nice writing instrument for penning future assignments!

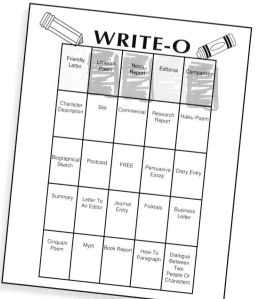

Personal Rubrics

Turn the assessment tables by challenging each student to design a rubric for evaluating a piece of her own writing. Pull out several examples of rubrics you've previously used with the class. Point out how the rubrics vary according to the different types of writing they assess. For example, a rubric that evaluates a poem differs from one that assesses a folktale. Call attention to the purpose of different writings and how the purpose influences each rubric's content. Next have students help you design a simple, five-part rubric for assessing a personal essay (see the illustration). Afterward challenge each student to develop a rubric that assesses her most recent writing assignment. If desired, continue this process when making future writing assignments and expect the quality of your students' writing to greatly improve!

My Personal Rubric

Does my essay have a title?
    yes   no

Did I indent each paragraph in my essay?
    yes   no

Does each paragraph in my essay have a topic sentence?
    yes   no

Does my essay provide supporting details?
    yes   no

Does my essay use correct capitalization and punctuation?
    yes   no

For additional ideas about student checklists and evaluation forms, see pages 171–173.

Whether it's a party or a picnic, planning is the key to any event's success. Ask students what they would include if they were planning a party (invitations, food, party supplies, entertainment, etc.). Begin writing an outline on the board with student responses. Then ask students to give specific examples for each category (such as games and music for entertainment). List these as subheadings on your outline. Use the party-planning outline to discuss the basic elements of an outline—a title, main headings, subheadings, and details—with your students.

Next have each student imagine that for one day he could go anywhere in the world—on safari in Africa, mountain climbing in Canada, or picnicking with the queen of England. Direct each student to follow the example on the board to create an outline of his day. Have the student include information necessary to prepare for and take part in the activity.

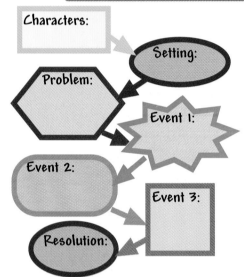

Picture This: Story Maps

Explain to students that a *story map* is a plan or an outline used for understanding or writing fictional stories. Discuss how every fictional story includes characters, setting, plot (sequence of events including problem, rising action, and resolution), and theme. Tell your students that a writer uses a story map like the one shown to help build these elements into a story. It helps her organize its beginning, middle, and end.

Display various magazine pictures that show a person or group of people within a setting. Instruct each student to choose a picture that appeals to her. Then direct the student to use the character(s), setting, and action in the picture to help her create a story map. Finally have each student share her picture and accompanying story map with her classmates.

Building A Paragraph

What could be handier than a visual aid that reminds students how to write a good paragraph? Copy the drawing of a paragraph's basic structure shown at right onto a sheet of poster board. Then follow these steps to point out how writing a good paragraph is much like building a house:

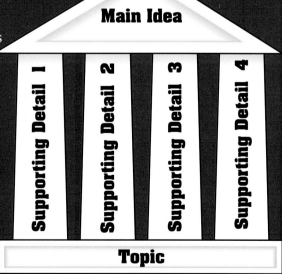

1. Tell students that the first step in building a house (writing a paragraph) is pouring the foundation (deciding on a topic).

2. Ask students to suggest a topic for writing a paragraph. Record the topic on the board.

3. Explain that the next step in building a house is setting beams (supporting details) on the foundation to support the roof (main idea).

4. Write a main-idea sentence on the board just below the topic. Read the sentence aloud.

5. Add four sentences that support the main idea. Read the resulting paragraph aloud.

6. Point out that the walls, windows, doors, and other parts of a house (the writer's choice of words, phrasing, and types of sentences) give the house its finishing touch (define the paragraph's style).

Review the six steps; then challenge each student to build a good paragraph about a topic of his choice.

Wall-To-Wall Stories
(Narrative Writing)

Let your students have some fun by creating wall-to-wall stories! First review the purpose of narrative writing. Next tape a length of white bulletin-board paper to a classroom wall, stretching the paper from one wall to another. Position a small table at the left end of the paper. On the table place colored markers and three decorated coffee cans labeled "Character," "Setting," and "Event." Write the ten topics shown for each category on different slips of paper, fold the papers once, and store them in the appropriate cans.

Each morning have one student draw a paper from each can and read the papers aloud. If, for example, papers with the words *magician, haunted house,* and *blizzard* are read, explain that the main part of the story must take place in a haunted house, the main character must be a magician, and the plot must include a blizzard. Direct the student who read the papers aloud to begin the story by writing one sentence with any colored marker. Establish that the rest of the story will be written throughout the day as other students in turn add one more sentence at a time with the same marker. Point out that the story must be finished by the time students reach the end of the paper. As one story is completed, allow students to start a new story by choosing three more papers and a different-colored marker, beginning the next story right under the first one. Save some time at the end of the day for sharing the completed stories aloud!

| magician | haunted house | blizzard |

Marty the magician decided to present a magic show in a haunted house. He thought it would be really creepy. The show took place at midnight on a night with a full moon. One of Marty's tricks involved making snow. He made the snow, but he couldn't stop it! Before he knew it, there was a blizzard!

Characters: magician, mail carrier, baby-sitter, juggler, teacher, Boy Scout, acrobat, horseback rider, cowboy, nurse

Settings: airplane, haunted house, desert, cruise ship, Disneyland®, beach, high-rise apartment building, farm, zoo, school

Events: power failure, blizzard, Martian invasion, rodeo, circus, flood, rock concert, Halloween party, campout, drought

(Expository Writing)

Help students recognize and use different signal words in expository writing with this fun team game. First use four different-colored markers to write the four groups of signal words at right on a sheet of chart paper. Next write each signal-word category in its corresponding color on a different index card. Spread the cards facedown on a table at the front of the classroom. Review the purpose of expository writing; then divide the class into four teams, give each team paper and a pencil, and write one of the suggested topics below on the board. Guide the teams through the following steps:

1. Pick one team member to be the runner.
2. At your teacher's signal, have your runner go to the table, grab a card, and return to your group.
3. As a group, read the category written on your card; then write a paragraph about that topic using all four of the category's signal words.
4. Yell "Done!" when your paragraph is finished.

Direct one member of the first team to finish to share its paragraph aloud with the class. If the para-graph contains all four signal words and is reasonably well-written, give that team one point. Collect the cards and shuffle them before playing another round. Play until one team earns five points or until a set amount of time passes, declaring the team with the highest score the winner.

Sequence	first, next, then, finally
Description	for example, in addition, also, in other words
Comparison	different, alike, same as, on the other hand
Cause/Effect	because, as a result, therefore, if...then

Suggested Topics: Eating A Pizza, Learning To Skateboard, Planning A Birthday Party, Making A New Friend, Talking On The Telephone, Choosing A TV Show

Crystal-Clear Explanations

(Expository Writing)

Understanding how to do something will be crystal clear with this writing activity! Make a transparency of the cube pattern on page 147 for yourself; then give a paper copy of the pattern, scissors, tape, an overhead marking pen, and a blank transparency to each student. Direct each student to trace his cube pattern on the blank transparency, then cut it out as you cut out the pattern on your transparency. Display the pattern you cut out on an overhead projector. Have each student label five faces of his transparency cube with the numbers 1–5 as you number yours, turning the pattern as needed. Next announce that you are going to write the steps on your pattern that clearly explain how to draw a happy face. Then write the title in the blank face and the five steps in their appropriate places. Afterward fold the pattern along the dotted lines and use clear tape to hold the faces in place. Hold up the resulting cube so that students can see its faces clearly. Students should agree that your explanation is crystal clear! Finally have each student write the directions for drawing something equally simple on his crystal-clear pattern. If desired, display the completed cubes in a free-time drawing center.

How To Draw A Happy Face

1. Draw a large circle about 4 cm in diameter.
2. In the center of the circle, make two points side by side about 1/2 cm apart.
3. Enlarge the points so that they become two oval-shaped eyes that are vertically parallel.
4. Draw a U-shaped line, beginning about 1/2 cm below the left oval and stopping 1/2 cm below the right oval.
5. If desired, write "Smile!" on the drawing, centered above the eyes.

Describing The Unknown
(Descriptive Writing)

Fine-tune your students' descriptive-writing skills with this mystery-bag activity. Gather and number a class supply of lunch bags. Fill each bag with a 3" x 5" index card and a different common item, such as a button, a paper clip, a rubber band, etc. Give a bag to each student, instructing him to remove the index card, write the number from the bag on his card, and peek inside the bag to identify the object. Leaving the object in the bag, have him write a paragraph on the card that answers the following questions:

- What does it look like?
- What is it used for?
- What is it made of?
- Why is it important?

Collect the mystery bags and spread them on a table. Then collect, shuffle, and redistribute the index cards so that no student gets his own card. Give each student a sheet of paper on which to draw and label the object described on his index card. Afterward have each student claim the bag that matches the number on his card, read his card's description aloud to the class, then hold up the drawing he made and the object inside the bag so the class can make a comparison. The comments and suggestions for improvement will become immediate feedback to the author—who can remain anonymous since the cards have numbers and no names!

What does it look like?

What is it used for?

What is it made of?

Why is it important?

My object is light tan, but it can be other colors, too. It's round, very flexible, and can stretch easily. You can wrap this object around other things to hold them together. It's made of rubber and is quite handy in offices and classrooms.

Directions:
1. Spread one brand or kind of peanut butter on one of your crackers.
2. Record the peanut butter's name, cost, and list of ingredients on your sheet.
3. Taste the sample. Use your five senses to notice the sample's taste, texture, appearance, smell, and sound.
4. Record your observations on the sheet.
5. Repeat Steps 1–4 with another kind of peanut butter.

The Taste Test
(Comparative Writing)

Unleash your students' taste buds to help complete this comparative-writing assignment! Gather a large box of saltine crackers, four plastic knives, and four different types of peanut butter—crunchy, smooth, brand-name, generic, etc. Copy the directions at left onto the chalkboard; then label each brand of peanut butter with its cost. Have each student pretend that she's been asked by a leading consumer magazine to compare two different brands of peanut butter. Give each student two crackers and a copy of page 174. Instruct each student to follow the directions on the board.

After the testing has been completed, direct each student to use the data recorded on her "Consumer's Choice" sheet to write a paragraph comparing the two brands she tested, then share it with the class. Vary the activity by having students test two different brands of another food.

Sitcom (And Other) Summaries
(Writing A Summary)

Summaries help students understand important ideas, and also help you evaluate their understanding of a topic. Explain to students that a *summary* is a paragraph with a topic sentence and several supporting details. Next have your students name some of their favorite TV shows. Share several summaries of these shows from a recent issue of a television guide. Ask students what kinds of information the reviewer shares with the reader (setting, characters, and plot events). As a class, write a new review for one program. Have each student—with his parents' guidance—select a show to watch and write a summary about to share with the class. Compile the summaries together in a classroom television guide titled "Kids' Guide To Nighttime Television."

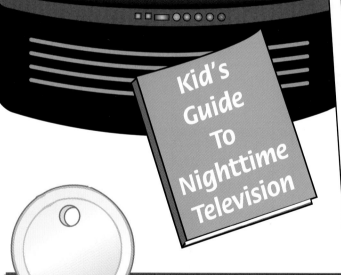

Kid's Guide To Nighttime Television

Telegram Summaries
(Writing A Summary)

Help your students understand that only the most important information should be included in a summary by having them write telegrams. Begin by explaining that a telegram is a short message that is electronically transmitted, then delivered on paper. Further explain that a person must pay to have the message sent, so telegrams are usually very short. Share the example shown. Then have each student summarize his favorite story in the form of a telegram, giving sufficient detail but using as few words as possible.

Next, divide students into small groups. Direct each group member to calculate the cost of her summary at ten cents a word. Then have each group identify which summary is the least expensive yet gives enough information about the story.

Telegram

Send message to:
Lindsay Smith
Cold Spring Elementary School
2241 Cold Spring Road
Coldville, AK 23454
Message from: Beth Willet

Message: Stone Fox by John Reynolds Gardiner. Willy's grandfather very ill. Willy discovers grandfather owes $500 in taxes for farm. Stone Fox helps Willy. Enters dog-sled race to raise money. Willy wins race with Stone Fox's help. Willy saves farm.

Locating Important Details
(Writing A Summary)

Help students learn how to take notes by focusing on the key words in paragraphs. As a student reads a chapter for science or social studies, direct him to list the most important words in each paragraph of that chapter on paper. Then have him close his book and write one or two sentences that use those key words to summarize what he's read. If the assigned chapter is a long one, divide it into smaller sections and have each student summarize only a certain number of paragraphs. Studying the resulting notes will be a valuable way for students to review a chapter's material.

Compliments Vs. Complaints

(Letter Writing)

Junk food is a hot topic. Use it to motivate your students to write business letters. First review the parts of a business letter; then draw five large boxes on the chalkboard. Label the boxes "Sight," "Sound," "Smell," "Taste," and "Texture." Divide each box in half with a vertical line; then put a *plus* sign at the top of one column and a *minus* sign atop the other. Have students brainstorm words with positive and negative food connotations for each category and list them on the board under the appropriate column. Continue until five words are listed in each column for every category.

Have students pretend that their congressman is proposing a bill to ban junk food. Divide the class in half, one group representing the kids who are against the bill and the other representing parents who are in support of the bill. Instruct each student in each group to write a letter to the congressman supporting or opposing the bill. In his letter have the student name a junk food of his choice, and use as many of the positive or negative words generated by the class as he can to describe that food and support his stance. Display the letters on a bulletin board titled "Where Do You Stand?"

Sight +	Sight –	Sound +	Sound –	Smell +	Smell –	Taste +	Taste –	Texture +	Texture –
beautiful	ugly	soft	crunching	fragrant	stinky	sweet	sour	fluffy	gooey
clean	dirty	pleasant	annoying	mild	rotten	fresh	stale	silky	slimy
colorful	dull	peaceful	grinding	fresh	stale	delicious	greasy	creamy	lumpy
mouthwatering	nasty	contented	deafening	delicious	spoiled	juicy	dry	smooth	gritty
fancy	plain	quiet	crackling	spicy	rank	spicy	bitter	meaty	grainy

1890   1950   1998

Time-Traveling Pen Pals

(Letter Writing)

Integrate science and social studies with this creative letter-writing project. Pair students; then direct one student in each pair to choose a topic from the past, and have the other student choose a topic from the future (see the example). Once a week have each student write a letter to his partner from his assigned perspective that answers a specific question posed by you such as, "What do you do for entertainment?" Tell the "past" partner to research facts to include in his letter. Tell the "future" partner to write creatively and imaginatively. At the end of the week, have each pair share its letters with the class. After writing two letters, allow the partners to trade roles for the next two letters so that each student gets to practice both types of writing.

10/12/1890

Dear Ben,
  Today we are having a barn dance. Pa is going to play his fiddle and there will be lots of square dancing. Hope you can come.

                Sincerely,
                Sam

10/12/1998

Dear Sam,
  Tonight we plan to go to the arcade and play video games, then go to see the new science fiction movie. Can you join us?

                Sincerely,
                Ben

Fun Formulas
(Writing Poetry)

Could a simple rhyming poem help students memorize the different formulas they use in math? Why not give it a try? Each time you introduce a new math formula, challenge your students to compose a poem to help them remember it. Then display the poem on an attractive banner or an interesting shape as a visual reminder throughout the year!

When the area of a triangle Is what I have to face, All I need to remember is, "Multiply the height times the base!"

Word Poems
(Writing Poetry)

Make poem-writing easier by allowing each student to create a poem from a single word! Together brainstorm a list of words based on different themes—such as foods, animals, seasons, activities, etc. Then have each student choose one word, spell it vertically down his paper, and then think of words or phrases that begin with the letters used to spell that word. To display the poems, ask each student to copy his completed poem onto a cutout of the object he wrote about as shown.

Icy
Creamy
Eaten slowly

Cold
Refreshing
Everyone's
All-time
favorite
Mmm...

Adventurous Avenue

Dorothy
Young, brave
Dreaming, befriending, journeying
Longing to return home
Homesick

Cinquain Characterizations
(Writing Poetry)

Turn the writing of a cinquain poem into a lesson on characterization and an interesting display. Have each student choose a different literary character and write a cinquain (see the formula) describing that character's unique traits.

Formula For A Cinquain
Line 1: Name of character
Line 2: Two adjectives that describe the character
Line 3: Three verbs that describe the character and end in -ing
Line 4: Four words that express the feeling of the character
Line 5: One word that describes the character other than his/her name

Have each student read her cinquain aloud so the class can note all the characters' similarities. Sort the characters into categories according to students' comments.

To make an interesting display, have each student copy her cinquain onto a pentagon or house shape cut from light-colored paper. Direct student volunteers to cut out construction-paper streets and street signs labeled with names such as "Courageous Court" and "Adventurous Avenue." Arrange the pentagon-shaped cinquain houses on a bulletin board titled "A Who's Who Of Characters" so that characters with similar traits reside on the same street.

Parts-Of-Speech Poem
(Writing Poetry)

What better way to review parts of speech than by having students fill in the missing parts of a skeleton poem! After students have worked with noun determiners, adjectives, verbs, nouns, adverbs, and prepositions, give each student a copy of the bottom half of page 175. If desired you can revise the poem frame later on to include literary devices such as metaphors and similes.

Parts-Of-Speech Poem

Fluffy Kitten
Title (adjective, noun)

The kitten
(noun determiner, noun)

Soft and
(adjective)

furry
(adjective)

Sits quietly
(verb, adverb)

On the windowsill.
(preposition, noun determiner, noun)

Charity H.
Student's name

* Who will operate the video camera?
* What should we title the video?
* How long should the video be?
* Which poems should be in the video, and in what order?
* Where should we tape the video?
* What should we use as a background and as props?
* What should be edited out of the video?
* What should we do to make a smooth transition from one poem to the next?

Poetry Video
(Poetry)

If a picture is worth a thousand words, then a class-produced video featuring choreographed poems could fill volumes! Involve your students in every stage of this production, from the planning to the performing. Use the suggested tips at left as a starting point. Then have each student be responsible for memorizing his poems, choreographing them, making or bringing in the props he'll need, and practicing on his own so that the actual videotaping will go more smoothly. Once the final version of the video is complete, enjoy it as a class; then route it to other classes for their convenience in viewing.

Connecting
READING AND WRITING

It All Depends On Your Point Of View

Help your students understand and appreciate different perspectives by rewriting fables. First show the class a glass that's half-full of water. Ask, "Is this glass half-full or half-empty?" Expect responses that represent both possibilities. Then read Judy Blume's *The Pain And The Great One* (Simon & Schuster) twice—once from the sister's point of view and then from the brother's. Afterward ask students to share their own experiences about how two people can have different perceptions of the same thing.

Next read aloud *The Tortoise And The Hare* (Living Books), a familiar Aesop fable. Ask students to think about how the tortoise's version of that story would differ from the way the hare would tell the tale. Challenge each student to rewrite the fable from two different perspectives, the tortoise's point of view and the hare's. After writing both perspectives, ask students to tell if their opinions of the characters changed after having "walked" in the other character's shoes!

SHOEBOX REVIEW

This novel idea is sure to make book reviews a "shoe-in" with your students! Obtain six same-size shoeboxes. Cover each box with colorful paper; then label each box with a different genre of literature: mystery, fantasy, adventure, historical fiction, realistic fiction, and nonfiction.

Discuss with your students the purpose of a book review: to inform a potential reader about the plot of a story. Point out that a review should not tell too much about the plot, but give enough detail so the reader will want to find out more about the book. Share several book reviews of your children's favorite books. Have the students identify specific information included in a review, such as the title, author, character information, a story summary, the theme or message, and the reviewer's opinion of the story.

Next give each student a 4" x 6" index card. Have her choose a book that fits one of the genres. Direct the student to read the book, then write a book review on the index card. After each student completes her review, have her place it in the appropriate shoebox. Put the shoeboxes in a special area of your classroom. Each time one of your students reads a new book, have her write a review and add it to a box. Encourage students to use the boxes as a handy reference when searching for a good book to read.

MYSTERY

Book Authors For Little Friends

Allow your budding authors to supply the text for wordless picture books and share the result with younger friends. First give students a better understanding of what an author's job entails by reading aloud *What Do Authors Do?* by Eileen Christelow (Houghton Mifflin Company). Then guide your class through the five steps below to become children's book authors.

 1 Have the class brainstorm a list of multiple-choice interview questions that will help a very young child think of an idea for a children's book. For example, "Which do you like better, real-life stories or make-believe stories?" and, "Which do you like better, stories about people or stories about animals?"

 2 Make arrangements with a kindergarten or first-grade teacher to pair each of your students with a younger child for an interview session; then schedule the interviews.

 3 Gather a large supply of wordless picture books such as those listed below. Using the information gained during the interview, have each of your students choose a book that would appeal to his younger partner.

 4 Direct each student to use the pictures in the book he selected to help him write an imaginative narrative that could accompany those pictures.

 5 When the story is completed, allow each student to visit his little friend and share his special book and story.

Suggested WORDLESS PICTURE BOOKS:

Changes, Changes by Pat Hutchins
(Simon & Schuster For Young Readers)

Free Fall by David Wiesner
(William Morrow And Company, Inc.)

Frog Goes To Dinner by Mercer Mayer
(Dial Books For Young Readers)

Hiccup by Mercer Mayer
(Puffin Books)

Paddy Under Water by John Goodall
(Simon & Schuster For Young Readers)

Pancakes For Breakfast by Tomie dePaola
(Harcourt Brace & Company)

Sunshine by Jan Ormerod
(William Morrow And Company, Inc.)

The Angel And The Soldier Boy
by Peter Collington
(Alfred A. Knopf Books For Young Readers)

Tuesday by David Wiesner
(Houghton Mifflin Company)

The Tall-Tale Trail
(Writing Tall Tales)

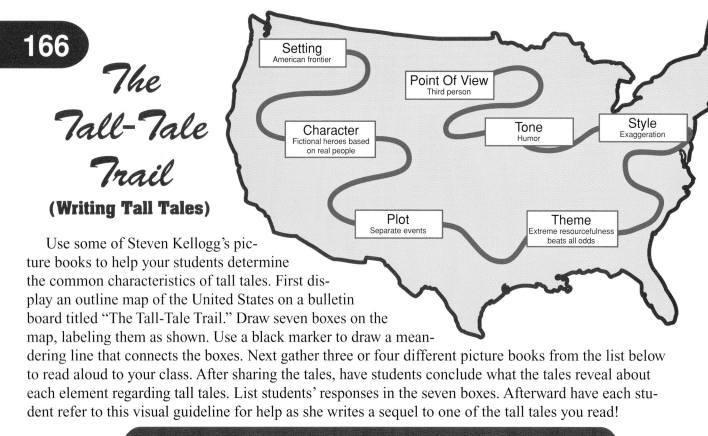

Setting
American frontier

Point Of View
Third person

Character
Fictional heroes based
on real people

Tone
Humor

Style
Exaggeration

Plot
Separate events

Theme
Extreme resourcefulness
beats all odds

Use some of Steven Kellogg's picture books to help your students determine the common characteristics of tall tales. First display an outline map of the United States on a bulletin board titled "The Tall-Tale Trail." Draw seven boxes on the map, labeling them as shown. Use a black marker to draw a meandering line that connects the boxes. Next gather three or four different picture books from the list below to read aloud to your class. After sharing the tales, have students conclude what the tales reveal about each element regarding tall tales. List students' responses in the seven boxes. Afterward have each student refer to this visual guideline for help as she writes a sequel to one of the tall tales you read!

Suggested Steven Kellogg Books:
Johnny Appleseed (William Morrow and Company, Inc.; 1988)
Paul Bunyan (William Morrow and Company, Inc.; 1992)
Pecos Bill (William Morrow and Company, Inc.; 1986)
Sally Ann Thunder Ann Whirlwind Crockett: A Tall Tale
    (William Morrow and Company, Inc.; 1995)
Mike Fink (William Morrow and Company, Inc.; 1992)

Star Reporters
(Writing A Newspaper Article)

Transform your students into top-notch journalists with the following activity. First review the 5 Ws *(who, what, when, where, why,* and *how)* of a newspaper article and why they are so important to a reader. Then draw a large star on the board. Fill in each part of the star with all the important facts about an upcoming event at your school. Afterward model how to translate that information into a well-written news article.

Next give each student a copy of the star-shaped guide on page 176. Have the student complete the guide, as directed, with information about any current event. After each student has finished writing his news article, instruct him to cut out his star pattern. Collect the patterns and place them inside a construction-paper pocket stapled to one corner of a bulletin board titled "The Proof Is In The Reporting!" Then post on the board each student's news article. During free time, invite students to pull a guide from the pocket, read its information, and pin it to the corresponding article to show a correct match. A student will know he's done a good reporting job if a classmate easily matches his article and star!

Ready Reference

Editing Symbols

Writers use special marks called *editing symbols* to help them edit and revise their work. Editing symbols are used to show what changes a writer wants to make in his or her writing.

Symbol	Meaning	Example
	Correct spelling	animl
	Delete or remove.	dogg
	Close the gap.	fi sh
^	Add a letter or word.	lives in tree a
#	Make a space.	fliessouth
	Reverse the order of a letter, a word, or words.	plants eats
	Insert a comma.	the crab an arthropod
	Insert end punctuation.	Cats purr
	Insert an apostrophe.	a deers antlers
	Insert quotation marks.	She said, Look at the pig.
≡	Make the letter a capital.	birds eat seeds.
/	Make the letter lowercase.	a Snowshoe hare
¶	Start a new paragraph.	¶Some dogs have tails.

Journal Topics

September

September is Self-Improvement Month. This month celebrates the importance of lifelong learning and self-improvement. Name something about yourself that you'd like to improve, and then list the steps you will take to do this.

Apples abound this month! How many dishes can you think of that are made with apples? List them.

National Pet Memorial Day falls annually on the second Sunday in September. Write a description of a pet you have now, one you have had in the past, or one that you would like to have in the future. Include a message that recognizes the pet's best qualities.

The summer has come to an end and it's time for heading back to school. If you were commissioned to design "the ultimate" school, what would your school be like?

The planet Neptune was first discovered on September 23, 1846. Pretend that a unique species lives on the planet. Describe the physical characteristics of these creatures, and then tell what a day in their life is like.

October

National Dessert Month is held each year in October. Describe the best dessert imaginable.

Create a new monster for Halloween. Describe what the monster looks like; then tell what it would do on Halloween night.

Peace, Friendship And Good Will Week falls annually the last seven days in October. Its purpose is to establish good human relations throughout the world. Write a letter to the people of the world telling them five ways they can make the world a friendlier place to live.

October celebrates Get Organized Week. Think of the most unorganized person you know. Describe what this person can do to get himself or herself organized.

Germany, once a divided country, was reunited on October 3, 1990. How would you feel if the United States were a divided nation? How do you think your life would be different if this happened?

November

National Authors' Day is observed on November 1. Write a letter to your favorite author telling what you like about his or her books. Give the author some suggestions on what he or she could write about in an upcoming book.

November 3 is the birthday of John Montague, the Earl of Sandwich. What did he invent? The sandwich, of course! Write a recipe for a new and unusual sandwich.

Mickey Mouse first appeared in a cartoon on November 18, 1928. Draw a cartoon featuring a new kind of mouse.

Hunting is a very popular sport this time of year. Write a paragraph telling why you are for or against this sport.

Write about your favorite family Thanksgiving Day tradition.

The Christmas shopping season traditionally begins on the Friday after Thanksgiving. If you could get the *perfect* gift for everyone in your family, what gift would you get each member, and why?

December

Many people celebrate the holiday season by decorating a freshly cut tree. Imagine you are a tree that is just about to be cut down. Write a dialogue between yourself and a tree cutter.

Emily Dickinson is considered to be one of America's greatest poets. Most of her poems—published after her death in 1886—were found written on such things as scraps of paper and the backs of envelopes. Write your own poem on an unusual material in honor of her birthday (December 10, 1830).

Underdog Day falls annually on the third Friday in December. Name a book character that you think is an *underdog,* or someone predicted to lose. Tell why you think this character is an underdog.

Winter begins in December with the coming of the *winter solstice,* the shortest day of the year. Curling up in front of a fire with a good book, steam from a cup of hot cocoa—what are some of the things that remind you of winter?

December 31 is New Year's Eve. Before setting goals for the New Year, list all the things you have accomplished this past year.

January

If you could have one wish for the New Year, what would it be?

Z Day on January 1 honors people whose names begin with the letter *Z* and are usually thought of as last. Describe what your day would be like if everything suddenly started going in reverse order.

January 11 is International Thank You Day. Write a letter to yourself expressing thanks for something you did for someone else.

Civil rights leader, minister, and Nobel Peace Prize winner Dr. Martin Luther King, Jr., was born on January 15, 1929. Explain what the word *prejudice* means to you; then decide if you think you are or are not prejudiced. Write your response.

Begin the New Year with some innovative thinking! Describe an innovative way of doing an ordinary activity, or a new invention you'd like to create.

February

Responsible Pet Owner Month is celebrated in February. Write a broadcast for a local radio station reminding pet owners how to care for their pets.

Need an excuse to just do nothing all day long? Since Nothing Day is celebrated in February, here's your chance! Describe a day in which you had nothing to do except what you wanted.

Many animals have a difficult time finding adequate food and shelter during the cold winter months. Write about the kind of animal you'd like to be during the wintertime. What would you do to survive?

February 16 is Heart 2 Heart Day. Write a heart-to-heart conversation that you'd like to have with your parent.

The Chinese celebrate their New Year during the month of February. If you could go back to the old year and change one thing, what would it be?

March

People magazine was launched on March 4, 1974. Imagine yourself on the cover of the magazine 20 years from now. Why would you be chosen as the magazine's Person Of The Year?

Theodor Seuss Geisel, better known as *Dr. Seuss,* was born on March 2, 1904. Write the title of your favorite Dr. Seuss book, and then tell why it is your favorite.

Write about what life would be like if the color green were made illegal.

On March 18, 1995, Michael Jordan announced he was returning to professional basketball after resigning 17 months earlier. Is there something you quit that you wished you hadn't? Explain.

List the things about spring that make you feel happy.

April

April Fools' Day is observed on April 1. Who in your family has the best sense of humor? Describe something funny this person said or did.

Eggs are a popular food this month. Name a food that you absolutely hate. Describe the taste, texture, appearance, and smell of the food.

Earth Day was first celebrated on April 22, 1970, with the slogan "Give Earth A Chance." Its purpose was to bring attention to our need to care for the earth. Think of a slogan for this year's Earth Day; then tell how you would promote the day.

National Library Week is celebrated in April. If you could ask anyone in the world to read a book to you, whom would you ask? What book would you read together, and why would you choose that book?

In 1910, President William Howard Taft began a new sports tradition by throwing out the first baseball of the season. If you could be a star at any sport, which one would it be, and why?

May

America's premier Thoroughbred horse race, the Kentucky Derby, first began on May 17, 1875. Describe an animal that you consider to be truly beautiful.

National Teacher Day falls annually on the Tuesday of the first full week in May. List all the duties your teacher has to perform within a year. Then pay tribute to your teacher through a kind word or action.

Limericks, funny five-lined poems, were made popular by a man named Edward Lear. Limericks follow a specific rhyming pattern: the first, second, and fifth lines rhyme; and the third and fourth lines rhyme. In honor of Lear's May 12 birthday, write a limerick of your own.

Memorial Day (the last Monday in May) pays tribute to those who have died, especially those who have died in battle. Do you think America should get involved in wars with other countries? Why or why not?

With the end of May approaching, summer is in the forecast! Plan a summer vacation for yourself and your best friend.

Tell Me What You Think!

As you read the attached writing, complete the following checklist.

Name Of Author   **Name Of Editor**

_____   _____

Title Of Work

_____

Mechanics
	YES	NO
Did the author indent each new paragraph?	___	___
Did the author begin each sentence with a capital letter?	___	___
Did the author capitalize the names of specific people, places, and things?	___	___
Did the author end each sentence with the correct punctuation mark?	___	___
Did the author correctly use quotation marks for any dialogue?	___	___
Did the author use commas to separate items in a series?	___	___
Did the author use apostrophes to show ownership or contractions?	___	___

Composition
Did the paper have a main idea?	___	___
Did the author stick to the topic?	___	___
Did the author use complete sentences?	___	___
Did the author use details to support the main idea?	___	___
Did the author provide a concluding sentence?	___	___

Style
Did the author use a variety of sentence types?	___	___
Could you tell how the author felt from his/her writing?	___	___
Did the author use specific words that helped you visualize the writing?	___	___

A Last Look

What did you like best about this paper? _____

_____

_____

What suggestions for improvement would you make to the author? _____

_____

_____

Edited By   **Date**

_____   _____

Note To The Teacher: Use with "Outside Input" on page 155. Give each student a copy of this editing checklist to attach to his writing. Then have him ask a student in another classroom, a faculty member, a parent, a sibling, or an older relative to complete the checklist, providing him with feedback.

Check It Out!

Inside every writer's portfolio is a checklist. A checklist helps a writer keep track of each step of the writing process. Add the checklist below to your writing portfolio. Use it each time you begin writing.

Writer's Checklist

Put a check in the box after you complete each step.

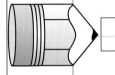 **Step 1: Plan—Think about what you will write.**
To help you get started, ask yourself the following questions:
- What is my purpose—to explain, describe, persuade?
- What is my subject—who or what am I writing about?
- How am I going to organize my paper—paragraph, letter, poem?
- Who is my audience—teacher, classmates, business person?

Then get your ideas together. Brainstorm and create a list, a web, or an outline to organize your writing.

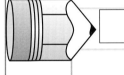 **Step 2: Write—Focus your writing.**
Write down your ideas. Begin with a main-idea sentence and add detail sentences. Keep writing. Don't worry about things like spelling or neatness yet.

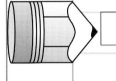 **Step 3: Polish—Make your writing better.**
Use an editing checklist to help you make changes. Then rewrite your work neatly.

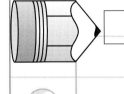 **Step 4: Check And Share—Make the final touches.**
Check your work one more time and make any necessary corrections. Then share what you've written.

Remember: Plan, Write, Polish, Check and Share!

Note To The Teacher: Duplicate several copies for each student to put into his writing portfolio.

Polishing Your Writing

Ask any writer you know, and she'll tell you that writing takes some "elbow grease"! An important part of writing is *revising.* Revising means changing your writing to make it better. A good writer reviews her writing and makes notes of the changes she wants to make.

Use the questions below to help you revise your writing. Check *yes* or *no* for each question. Make note of the changes you want to make on your paper; then rewrite your paper. Always remember, with just a little extra cleaning and polishing, your work will shine!

Do you, madam, feel you have polished your writing to the best of your ability?

I do!

Editor's "Do I?" Checklist

Organization:

	yes	no
Do I have a beginning, a middle, and an end?	☐	☐
Do I arrange my ideas in the best order?	☐	☐
Do I have a catchy title?	☐	☐

Details:

	yes	no
Do I have a main-idea sentence?	☐	☐
Do I have sentences that support the main idea?	☐	☐
Do I have enough details and examples?	☐	☐
Do I have a concluding sentence that wraps up my writing?	☐	☐

Style:

	yes	no
Do I write clearly and is my writing easy to follow?	☐	☐
Do I use a variety of sentences—some long, some short?	☐	☐
Do I have sentences with different beginnings?	☐	☐
Do I use specific nouns, strong verbs, and colorful adjectives?	☐	☐

Mechanics:

	yes	no
Do I end all my sentences with the correct punctuation?	☐	☐
Do I use commas, apostrophes, and quotation marks correctly?	☐	☐
Do I begin all my sentences and names of specific people and places with capital letters?	☐	☐
Do I spell my words correctly?	☐	☐

Note To The Teacher: If desired, duplicate a copy of the editing symbols on page 167 for each student to use with this checklist when editing and revising her work.

Tools Of The Trade

The right kinds of tools—everybody needs them! Carpenters, mountain climbers, doctors, and students all have special tools to help them get the job done. One tool a writer uses to keep his work organized is a *portfolio*. Whether it's a binder, folder, or other organizer, your portfolio will help you keep your writing together!

Write your name on the portfolio tag below. Then color and cut it out. Glue the tag to the front of an organizer. Use the portfolio to keep all your writing organized.

Writer's Portfolio

_____
(writer's name)

©1997 The Education Center, Inc. • *The Mailbox® Superbook • Grade 4 • TEC453*

Writer's Evaluation Sheet

Evaluating your work will help you become a better writer. After you've written a piece, complete this form. Use the back of this sheet if you need more space. After you've completed the evaluation, attach it to your writing and place it in your portfolio.

1. Date this piece was written: _____

2. Title of this piece: _____

3. Subject of this piece: _____

4. Type of writing (poem, letter, short story, etc.): _____

5. I'm proud of this piece because _____
   _____
   _____
   _____

6. The strengths of this piece are _____
   _____
   _____
   _____

7. Some difficulties I had with this piece were _____
   _____
   _____
   _____

8. If I wrote this piece again, one thing I'd do differently is _____
   _____
   _____
   _____

©1997 The Education Center, Inc. • *The Mailbox® Superbook • Grade 4 • TEC453*

Note To The Teacher: Provide each student with a pocket folder or other inexpensive organizer. Duplicate one copy of the portfolio tag for each child. Provide glue, scissors, and markers so the child can complete his portfolio tag. Duplicate several copies of the bottom portion of the page for each student to put into his writing portfolio. 173

Consumer's Choice

Consumer's Name: _____

Product: _____

Brand Name: _____   Brand Name: _____

Taste

Texture

Appearance

Smell

Sound

Price

$

Ingredients

Note To The Teacher: Use this sheet with "The Taste Test" on page 159.

WRITE-O

Comparison	Editorial	News Report	Limerick Poem	Friendly Letter
Haiku Poem	Research Report	Commercial	Skit	Character Description
Diary Entry	Persuasive Essay	FREE	Postcard	Biographical Sketch
Business Letter	Folktale	Journal Entry	Letter To An Editor	Summary
Dialogue Between Two People Or Characters	How-To Paragraph	Book Report	Myth	Cinquain Poem

---

Name _____

Writing Frame: parts-of-speech poem

Parts-Of-Speech Poem

_____
Title (adjective, noun)

_____
(noun determiner, noun)

_____ and _____
(adjective)   (adjective)

_____
(verb, adverb)

_____
(preposition, noun determiner, noun)

_____
Student's name

Note To The Teacher: Use with "Parts-Of-Speech Poem" on page 163.

Pattern
Use with "Star Reporters" on page 166.

Star Reporters Guide

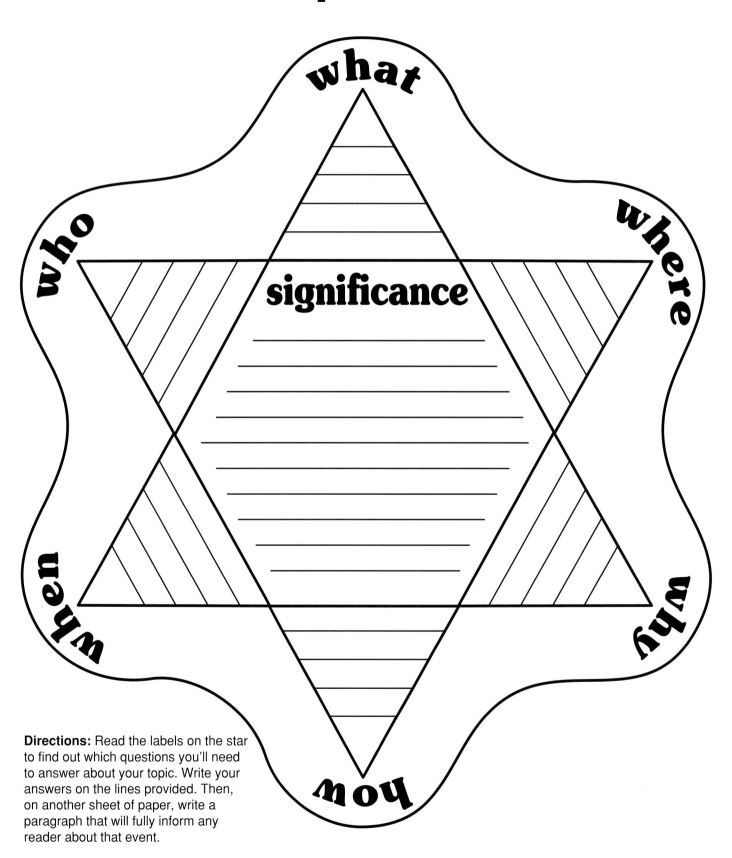

Directions: Read the labels on the star to find out which questions you'll need to answer about your topic. Write your answers on the lines provided. Then, on another sheet of paper, write a paragraph that will fully inform any reader about that event.

©1997 The Education Center, Inc. • *The Mailbox® Superbook* • Grade 4 • TEC453

LITERATURE

Ideas To Use
WITH ANY BOOK

CHAIN OF EVENTS

Use this 3-D activity to help students sequence book events. After reading a story, provide each child with several 1" x 6" strips of construction paper. Direct each student to write each of the following items on a separate strip—her name, the book's title, the author's name, and each of the major events in the story. Direct the student to then staple the strips to make a chain that demonstrates the sequence of events in the story. Hang the chains from the ceiling in your classroom.

Vocabulary READ-O

Learning new words has never been easier! Duplicate a 5 x 5 grid for each student. Ask each student to fill each square with a different vocabulary word from your current novel. Give each child beans or plastic chips to use as markers. Then read a definition aloud, keeping track of each one you call by listing its corresponding word on paper. Instruct each student to cover the word that corresponds to the definition called on his grid. Have a student call out, "READ-O!" if he gets five markers in a row; then have everyone clear his board and begin the game again. Add variety by changing the winning pattern from five in a row to four corners or another bingo combination.

READ-O

deprived	indignant		ordeal	disposition
pewter	stout	tuft	solitary	gaunt
flint	finicky	m	s	prowess
heather	detested	wary	boggy	shambles
trenchers	medley	persisted	nudge	

Character-Trait Collage

Spice up your study of character traits with this fun activity! Brainstorm a list of character traits with your students. List these traits on chart paper. Next have each child select a character from the novel your class is reading. Have the student write his character's name in the center of a sheet of construction paper and the novel's title at the top. Then direct the student to cut out words and pictures related to his character from old magazines, and glue them collage-fashion on the construction paper. Display the collages on a bulletin board titled "Creative Character Collages."

Flip-Up Sequence Report

Review the sequence of events in a short book or a chapter of the novel you're reading with this unique project. Direct each student to fold an 8 1/2" x 8 1/2" paper into fourths. Next have her open the paper and fold each point toward the center of the square. Have the student number the four flaps as shown. On each flap have her write a sentence about one of four major events of the chapter or story. Then have her illustrate each event under its flap. Finally have the student write her name and the story's title and author on the back of the report. Store the reports in a basket in your classroom library.

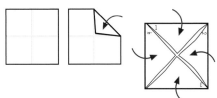

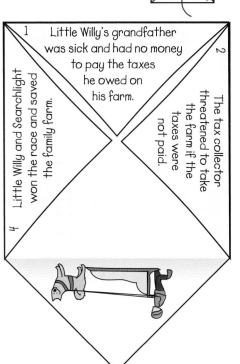

1
Little Willy's grandfather was sick and had no money to pay the taxes he owed on his farm.

2
The tax collector threatened to take the farm if the taxes were not paid.

4
Little Willy and Searchlight won the race and saved the family farm.

Teaching STORY ELEMENTS

Need help teaching basic story elements? Picture books can do the trick! Read aloud a fairy-tale picture book—such as *Cinderella* by Charles Perrault (Puffin Books, 1993). Then read a similar book, such as *Mufaro's Beautiful Daughters: An African Tale* by John Steptoe (Lothrop, Lee & Shepard Books, 1987). Using a chart as shown, have students point out the setting, characters, problem, and solution in each story. Then ask each child to write a new version of the story, changing several elements while following the basic plotline. Encourage each child to share his revamped tale aloud. Ask students to point out the story elements in each classmate's story.

	Cinderella	Mufaro's Beautiful Daughters
settings	Small village in France	Small village in Zimbabwe, Africa.
characters	Cinderella Prince Stepmother Stepsisters Fairy Godmother	Nyasha Nyoka Manyara The King Mufaro
problems		
solutions		

CHARACTER ANALYSIS WHEELS

Chug right through character analysis with this fun activity! After reading a novel, assign each student a character. Then have her follow these steps to make a one-of-a-kind project:

1. Trace a six-inch circle on a sheet of construction paper. Cut out the circle.
2. Draw a smaller three-inch circle in the center of the circle. Write the character's name, the book's title, and the author in the smaller circle.
3. Draw spokes on the wheel as shown. Then write a personality trait describing your character in each spoke.

To display the projects, post several cut-out train cars on a bulletin board titled "All Aboard For Characterization!" Staple the wheels to the cars.

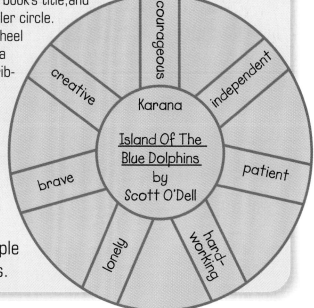

courageous / independent / patient / hard-working / lonely / brave / creative

Karana
Island Of The Blue Dolphins
by
Scott O'Dell

Add a little intrigue to your review of a novel's characters with this fun game! Pair students who have read the same novel; then provide each pair with index cards, markers, and the following instructions:

1. Write the name of each character from the novel on a separate card.
2. Shuffle the cards. Player 1 deals one card to himself/herself and one to Player 2. Place the remaining cards facedown.
3. Player 1 tries to guess the character card being held by Player 2 by asking a yes/no question, such as "Is your character a good friend?" or "Was your character in the school play?"
4. If Player 2 answers the question with a yes, then Player 1 must guess the character named on Player 2's card. If Player 1 guesses correctly, he/she keeps that card. Then Player 1 goes again after Player 2 has drawn another card from the pile.
5. If the answer to the question is no, play continues with Player 2 taking a turn.
6. The game continues until all the cards from the pile are gone. The player with the most cards at the end of the game wins.

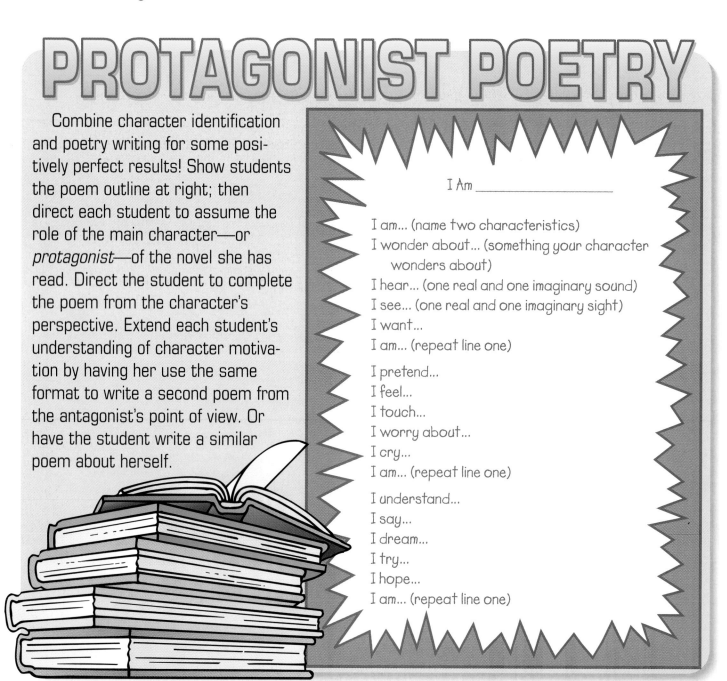

PROTAGONIST POETRY

Combine character identification and poetry writing for some positively perfect results! Show students the poem outline at right; then direct each student to assume the role of the main character—or *protagonist*—of the novel she has read. Direct the student to complete the poem from the character's perspective. Extend each student's understanding of character motivation by having her use the same format to write a second poem from the antagonist's point of view. Or have the student write a similar poem about herself.

I Am _____

I am... (name two characteristics)
I wonder about... (something your character
    wonders about)
I hear... (one real and one imaginary sound)
I see... (one real and one imaginary sight)
I want...
I am... (repeat line one)

I pretend...
I feel...
I touch...
I worry about...
I cry...
I am... (repeat line one)

I understand...
I say...
I dream...
I try...
I hope...
I am... (repeat line one)

Reflective Reading Record

Tired of the traditional book report? Then try this brain-boostin' alternative! Provide each student with several copies of page 192. Ask her to end each reading session by *reviewing* (summarizing what she's read that day), *reflecting* (relating what has happened in the novel to her own life experiences), and *predicting* (guessing what will happen next in the story). Have the student record this information on her copy of page 192. As each student reflects, encourage her to consider these questions:

- How believable are the story's characters and events?
- Is the writer's choice of subject matter and story line interesting? Why or why not?
- In what ways could the author make the novel better?

Baggy Book Jackets

Foster independent reading by sponsoring a contest that looks a lot like a fashion show! Direct each student to cut a vest from a paper grocery bag as shown. Have the student write the book's title and author, as well as a short summary, on the bag. Then encourage her to decorate the bag using characters and scenes from the book she has read. Invite each student to wear her book jacket while giving a talk on the featured novel.

IT'S IN THE BAG

This fun book-report idea is guaranteed to be a "shoe-in" with your students! Direct each student to bring in an empty shoebox from home. Provide the student with arts-and-crafts supplies; then direct him to use the supplies to transform the inside of the box into a scene from a novel he recently read. Next have the student use the verse pattern below to describe the scene illustrated in the box. Display the boxed scenes and verses around your room. For an extra challenge, separate each verse from its corresponding box; then have students try to match each poem with its scene.

line 1   **book's title**
line 2   **name the main characters**
line 3   **summarize the story theme**
line 4   **describe the setting**
line 5   **write an opinion about the book or a lesson learned from the book**

Shiloh
Marty Preston and Shiloh
Loyalty between a boy and dog
A country town in West Virginia
Always be kind to animals

TIME-OUT FOR A TABLEAU

Your class has just finished a great novel—now what? Try this terrific book-ending activity. Explain to students that a *tableau* or *tableau vivant* is a living scene usually presented on stage by silent, motionless, costumed participants. Next divide your students into groups. Have each group work together to physically re-create a scene from the novel just completed. Assign one student in each group to act as the director, arranging the remaining group members in the scene re-creation. Encourage each group to make props and costumes from art supplies. Then have each group present its scene to the rest of the class as its director explains its significance in the story. Take a photo of each tableau to create an interesting display!

COOPERATIVE CONTRACT

Your students will sail right through their reading with the help of this cooperative book-reporting activity! Pair students and direct each pair to select a novel to read together. Then provide each student with a copy of the cooperative book-report contract on page 193. Have each pair read its novel and complete the contract as a team. Display the completed projects, and encourage other students to use them as references when selecting future reading material.

Freedom-Of-Choice Book Reports

Give your students plenty of book-reporting options with this simple suggestion:

1. Select five to ten book-report projects (see the list on pages 186–187).
2. Write or type each project's directions several times on a sheet of paper; then cut the copies apart. Glue one copy to the front of a 5" x 7" envelope; then place the remaining copies inside the envelope.
3. Store the envelopes in a shoebox.
4. Have each student read the directions on the envelopes and select a project that interests him. Then have him take a copy of the directions from the selected envelope and complete the project.
5. Display the finished project so students can see examples of the book-report options they have.

Design

Making A Book Mobile

...ng A Book ...Bag

Motivating STUDENTS TO READ

GREAT WALL OF BOOKS

Help your students build great reading habits with this motivational activity! Cut a supply of 3" x 5" red construction-paper bricks. After each student finishes reading a novel, have her write the book's title and author, a short summary of the book, and her name on the front of a paper brick. Then have her tape the brick to a wall in your classroom. Explain that once the reading wall reaches certain predetermined heights—such as two feet, four feet, and six feet—those contributing bricks to it will receive a special treat.

David Reitz

Charlie And The Chocolate Factory by Roald Dahl
This book was about a poor boy named Charlie. He found a golden ticket inside a candy-bar wrapper. The ticket allowed him to visit the factory of the great candy maker, Willy Wonka. There were also four other children who found tickets. The other four children broke the rules Mr. Wonka gave before the tour. They didn't make it to the end. Because Charlie was a good and honest person, Mr. Wonka gave him the candy factory.

Reading Punch Cards

Put a little punch into your reading program with easy-to-make incentives! Cut a small tagboard card for each student. Have each student decorate his card with a special reading message; then have him number 1 to 5 along the left edge of his card and 6 to 10 on its right edge. Help each student set an individual reading goal by writing the number of books (between one and ten) he wants to read on the back of the card. When each child finishes reading and reporting on a book, punch out the lowest number on his card. Continue punching numbers as the student reads books until he has reached his goal. Celebrate the accomplishment by rewarding the student with a special treat.

READING IS G-R-REAT!
6 7 3 8 4 9 5 10

Kid Critiques

Who are the best critics of children's books? Kids, of course! Give students opportunities to recommend their favorite titles or authors to classmates. Keep a notebook at your reading center or a listing on your computer database. As a student finishes a book that she enjoyed, have her list its title and author, then write a brief summary to entice others to read it.

KICK BACK WITH A GOOD BOOK!

Kick Back And Read!

Excite students about reading with this toe-tappin' bulletin board! Enlarge and color the pattern on page 194. Then attach the pattern to a bulletin board titled "Kick Back With A Good Book!" On the board, display book jackets or copies of book covers along with short summaries or teasers to capture student interest. (Be sure to let students add book covers they've drawn and their own recommendations, too.) Place several copies of each featured book in a tub below the display. Then watch the books quickly disappear into the hands of eager readers!

Book Exchange

Encourage your students to make reading part of their daily routines by hosting a book exchange. Ask each child to bring (with parental permission) at least one recommended book from his personal collection to exchange with a classmate. Provide each student with a redeemable book ticket for each book he brings in for the exchange. Then display the collection of books and allow each student to exchange his ticket for a book he would like to read. Repeat this several times throughout the year. What a great way to help students get new reading material without the cost!

BOOK TICKET
Redeemable f

BOOK TICKET
Redeemable for one book at the book exchange.

John Newbery Award Winners
1970–1997

1997—*The View From Saturday* by E. L. Konigsburg

1996—*The Midwife's Apprentice* by Karen Cushman

1995—*Walk Two Moons* by Sharon Creech

1994—*The Giver* by Lois Lowry

1993—*Missing May* by Cynthia Rylant

1992—*Shiloh* by Phyllis Reynolds Naylor

1991—*Maniac Magee* by Jerry Spinelli

1990—*Number The Stars* by Lois Lowry

1989—*Joyful Noise* by Paul Fleischman

1988—*Lincoln: A Photobiography* by Russell Freedman

1987—*The Whipping Boy* by Sid Fleischman

1986—*Sarah, Plain And Tall* by Patricia MacLachlan

1985—*The Hero And The Crown* by Robin McKinley

1984—*Dear Mr. Henshaw* by Beverly Cleary

1983—*Dicey's Song* by Cynthia Voight

1982—*A Visit To William Blake's Inn* by Nancy Willard

1981—*Jacob Have I Loved* by Katherine Paterson

1980—*A Gathering Of Days* by Joan W. Blos

1979—*The Westing Game* by Ellen Raskin

1978—*Bridge To Terabithia* by Katherine Paterson

1977—*Roll Of Thunder, Hear My Cry* by Mildred D. Taylor

1976—*The Grey King* by Susan Cooper

1975—*M. C. Higgins, The Great* by Virginia Hamilton

1974—*The Slave Dancer* by Paula Fox

1973—*Julie Of The Wolves* by Jean Craighead George

1972—*Mrs. Frisby And The Rats Of NIMH* by Robert C. O'Brien

1971—*Summer Of The Swans* by Betsy Byars

1970—*Sounder* by William H. Armstrong

Suggested Read-Alouds

- *Jumanji* by Chris Van Allsburg
- *Falling Up* by Shel Silverstein
- *Something Big Has Been Here* by Jack Prelutsky
- *The Best School Year Ever* by Barbara Robinson
- *The Incredible Journey* by Sheila Burnford
- *The Indian In The Cupboard* by Lynne Reid Banks
- *Mrs. Frisby And The Rats Of NIMH* by Robert C. O'Brien
- *Sounder* by William H. Armstrong
- *The BFG* by Roald Dahl
- *An Occasional Cow* by Polly Horvath
- *From The Mixed-Up Files Of Mrs. Basil E. Frankweiler* by E. L. Konigsburg
- *Island Of The Blue Dolphins* by Scott O'Dell
- *Hatchet* by Gary Paulsen
- *Bridge To Terabithia* by Katherine Paterson
- *The Castle In The Attic* by Elizabeth Winthrop
- *The Boggart* by Susan Cooper
- *Shiloh* by Phyllis Reynolds Naylor
- *Bull Run* by Paul Fleischman
- *Poppy* by Avi
- *The War With Grandpa* by Robert K. Smith

Better Than A Book Report!
Creative Ways To Share About The Book You Just Read

Directions: When you finish reading a novel, choose a project from the list below to complete. When your project is finished, place a check in the box next to it.

_____ Write a newspaper with stories describing events that happened in the novel you read. Include articles that describe interesting details about one of the book's main characters or its setting.

_____ Create a time capsule for the main characters in your story. In the time capsule, include important items from the story that help tell what happened in the book. Present your time capsule to the class and explain why each item it includes is important.

_____ Design a set of finger puppets to represent the main characters in your favorite scene in the story. Act out the scene for your classmates using the puppets.

_____ Select a scene from the novel to act out. Rewrite the scene in script form. Ask classmates to act out the roles of characters in the scene. Practice the scene; then perform it for your classmates.

_____ Design a travel brochure that advertises the setting of the story as a tourist spot. Fold an 8 1/2" x 11" sheet of white paper into thirds. Fill the brochure with information on sites and activities of interest, dining and lodging establishments, and any information that would help tourists.

_____ Design a poster to advertise your book to other readers. Use lots of colorful adjectives to capture the reader's interest. Be sure to include the story basics—such as the title, the author's name, the illustrator's name, and a short summary of the book—on the poster.

_____ Construct a diorama that shows an important scene from the story. Make the diorama three-dimensional with the help of various arts-and-crafts materials.

_____ Write a short commercial advertising the book. Then record it on an audiocassette tape. At the beginning of the tape, be sure to give your name, the book's title, and the author; then record your commercial.

_____ Find 15 new vocabulary words introduced in the novel. Create a glossary in which you define each word and draw an illustration to go with the definition.

_____ Create a mobile featuring cutouts and pictures that show the major events of the novel. Be sure to arrange the hanging shapes in the order they happened in the story.

_____ Design a coat of arms to represent the main character of the story. Decorate the coat of arms with symbols that represent the character's personality. On the back of the coat of arms, write a paragraph that gives your reasons for including each item.

_____ Write an acrostic poem to represent the main character of your story. To do this write the letters in the character's name vertically on a sheet of paper. Then, after each letter, write an adjective describing the character that begins with that letter.

_____ Dress as your favorite character from the book. Present a short summary of the book to your classmates. See if they can determine your identity based on your costume and speech.

_____ Pretend you are a news reporter interviewing the main character from the story. Write a list of questions and the responses you think the interviewee would give.

_____ Design a creative book jacket for the story. Be sure to make your design appealing so that it interests readers. Include the title, the author's name, the illustrator's name, a short summary of the novel, and illustrations on the book jacket.

_____ Create a collage to represent one of the characters in the story. Cut pictures and words from magazines. Glue them to paper to create a collage that describes the character.

_____ Write a sequel to the story. Use the information you learned about the characters as you read the book.

_____ Decorate a paper bag with scenes from the book. Write the title, the author's name, and a brief summary on the bag. Then place three items relating to the story inside the bag. Present the bag to your class and explain the items it contains.

_____ Cover a square box with paper. On one side of the box, write the title and author of the book you read. Record the five Ws—who, what, when, where, and why—on the other sides.

_____ Design a "Wanted!" poster featuring one of the characters in the story. Be sure to mention the character's name, a description, and what he or she is wanted for; then draw the character on the poster.

_____ Design a bookmark that advertises the novel. Write the title, the author's name, and a summary of the story on the bookmark. Also add an illustration of an important scene from the book.

BOOKS WORTH BARKING ABOUT!

Digging around for a great book? Make no bones about it,
these titles are worth barking about!

REALISTIC FICTION

Maniac Magee
by Jerry Spinelli

The Pinballs
by Betsy Byars

Strider
by Beverly Cleary

Shiloh
by Phyllis Reynolds Naylor

The Great Gilly Hopkins
by Katherine Paterson

ADVENTURE/ FANTASY

Stone Fox
by John R. Gardiner

The Indian In The Cupboard
by Lynne Reid Banks

My Teacher Fried My Brains
by Bruce Coville

The Whipping Boy
by Sid Fleischman

The Forgotten Door
by Alexander Key

HUMOR

Matilda
by Roald Dahl

Charlie And The Chocolate Factory
by Roald Dahl

How To Eat Fried Worms
by Thomas Rockwell

Skinnybones
by Barbara Park

Soup
by Robert Newton Peck

The Best Christmas Pageant Ever
by Barbara Robinson

Pippi Longstocking
by Astrid Lindgren

HISTORICAL FICTION

The Slave Dancer
by Paula Fox

Number The Stars
by Lois Lowry

Roll Of Thunder, Hear My Cry
by Mildred D. Taylor

Who Comes With Cannons?
by Patricia Beatty

Shades of Gray
by Carolyn Reeder

The Sign Of The Beaver
by Elizabeth George Speare

MYSTERY

Incognito Mosquito, Private Insective
by E. A. Hass

The Dollhouse Murders
by Betty Ren Wright

The Ghost Wore Grey
by Bruce Coville

The Case Of The Baker Street Irregular
by Robert Newman

BIOGRAPHY/ AUTOBIOGRAPHY

Lincoln: A Photobiography
by Russell Freedman

The Double Life Of Pocahontas
by Jean Fritz

Helen Keller's Teacher
by Margaret Davidson

Boy: Tales Of Childhood
by Roald Dahl

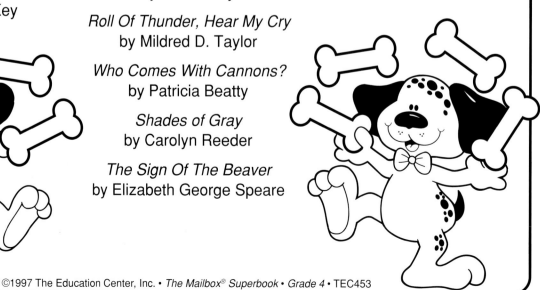

Name_____

Help the reporters at the Readers' Gazette meet their deadline! Using information from the novel you just read, write several articles for the upcoming issue of the newspaper in the spaces provided. Add an illustration in the box.

The Readers' Gazette

_____

_____

_____

_____

_____

_____

_____

_____

_____

Photo: Draw an illustration to go with the lead article.

Lead Article: Write about the most exciting part of the book. Write a headline; then write an accompanying article that includes the *who, what, when, where,* and *why* in your story.

Dear Editor:

_____

_____

_____

_____

_____

_____

_____

Editorial: Write a letter to the editor stating your opinion of one of the book's characters or events.

Feature Story: Write a feature story on a character or event of your choice from the story.

Name _____

190

A Whale Of A Tale

Directions: Cut out the whale parts below and glue them together to form a whale. Then fill in each part of the whale with information from the story or book you just read.

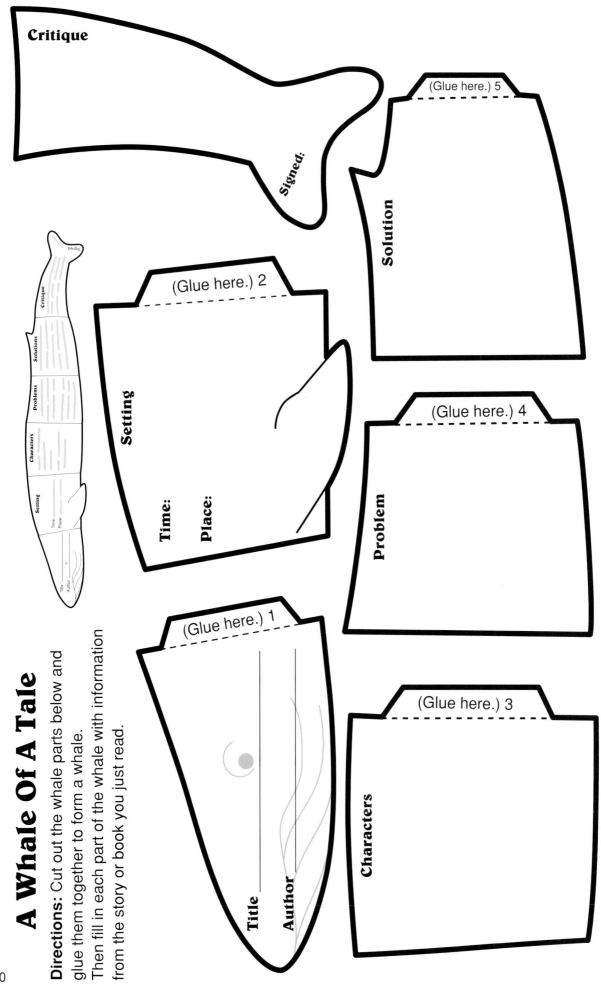

Critique

Signed: _____

(Glue here.) 5

Solution

(Glue here.) 2

Setting

Time: _____

Place: _____

(Glue here.) 4

Problem

(Glue here.) 1

Title _____

Author _____

(Glue here.) 3

Characters

Note To The Teacher: Provide each student with scissors and glue. Display the completed whales on a bulletin board titled "A Whale Of A Tale." During free time have students use arts-and-crafts materials to create an underwater scene on the board.

Lights, Camera, Sequence!

Directions: Cut out the filmstrip pattern below; then separate the strips by cutting along the center dotted line. (Save the bottom section of this sheet for later.) Glue the right end of the top strip to the left end of the bottom strip to create one longer strip. Use the filmstrip frames to retell the major events of the story you read. To do this, illustrate a scene and write a one-sentence summary of the event in each frame. Be sure your scenes are in the correct order.

(Glue here.)

Construct a film projection screen by cutting out the pattern below. Slit the two dotted lines as directed and slide your completed filmstrip in the slots so that one frame at a time is displayed in the center of the viewer. Show your finished filmstrip to a classmate.

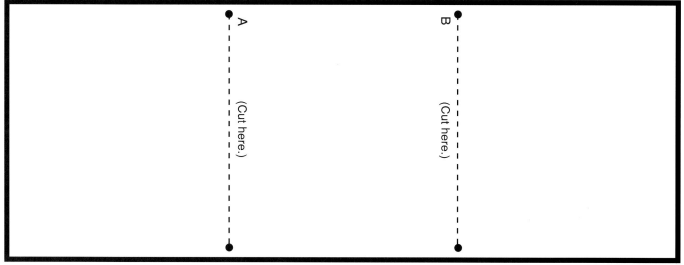

A

(Cut here.)

B

(Cut here.)

Note To The Teacher: Provide each student with scissors and glue.

REFLECTIVE READING RECORD

for _____
title

written by _____
author

REVIEW	REFLECT	PREDICT
What did you read today?	What did you think about what you read?	What do you think will happen next?
date		
date		
date		

Note To The Teacher: Use this sheet with "Reflective Reading Record" on page 181. Give each student one copy on which to record his responses to the novel he is currently reading. Provide each student with additional copies as needed.

Name _____

Partner _____   Due Date _____

"Two-Can" Do It!

Book Title _____   **Author** _____

Directions: When you and your partner have finished reading the novel you selected, work together to complete the activities outlined on each island. Color in each island after you complete the activity it describes.

Pick five interesting words from the novel you read. Illustrate the meaning of each on unlined paper.

Make a coat of arms for the main character of the story. Include important details about the character's personality.

On unlined paper, draw a detailed map of where the story takes place. Be sure to include a map key or legend.

Write a summary of your story as a cartoon strip. Fold a sheet of unlined paper into thirds lengthwise and then in half widthwise to make six blocks. Decide on the six most important events from the story; then illustrate each in cartoon fashion in one of the blocks.

Design a new book cover for your novel that shows both the main character and an important event from the story. Be sure to include the book's title and the author's name on the cover, too.

Note To The Teacher: Divide students into pairs that will read the same novel. Make one copy of this contract and program the due date on the appropriate line. Then duplicate and distribute one copy to each student. Have student pairs complete the contract together.

Pattern
Enlarge and use
With "Kick Back
And Read!" on
page 184.

©1997 The Education Center, Inc. • *The Mailbox® Superbook* • *Grade 4* • TEC453

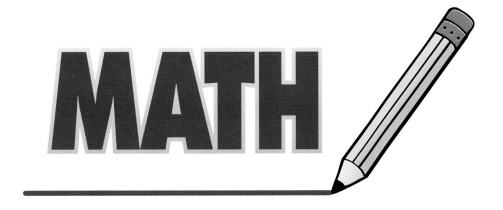

NUMERATION

Number Books

"How do I represent a number? Let me count the ways!" Strengthen understanding of the different ways to represent a number with this fun activity. Give each student several half-sheets of 9" x 12" construction paper and scissors. Instruct the student to select a number between 20 and 100, then write as many mathematical representations of that number as she can, each on a different sheet of construction paper (see the illustration). Have her create a title page and staple the booklet pages together. Place the completed number booklets in a learning center or reading corner for students to look through. As larger numbers are studied, challenge your students to make books for them, too!

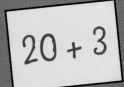

Place-Value Pictures

Put a little artistic expression into your study of place value with this simple project. Give each student one 9" x 12" sheet of construction paper, several copies of the patterns below, scissors, crayons, and glue. First have the student cut out his patterns and use them to design a picture on his construction paper. Then have him glue down each piece and add color to his picture. Next have him calculate the total value of his picture by adding the value of each piece used. Finally direct the student to use the total calculated value of his picture to give it a title. Post the completed pictures on a bulletin board.

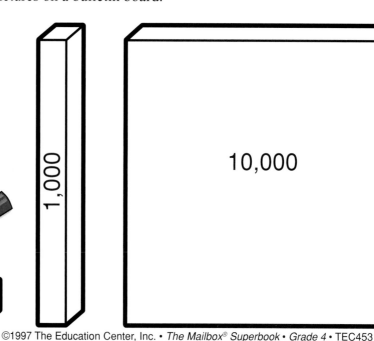

Go Fish!

Reel in addition and subtraction practice with this two-player variation of Go Fish! The object of the game is to create a larger numeral than your opponent by taking digits from him. Begin by having each partner secretly write a six-digit numeral with no repeating digits on a sheet of paper (for example, 926,184). Instruct Player A to ask Player B for a digit (for example, "Do you have an *8?*"). If Player B has an *8* in his six-digit numeral, have him announce its place value *(80)*. Then have Player A add that value to his six-digit numeral and Player B subtract it from his numeral (see the example). If Player B does not have the digit, he says, "Go fish!" and Player A scores a zero for that round. If the same numeral appears more than once in Player B's numeral, Player B may choose which place value to give away. The player with the larger numeral at the end of six rounds is the winner.

$$
\begin{array}{r}
537{,}185 \\
+80 \\
\hline
537{,}265 \\
-500{,}000 \\
\hline
37{,}265 \\
+20{,}000 \\
\hline
57{,}265 \\
\end{array}
\qquad
\begin{array}{r}
926{,}184 \\
-80 \\
\hline
926{,}104 \\
+500{,}000 \\
\hline
1{,}426{,}104 \\
-20{,}000 \\
\hline
1{,}406{,}104 \\
\end{array}
$$

In The Can!

Pair up a chalkboard eraser and a trash can for this whole-class game! Divide your class into two teams. In turn, have one player from each team stand 20 feet from the trash can and try to throw a chalkboard eraser into it. If the student tosses the eraser into the can, have her teammates make up an addition or a subtraction problem for her to solve on the chalkboard. If the eraser does not go in the can, have the opposing team make up the problem for her to solve. Give each team one point for each problem it correctly solves. Continue play until every student has had a turn. Reward the team with the most points at the end of the game with inexpensive prizes or homework passes.

Math Shuffleboard

Shuffle on down to addition and subtraction expertise with an exciting game of shuffleboard! Write six to ten addition and subtraction problems in a row on the chalkboard; then divide your class into two teams. Have one player from each team stand at opposite ends of the board. Instruct one player to slide the eraser along the chalk tray and solve the problem closest to where it stops. If he solves the problem correctly, award his team one point. If an incorrect answer is given, no points are awarded. Continue play with the other student. If a player slides the eraser closest to a previously solved problem, he loses his turn. Invite two different team members to the board and play another round. When only two problems remain unsolved, erase the solved problems and write new ones. Continue play until each student has had a turn; then declare the team with the most points the winner.

$$
\begin{array}{r}
5{,}623 \\
+7{,}842 \\
\hline
\end{array}
\qquad
\begin{array}{r}
9{,}654 \\
+2{,}300 \\
\hline
11{,}954 \\
\end{array}
\qquad
\begin{array}{r}
9{,}826 \\
-5{,}731 \\
\hline
\end{array}
\qquad
\begin{array}{r}
11{,}267 \\
-2{,}985 \\
\hline
\end{array}
\qquad
\begin{array}{r}
8{,}795 \\
+2{,}234 \\
\hline
\end{array}
$$

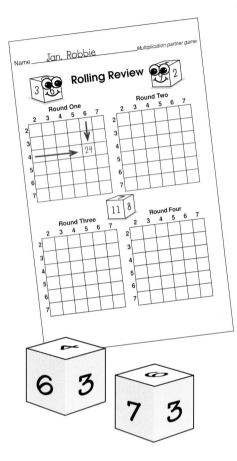

Rolling Review

Get the dice rolling for this kid-pleasin' multiplication facts game!

1 For each pair of students, duplicate two copies of the reproducible die on page 147 on white construction paper. Have students program the faces of one die 2–7 and those of the other die 7–12. Then have them follow steps 3–5 on the page to make each die.

2 Duplicate the reproducible gameboards on the top half of page 212 for each student.

3 Have each pair of students take turns rolling the dice, finding the product of the two numbers, and then writing it in the box where the two numbers intersect on his gameboard (see the illustration).

4 Have the first student to write four consecutive products in a horizontal, vertical, or diagonal row use a multiplication table to check his answers. If all four products were correctly placed, he wins that round.

5 To change the multiplication facts being reviewed, reprogram the numbers on the dice and the numbers along the horizontal and vertical axes of the gameboards.

Math Facts Match

Take the ho-hum out of learning math facts with this game for two. Cut about 50 index cards in half. Use a blue pen to write a different multiplication fact in the upper right-hand corner of each card; then use a red pen to write a product that doesn't match that fact in the lower left corner. Be sure that each fact has a matching product on *another* card.

To play, Player A draws ten cards from the deck and places each one diagonally on the table as shown. Then he gives five more cards from the deck to himself and five cards to his partner, placing the remaining cards facedown in a pile. In turn, each player draws a card from the pile and tries to match it or one of the cards in his hand with one of the ten cards lying faceup. (He cannot match two cards that are in his hand.) If he makes a match, he earns one point. If he is unable to make a match, the player puts the drawn card in his hand and says "Pass." The player with the most points when all cards have been played wins. Try programming cards with division facts for a whole new game!

2 x 6 =
32

8 x 4 =
16

2 x 5 =
45

4 x 4 =
12

9 x 5 =
10

3 x 7 =
42

8 x 5 =
6

6 x 9 =
21

3 x 2 =
40

7 x 6 =
54

2 x 6 =

8 x 4 = 32

16

Targeting Multiplication

Reinforce your students' estimating and multiplication skills with this two-player game. For each pair of students, program each of 25 cards with a different range of numbers and a point value (see the illustration). Divide your class into pairs. Give each pair a set of the cards, two dice, a pencil, a calculator, and a sheet of paper. Explain the following directions:

1. Shuffle the cards and place them facedown in a pile.

2. Draw the top three cards and place them faceup in the center of the playing surface.

3. Player A chooses one of the range cards facing up, then rolls each die separately to create a two-digit numeral. For example, if the first die rolled shows a *5* and the second die rolled shows a *3*, then the two-digit numeral is *53*.

4. Player A estimates what number times 53 will produce a product that falls within the range written on the chosen range card. For example, if Player A chose the 100–120 card, then he can multiply 53 x 2 to get a product of 106, which falls within the range. Player B uses a calculator to check Player A's calculations. If he is correct, Player A keeps that card and draws another one to take its place on the playing surface; then player B takes his turn. If Player A is incorrect, the card remains with the other three cards, and Player B takes his turn.

5. When time expires, each player adds the total number of points on his cards. The student with the most points is the winner.

100–120	190–210
1 point	3 points

60–80		
70–90		
80–100	} 1 point	
90–110		
100–120		

110–130		
120–140		
130–150	} 2 points	
140–160		
150–170		

160–180		
170–190		
180–200	} 3 points	
190–210		
200–220		

210–230		
220–240		
230–250	} 4 points	
240–260		
250–270		

260–280		
270–290		
280–300	} 5 points	
290–310		
300–320		

Division Decision

Motivate your students to practice division with this small-group game. Divide your class into groups of two or three. Give each group one hundred board, a crayon, and a die. Have Player A choose and lightly color a number on the hundred board with a crayon. Instruct him to roll the die and divide the number displayed on the die into the number he colored on the hundred board. Then have him multiply the remainder from the division problem by the number on the die to determine the number of points earned. Instruct each student to show all of his work on his paper and to keep track of his points. Continue play until each number on the board is colored or until time is up. Declare the player with the most points at the end of the game the winner.

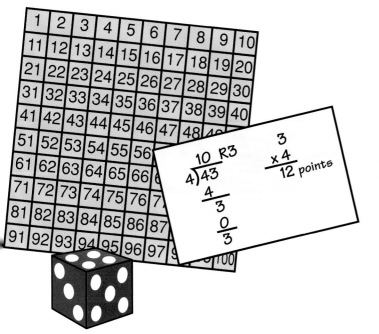

MONEY & TIME

FEES

desk rental = -$25.00
sharpening a pencil = - $2.00
using a textbook = - $4.35
throwing away one piece of trash = - $2.60
using the water fountain = - $5.75
using the dictionary = - $4.40
borrowing a pencil = - $3.85

PAYMENTS

turning in an assignment on time = + $5.20
answering a question = + $3.80
helping a friend = + $4.69
returning a note from home = + $6.78

Classroom Costs

Motivate your students to practice adding and subtracting money with this daylong math activity. Decide on a price list and a pay scale for various classroom activities (see the example). Write these prices on chart paper posted in the room. Instruct each student to write $100.00 at the top of her paper. Explain that the $100.00 is each student's imaginary salary for the day, and that everyone must keep track of her spending and earnings for the day. Direct each student to subtract $25.00 from her $100.00 balance and label it "desk rental." Throughout the day, have each student subtract the fees that she incurs and add any pay that she receives. Collect each student's paper at the end of the day and examine it for accuracy. Reward those students whose work shows few or no mistakes with a small treat or classroom privilege.

My, How Time Flies!

Have your students practice calculating elapsed time with this activity. First compile a list of at-home and at-school activities such as waking up, eating breakfast, and going to recess. Be sure that each activity is something that each child does every day. Then list the items on a chart as shown. Be sure to start with activities that can be completed during the remainder of the school day, and end with ones done the next morning. Duplicate a class set of the chart. Before lunch give each child a copy of the chart to start filling in at lunchtime.

During the next day's math class, divide your students into groups. Give each student a list of questions based on the chart information (see the questions below). Have each group use its members' completed charts to determine the answers.

Sample questions:

Which person from your group got up the earliest this morning?
Which person worked on homework the longest?
Which person slept the longest?
Which person ate dinner the latest?
Which person was on the bus for the least amount of time?

Activity	Time Started	Time Finished
lunch		
recess		
ride home		
dinner		
homework		
sleep		
breakfast		

FRACTIONS & DECIMALS

Roll To One Whole

Get students rolling their way to understanding equivalent fractions and fractional parts with a fun partner game! For each pair of students, cut file-folder labels to affix to all sides of a die. Label each die with the following fractions: 1/2, 1/4, 1/8, 2/8, 1/16, and 2/16. Pair your students; then give each pair one die and two copies of the fraction-strip patterns on page 213. Instruct each partner to cut out the "1 whole" fraction strip and place it in front of him. Direct the pair to cut out the remaining strips and place them in a pile between themselves.

To play, have the partners take turns rolling the die and placing a fraction strip that matches the fraction rolled on his 1 whole fraction strip. Continue play until one player has completely covered his 1 whole fraction strip without going over; then declare that player the winner.

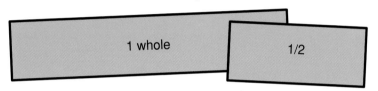

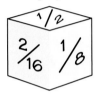

How Did You Solve That?

Need to give your class practice solving fraction and decimal word problems? Divide your class into groups of three students; then challenge the groups to solve each of the problems below. Instruct each group to explain its solutions and its method of solving each problem in a paragraph.

 Calvin and his three friends were working on a school project. Calvin went to the kitchen to get a snack for the group. He found only three cookies. If Calvin evenly divides the three cookies among the four group members, how much will each person receive? *(Each person gets 3/4 of a cookie.)*

 Calvin and his friends took a break and went outside to play. They found $0.50 lying on the ground. How can they fairly divide $0.50 among themselves? *(Each child gets $0.12, and there will be $0.02 left over.)*

The boys went back inside and wanted to color their school project. If Calvin doesn't mind breaking his crayons, how can he evenly divide his 22 crayons among the four boys? *(Each boy can get 5 1/2 crayons.)*

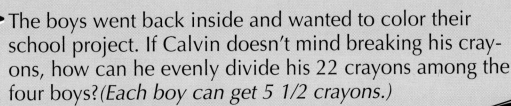

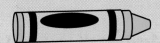

Fraction Collage

Send your students on a fraction hunt! Label and display a piece of poster board for each of the following fractions: 1/2, 1/3, 1/4, 1/6, 2/3, and 3/4. Then provide each student with a magazine to scour for pictures displaying parts of a set or parts of a whole for the various fractions. Instruct the student to cut out each picture that he finds and glue it to the appropriate poster. Students will begin to see that fractions are all around them!

Dividing Squares

Help your students recognize fractional parts of whole numbers with this thought-provoking activity. Create a full page of 4 x 4 dot squares; then duplicate a class set. Challenge each student to use a pencil to divide her squares into halves or fourths as many different ways as she can (see the illustration). Students will be amazed to see the unusual divisions that can be made. Extend this activity by giving students a page of 6 x 6 dot squares and having them divide the grid into thirds and sixths. What an "in-grid-ible" way to identify fractions!

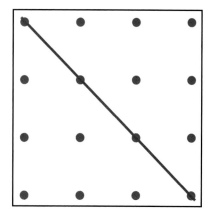
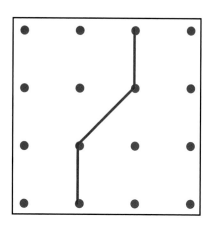

Decimal Draw

Practice addition to hundredths with this simple game. Divide your students into groups of two or three. Give each group one copy of the coin patterns on the bottom of page 215, a brown paper bag, and scissors. Instruct the group to cut out each pattern and place it in the bag. To play, have each player, in turn, draw three coins from the bag, write the value of each coin and their sum on a sheet of paper, and then return the coins to the bag. If a player draws a penalty card, she earns 0 points for that card. The player with the largest total after five rounds is the winner.

Round 1:	Round 2:
$ 0.10	$ 0.50
$ 0.05	$ 0.25
$ 0.25	$ 0.01
$ 0.40 Total	$ 0.76 Total

Geometry Flash Cards

Help students learn the names of geometric figures in a flash! Give each child 16 index cards, an old magazine, scissors, glue, and a rubber band. Instruct each student to peruse the magazine to find an example of each figure listed below. Have the student cut out and glue a different picture to one side of each index card, then write the name of that figure on the back of the card. Direct the student to use the rubber band to bind the cards together. During free time, have students use their flash cards alone or with a partner to practice identifying each geometric figure.

Geometric Figures:

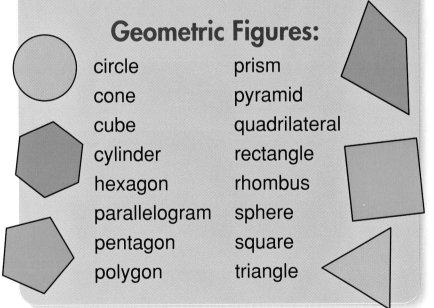

circle	prism
cone	pyramid
cube	quadrilateral
cylinder	rectangle
hexagon	rhombus
parallelogram	sphere
pentagon	square
polygon	triangle

Geo-Walk

Help your students see that geometry surrounds them by taking them on a "geo-walk" around your school. Give each student one copy of the bottom half of page 214 and a pencil. As you lead your class around your school, instruct each student to write down three objects she spots that match each figure shown on her paper. Explain that each player earns one point for each classmate who did not write the same object as she did.

After returning to the classroom, allow each student to share her findings; then calculate each child's point totals. Award the student with the highest point total a homework pass or other classroom incentive.

I See Something...

Play this whole-class game to give your students practice in identifying geometric shapes. Select one student to choose a geometrically shaped object in the room, such as a tissue box, for the class to identify. Then have the selected student use one of the geometric terms listed below to give a clue so that his classmates can identify the chosen object (for example, "I see something with eight vertices."). Call on students to identify the mystery object. If more clues are needed, have the student use another geometric term in a second clue (for example, "It has six faces."). Instruct the student who guesses the correct object to choose the next item and give clues to its identity.

Terms:

base

face

vertex/vertices

edge

side

angle

parallel lines

perpendicular lines

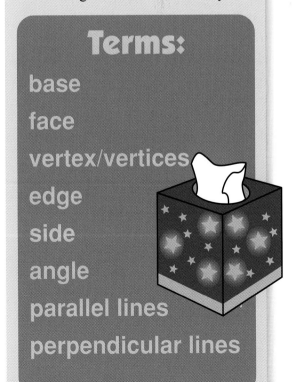

MEASUREMENT

Metric Conversions

Teaching metric conversions is easy with this method! Follow these steps:

1. Display a transparency of the staircase reproducible on the bottom half of page 212. Explain each step: the prefix, its value in comparison to the base, and the abbreviations for using it with grams, liters, and meters.

2. Write this conversion problem on the board: 4 m = _____ mm. Place your finger on the step labeled *meter*. Count the number of steps as you move your finger to the step labeled *millimeter*. Then move the decimal point the same number of places and in the same direction that you moved your finger (4 m = <u>4,000</u> mm).

3. Explain that by moving the decimal three places to the right, you are actually multiplying by 1,000 (1 m = 1,000 mm). When you move the decimal point to the left, you are actually dividing. Also point out that if you are moving up the staircase, your answer will be larger than the original number, but if you are moving down, your answer will be smaller.

4. Duplicate the staircase on page 212 for each child. On the board write several metric conversion problems for students to solve using the staircase.

5. Once students become familiar with the process, have each child create an acronym to remember how to label each step (for example, <u>K</u>atie *(kilo-)* <u>H</u>ates *(hecto-)* <u>D</u>ogs *(deka-)* <u>B</u>ecause *(base)* <u>D</u>ogs *(deci-)* <u>C</u>hase *(centi-)* <u>M</u>ailmen *(milli-)*.

milli-
0.001
mg
mL
mm

centi-
0.01
cg
cL
cm

deci-
0.1
dg
dL
dm

**gram
liter
meter
(base)**
1
g
L
m

deka-
10
dkg
dkL
dkm

hecto-
100
hg
hL
hm

kilo-
1,000
kg
kL
km

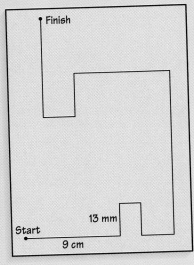

Use Your Ruler

Give your students practice in using a ruler with this partner game. Give each student a metric ruler and two sheets of drawing paper. Instruct him to use his ruler to create a design of ten line segments on one sheet of paper. Each line segment must start at the point were the previous one stopped and can only extend east, west, north, or south (see the illustration). Have each student place his second sheet of paper atop his design and trace the exact starting point with a pencil.

Next divide your class into pairs. Have one student give his partner the sheet labeled with the starting point of his design. Direct the student to give his partner oral directions on how to re-create his design from the starting point (for example, "Start at the labeled point and draw a 9 cm line segment heading east"). Have the student continue giving directions until the design is complete; then have him place the design on top of the original to see if they match. Instruct each pair to repeat this process using the other partner's design.

Finish

Start

13 mm

9 cm

"Graph-tastic" Ideas!

Looking for a way to spice up your graphing unit? Use the "graph-tastic" graphing topics listed in the following cooperative activity. Challenge each group of students to choose a topic, then conduct a survey on it. After the data is collected, have the group use the data it obtains to create bar graphs, pictographs, line graphs, or circle graphs. If desired, include data from other classes to make the graphs more complex and interesting. For example, for the topic "number of books read in a month," have students make the following graphs:

→ a bar graph displaying the number of books read by each class member in an average month

→ a double bar graph displaying the number of books read each month by two different classes

→ a line graph displaying the total number of books read by one class each month

→ a pictograph showing the number of books read by fourth graders in one month

Number Of Books Read Per Month

Graphing Topics

number of pencils in each student's desk
number of sips needed to drink a cup of water with a straw
number of pillows used at night
favorite season
type of shoes students are wearing (athletic, sandals, boots, dress, etc.)
number of students absent each week
number of pennies students can grab in one hand
height of fourth graders
whether or not students wear a helmet while riding a bicycle
number of books read in a month
number of different states visited
number of eyelets on students' shoes
number of raisins in each box
how many of each flavor in a bag of candy

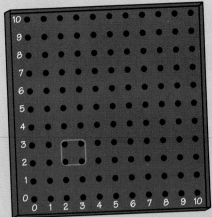

Ordered Pairs On The Geoboard

This ordered-pairs activity is sure to be a hit with your class! Give each student a numbered Geoboard, one rubber band, and a handful of Froot Loops® cereal. Then divide your class into pairs and share these steps:

1. Player A creates a square on his Geoboard by placing the rubber band around four pegs—without allowing his partner to see the rubber band's location.

2. Player B names one point on the Geoboard. Player A says "Hit" if the point named is one of the four points of his square or "Miss" if the point is not on his square.

3. If it is a "Miss," Player B marks the point he just called by placing one piece of cereal over that peg on his geoboard. If it is a "Hit," Player B loops his rubber band around that peg on his board.

4. Player B continues naming points until he finds all four points of his opponent's square. Once the square has been located, Player B counts the number of cereal pieces on his board, indicating his score.

5. Players switch roles, and Player A tries to find Player B's square. The player with the lowest score is the winner.

PROBABILITY

Random Outcomes

Chances are, your students will enjoy investigating probabilities with some hands-on fun! Choose from this collection of activities to provide your students with experience in random outcomes:

- Give each child one penny. Have her predict how many times she will have to toss the coin before she gets three heads or three tails in a row. Instruct each student to try the experiment and compare the actual number with her estimation.

- Give each group of three students two pennies. Have students take turns tossing the coins. Award five points to Player A each time *double heads* is tossed, five points to Player B each time *double tails* is tossed, and three points to Player C each time the pennies show *one heads and one tails*. Direct each group to play the game for 20 tosses each and record each player's points. After the game, instruct each player to write a paragraph telling whether or not she thinks this game is fair. *(The probability of tossing double heads, double tails, or one heads and one tails is the same. Therefore, the game is not fair, because one player is awarded only three points whereas the others are each awarded five.)*

- Give each student a die. Have her use tally marks to record how many rolls it takes before she rolls a *1*. Instruct her to repeat this process five times. Discuss each student's results as a class. *(Each time a student rolls the die, she has a one-in-six chance of rolling a 1.)*

Playing Around With Probability

Introduce the concept of probable outcomes to your students with this simple demonstration. Place a red, a blue, and a green crayon in a paper bag. Ask your students:

✳ How many crayons are in the bag? *three*
✳ How many different colors are there? *three*
✳ What are the chances of pulling out a red crayon? blue? green? *The chances of pulling out each color crayon are 1 out of 3, or 1/3.*
✳ Does each crayon have an equal chance of being pulled out? *yes*

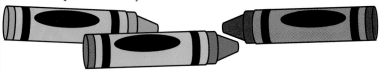

Now add another blue crayon to the bag. Ask:

✳ How many crayons are in the bag? *four*
✳ How many different colors are there? *three*
✳ What are the chances of pulling out a red crayon? *1 out of 4, or 1/4*
✳ What are the chances of pulling out a blue crayon? *2 out of 4, or 2/4*
✳ What are the chances of pulling out a green crayon? *1 out of 4, or 1/4*
✳ What are the chances of pulling out a yellow crayon? *0 out of 4, or 0/4*

Ask your students, "If you were to pull a crayon from the bag 30 times, how many times do you think the crayon would be red? blue? green?" Conduct the experiment and discuss the results. Explain to students that probable outcomes are what *probably* will happen and will *likely* happen, but don't necessarily happen.

Multiplication Table Patterns

Increase your students' understanding of multiples with this nifty patterning activity. Make 11 overhead transparencies of a multiplication table. Also make 11 paper copies of the table for each group. Divide your class into groups of three or four students. Give each group 10 copies of the multiplication table, crayons, and a calculator. Display one transparency of the table; then use an overhead pen to color in each multiple of 6. Discuss the patterns found on the table. Then instruct each group to color a separate table for each of the multiples of *2, 3, 4, 5, 7, 8, 9, 10, 11,* and *12*. Have students color each table a different color if possible. Allow students to use calculators as needed to help with the multiplication. Use the other ten transparencies to go over each group's findings. Have students discuss which tables have the same patterns or similar characteristics. Then look at each table individually and ask questions similar to those written below for the multiples of *6* table:

▷ Which rows are completely shaded? Why?

▷ Why is every other number shaded in the third row?

▷ Why are there only two numbers shaded in the fifth row?

1	2	3	4	5	6	7	8	9	10	11	12
2	4	6	8	10	12	14	16	18	20	22	24
3	6	9	12	15	18	21	24	27	30	33	36
4	8	12	16	20	24	28	32	36	40	44	48
5	10	15	20	25	30	35	40	45	50	55	60
6	12	18	24	30	36	42	48	54	60	66	72
7	14	21	28	35	42	49	56	63	70	77	84
8	16	24	32	40	48	56	64	72	80	88	96
9	18	27	36	45	54	63	72	81	90	99	108
10	20	30	40	50	60	70	80	90	100	110	120
11	22	33	44	55	66	77	88	99	110	121	132
12	24	36	48	60	72	84	96	108	120	132	144

Fibonacci Numbers

Patterns are everywhere! That's what inspired Leonardo Fibonacci to create a number series known today as *Fibonacci numbers.* This series of numbers was created by adding each number to the number on its left. The sum then becomes the next number in the series. The series starts like this: 1, 1, 2, 3, 5, 8, 13, 21, 34, 55, 89 (1 + 1 = 2, 1 + 2 = 3, 2 + 3 = 5, and so on). Create several number series as in the examples at right. Share the Fibonacci number series with your class; then have each student find the pattern in each of your series of numbers. After this activity challenge each student to create five number series of her own for a partner to solve.

Examples

5, 7, 11, 17, 25, 35
(+2, +4, +6, +8, +10)

3, 2, 6, 4, 9, 6, 12
(−1, +4, −2, +5, −3, +6)

5, 8, 11, 16, 21, 28, 35
(+3, +3, +5, +5, +7, +7)

PROBLEM-SOLVING Strategies

Make A Table

Tables can help solve a problem—especially when comparing and organizing different bits of information. Instruct each student to solve the following problem using the make-a-table strategy:

 Mrs. Weeden gave her class a choice of 85 minutes of free time or earning minutes as follows: zero minutes on the first day, two minutes on the second day, four minutes on the third day, six minutes on the fourth day, and so on for ten days. Which choice would give Mrs. Weeden's class more free time? *(The second choice of receiving zero minutes on the first day and adding two each day for the next ten days would give Mrs. Weeden's class more free time.)* How much more? *(Five minutes more—90 – 85 = 5)*

Day	1	2	3	4	5	6	7	8	9	10
Minutes	0	2	4	6	8	10	12	14	16	18

Draw A Picture

Sometimes it may be helpful to use an available picture or to draw a picture or diagram when trying to solve a problem. The picture helps the problem solver understand and manipulate the data in the problem. Assign the following problems to provide your students with practice using this strategy:

Mickey, the class's pet mouse, has escaped and is trying to get back to the safety of his cage. He is at the bottom of the stairwell, 14 steps below his cage. Every day he manages to climb two steps, but he falls back one step during the night. At this pace, how long will it take Mickey to reach his cage? *(It will take Mickey 14 days to reach his cage.)*

A team picture is 11" x 14". Leon wants to frame his picture so that there will be a three-inch-wide border around it. How large will the framed picture be? *(17" x 20")*

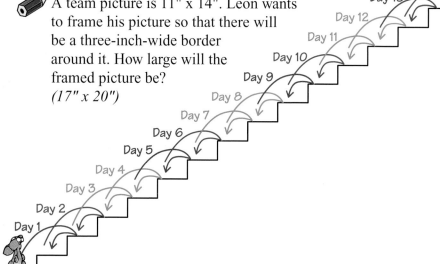

Guess And Check

Some problems can be solved by using the guess-and-check strategy. If the first guess is correct, the problem is solved. If not, try other possible solutions and recheck. Have your students solve the problems below using this problem-solving strategy:

Charleton has 9 coins totaling $0.58. If he does not have a half-dollar, what are the coins? *(Charleton has 1 quarter, 1 dime, 4 nickels, and 3 pennies; or 5 dimes, 1 nickel, and 3 pennies.)*

Three consecutive page numbers in a book add up to 198. What are the three pages? *(65, 66, 67)*

Make An Organized List

Sometimes the answer to a problem may have many parts. An organized list helps problem solvers organize their thinking about a problem. The list can help make sure that no choices are left out or repeated. Challenge your students to solve the following problems using the make-an-organized-list strategy:

 Shannon went to the store with $5.00. She spent $4.79 and put the change that she received in her pocket. Using dimes, nickels, and pennies, list all the possible coin combinations that can be in her pocket. *(See the chart below.)*

 Write A, B, C, and D on your paper. If A is always first in line, how many different ways can you line up the other three letters behind it? *(six)* List the ways. *(ABCD, ABDC, ACBD, ACDB, ADBC, ADCB)*

$0.21		
Number of Dimes	Number of Nickels	Number of Pennies
2	0	1
1	2	1
1	1	6
1	0	11
0	4	1
0	3	6
0	2	11
0	1	16
0	0	21

(See also the Ready Reference pages on pages 210–211.)

Working backward to solve a problem involves making a series of computations, starting with the data mentioned at the end of the problem and ending with the data mentioned at the beginning of the problem. Familiarize your students with this problem-solving strategy by challenging them to solve the problem below:

 There is a bowl of candy on your teacher's desk. There are twice as many lollipops as chocolate bars and one more stick of gum than lollipops. Eight pieces are either sticks of gum or mints. There are three mints. How many chocolate bars are in the bowl?
— If eight pieces are either gum or mints and there are three mints, then there must be five sticks of gum.
— There is one more stick of gum than lollipops, so there must be four lollipops.
— If there are twice as many lollipops than chocolate bars, then there have to be two chocolate bars.

Use Logic

Logical reasoning is a general problem-solving strategy that enables a person to see how several facts work together to make a solution. Displaying the data for this type of problem in a chart or matrix is very helpful. Assign the following problem to your students and have them use logical reasoning to find a solution:

 Spaltar, Chamtar, Ramtar, and Plaktar are visitors from the planet Tar. Each alien is allowed to bring one favorite Earth food back to his home planet. The aliens brought home sardines, peanuts, cheese, and raisins. Either Spaltar or Ramtar likes cheese. Neither Ramtar nor Chamtar likes fish. None has a favorite food with the same first letter as in his name. If Chamtar's favorite food is peanuts, what is Spaltar's favorite Earth food? *(Spaltar's favorite Earth food is raisins.)*

	SPALTAR	CHAMTAR	RAMTAR	PLAKTAR
sardines	X	X	X	
peanuts	X		X	X
cheese	X	X		X
raisins		X	X	X

Problem-Solving Strategies

Act It Out

To help you see a problem clearly, act it out or use manipulatives to help.

Example:

In a card game, Rob sits across from Meg, Drew is at Meg's right, and Kate complains that Rob's right elbow bumps her left arm. How are the friends arranged?

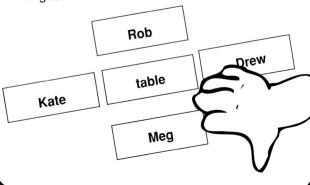

Draw A Picture Or Diagram

Use a picture or a diagram to help you solve a problem.

Example:

Kendra and Max live the same distance from the bridge. Kendra is upstream and Max is downstream. They live 1,258 feet apart. How far does each one live from the bridge?

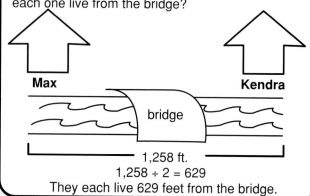

$1{,}258 \div 2 = 629$

They each live 629 feet from the bridge.

Use Logic

When several facts must work together to make a solution, use thinking skills to help you solve the problem.

Example:

A numeral has three digits. The first digit is an odd number. The last digit is two more than the first. Multiplying its digits gives a product of 70. What is the number?

1. The first digit can be 1, 3, 5, or 7. It cannot be 9.
2. The last digit can be 3, 5, 7, or 9. It cannot be 1 or an even number.
3. The second digit can be any numeral between 0 and 9.
4. Which three possible numerals will give a product of 70?

$5 \times 2 \times 7 = 70$. The answer is 527.

Guess And Check

Take a guess at a problem's answer and check it. If you're not correct, adjust your guess and try again.

Example:

The product of two numerals is 115. What are the two numerals?

Since 115 has a 5 in the ones place, you know it is a multiple of 5.

Guess: $5 \times 20 = 100$ *(The answer is too small.)*

Guess again: $5 \times 23 = 115$ *(Yes!)*

The numerals are 5 and 23.

Find A Pattern

Decide how you get from one numeral to the next numeral in a pattern. Then see if this rule works for the rest of the pattern.

Example:

Degas is making a picture. He places one tile in the first row, four tiles in the second row, and seven tiles in the third row. How many tiles will be in the sixth row?

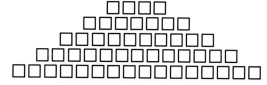

The pattern is *add three.*

The sixth row will have 16 tiles.

Problem-Solving Strategies

Make A List

Make an organized list when you need to show all the possible solutions.

Example:
How many different outfits could you make if you bought one red shirt, one blue tank top, one pair of tan pants, and one pair of gray shorts?

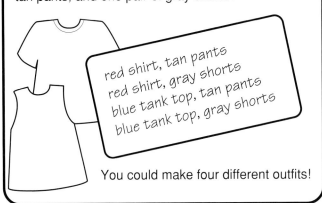

red shirt, tan pants
red shirt, gray shorts
blue tank top, tan pants
blue tank top, gray shorts

You could make four different outfits!

Work Backward

Read the problem. Identify the operations used. Then use *inverse* operations to work backward to the problem's beginning.

Example:
Bill returned from shopping with $3.00. He had spent $9.25 for snacks and $12.75 for comic books. How much money did he have before he went shopping?

Amount Bill had left:	Amount spent on snacks:	Amount spent on comic books:	He started with $25.00!
$3.00 +	$9.25 +	$12.75 =	

$3.00 + $9.25 + $12.75 = $25.00

Simplify

To help you understand a problem, decide on a way to make the numbers simpler.

Example:
At 7:00 A.M. on Friday, Carinda finds this note from her mom: "Your aunt will be here in exactly 1,500 minutes." On what day and at what time will Carinda's aunt arrive?

60 minutes = 1 hour
24 hours = 1 day
1,500 minutes ÷ 60 minutes = 25 hours
25 hours = 1 day and 1 hour.
Carinda's aunt will arrive at 8:00 A.M. on Saturday.

Brainstorm

Think of a new, creative way to look at a problem.

Example:
How do five and nine more make two?
If it's 5 o'clock and you move the hour hand ahead 9 hours, it will become 2 o'clock!

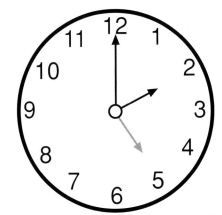

Make A Table, Chart, Or Graph

Use a table, chart, or graph when you need to keep track of data and see how it changes.

Example:
Bruce is 4 years old and Matt is 13 years old. When will Matt be twice as old as Bruce?

	years					
Bruce	4	5	6	7	8	9
Matt	13	14	15	16	17	18

Matt will be twice as old as Bruce in 5 years!

ROLLING REVIEW

Name _____

Round One

Round Two

Round Three

Round Four

Name _____ _Metric system_

Metric Conversions

When moving up the stairs, multiply by moving the decimal
    point to the right.
When moving down the stairs, divide by moving the decimal
    point to the left.

milli-
0.001
mg
mL
mm

centi-
0.01
cg
cL
cm

deci-
0.1
dg
dL
dm

**gram
liter
meter
(base)**
1
g
L
m

deka-
10
dkg
dkL
dkm

hecto-
100
hg
hL
hm

kilo-
1,000
kg
kL
km

Examples:

1. 4 m = <u>4,000</u> mm

2. 204 g = <u>2.04</u> hg

Note To The Teacher: Use "Rolling Review" with the idea on page 198. Use "Metric Conversions" with the idea
212 on page 204.

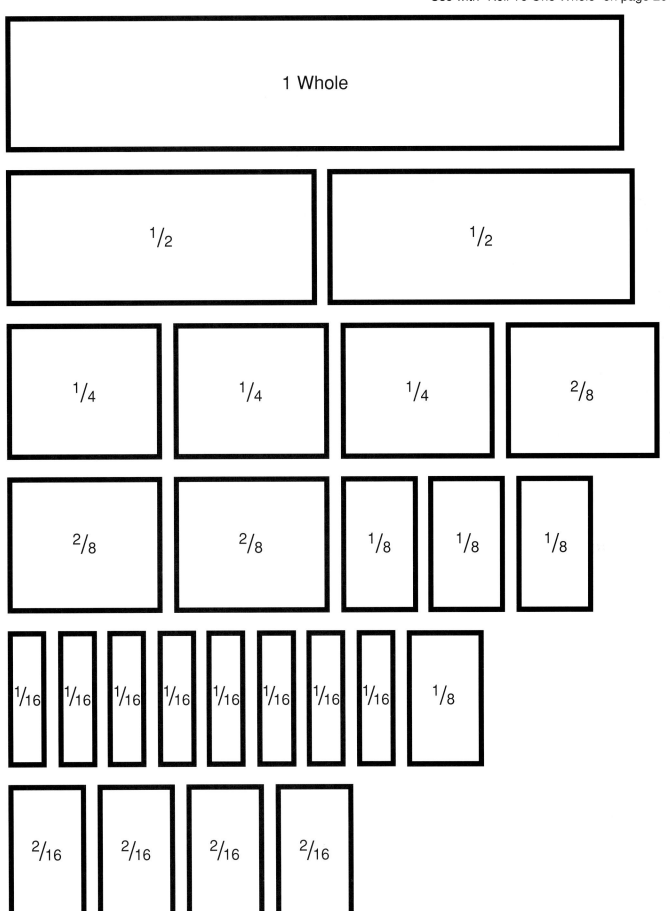

1 Whole

¹/₂   ¹/₂

¹/₄   ¹/₄   ¹/₄   ²/₈

²/₈   ²/₈   ¹/₈   ¹/₈   ¹/₈

¹/₁₆   ¹/₁₆   ¹/₁₆   ¹/₁₆   ¹/₁₆   ¹/₁₆   ¹/₁₆   ¹/₁₆   ¹/₈

²/₁₆   ²/₁₆   ²/₁₆   ²/₁₆

Club Confusion!

All the after-school clubs at Arthur Middle School signed up to meet at the same time in the gymnasium. To avoid any confusion, the principal gave each club a percentage of the gymnasium to use for its meeting. Use the percentages listed below to make a diagram on the 100-square grid showing how the gymnasium should be divided. Assign each club a different color; then use that color of crayon to color the correct number of squares on the grid.

		Color
Cheerleaders	26%	☐
Band	12%	☐
Drama Club	11%	☐
Student Council	14%	☐
Tutoring Club	16%	☐
Yearbook Committee	18%	☐

What percentage of space is left in the gymnasium? _____ %

Bonus Box: Suppose each club had to pay $1.25 for each of its colored spaces on the grid. On the back of this paper, write how much each club would have to pay for its total space in the gymnasium.

©1997 The Education Center, Inc. • *The Mailbox® Superbook* • Grade 4 • TEC453 • Key p. 316

Name _____ *Identifying geometric figures*

Geo-Walk

Figure	Object	Points	Figure	Object	Points
pyramid	1. 2. 3.		triangle	1. 2. 3.	
circle	1. 2. 3.		rectangular prism	1. 2. 3.	
pentagon	1. 2. 3.		cylinder	1. 2. 3.	
square	1. 2. 3.		hexagon	1. 2. 3.	

Bonus Box: On the back of this paper, write the name of one object listed above that you think will earn the most points for you. If you are correct, you will earn five bonus points.

Total [ ]

©1997 The Education Center, Inc. • *The Mailbox® Superbook* • Grade 4 • TEC453

214 **Note To The Teacher:** Use the bottom form with "Geo-Walk" on page 203.

Fruity Fractions

Fran's famous fruit salad was a big hit at her party. Now all her friends want the recipe! Help Fran reduce the recipe so that it fits each of her friend's needs.

Fran's Famous Fruit Salad
(serves 48 people)
24 oranges
1 honeydew melon
1 cup cherries
12 cups strawberries
36 apples

1.
Betty needs enough fruit salad for 24 people.
_____ oranges
_____ honeydew melon
_____ cup(s) cherries
_____ cup(s) strawberries
_____ apples

2.
Michael wants to make 1/3 of the recipe.
_____ oranges
_____ honeydew melon
_____ cup(s) cherries
_____ cup(s) strawberries
_____ apples

3.
Madison wants enough salad for her family of eight.
_____ oranges
_____ honeydew melon
_____ cup(s) cherries
_____ cup(s) strawberries
_____ apples

4.
Cassidy wants to make 1/4 of the recipe.
_____ oranges
_____ honeydew melon
_____ cup(s) cherries
_____ cup(s) strawberries
_____ apples

Bonus Box: How much of each ingredient would you need to serve Fran's famous fruit salad to 120 people? Write your answer on the back of this paper.

Patterns
Use with "Decimal Draw" on page 202.

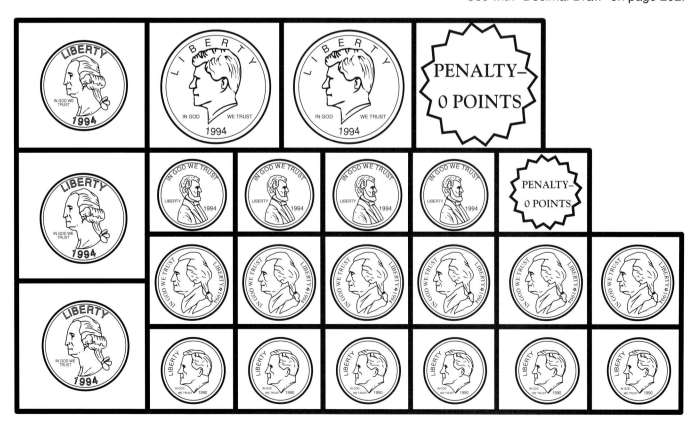

PLACE-VALUE PYRAMID

Carefully study the numerals in the pyramid below; then follow the directions to create a colorful pyramid.

1. Color the largest numeral *purple*.
2. Color the smallest numeral *yellow*.
3. Color all the numerals with a six in the hundreds or thousands place *red*.
4. Color all the numerals between 100,000 and 150,000 *green*.
5. Color all the numerals between 30,000 and 50,000 *orange*.
6. Color all the numerals between 150,000 and 800,000 *blue*.

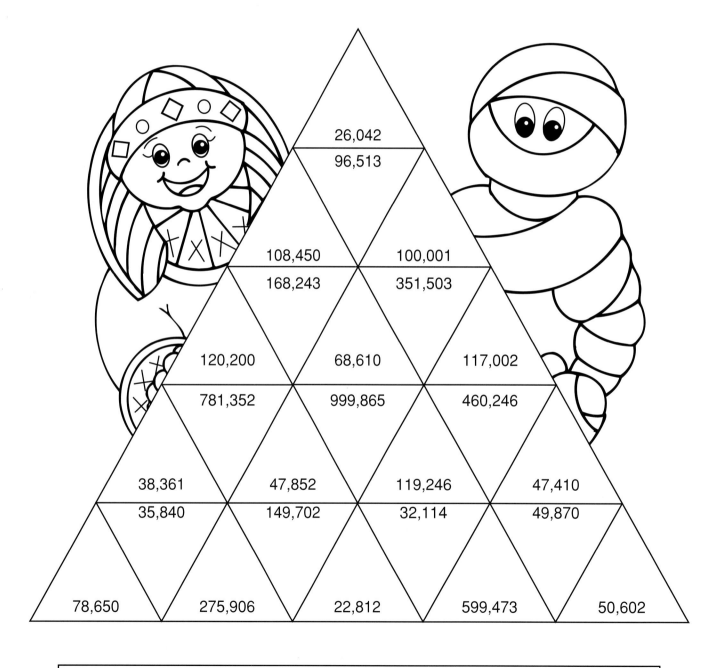

Bonus Box: On the back of this page, use any numerals from the pyramid to write two word problems. Then challenge a friend to solve the problems.

 ©1997 The Education Center, Inc. • *The Mailbox® Superbook* • Grade 4 • TEC453 • Key p. 317

Addition Shape-Up

It's time to get your addition skills in tip-top shape! Use the key to help you calculate the total value of each picture below. Show your work on the back of this paper; then write your answer on the line provided.

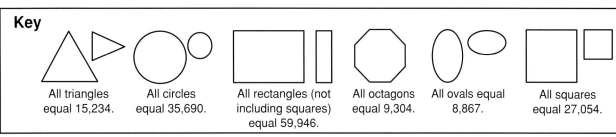

Key

All triangles equal 15,234.   All circles equal 35,690.   All rectangles (not including squares) equal 59,946.   All octagons equal 9,304.   All ovals equal 8,867.   All squares equal 27,054.

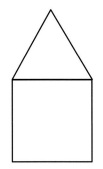

1. value = _____

2. value = _____

3. value = _____

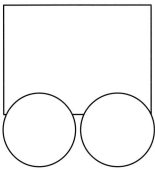

4. value = _____

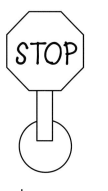

5. value = _____

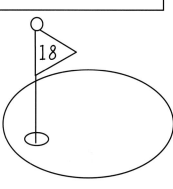

6. value = _____

7. value = _____

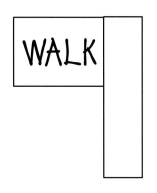

8. value = _____

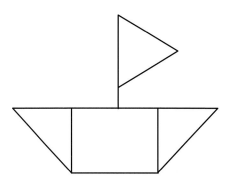

9. value = _____

Bonus Box: On the back of this paper, use the shapes in the key to create your own picture. Then challenge a friend to calculate its value.

☆ ☆ ☆ ☆ ☆ Abracadabra! ☆ ☆ ☆ ☆ ☆

You don't need magic to solve these problems—just a bit of brainpower! Solve each of the problems below. Write the answer to each problem in the box with the matching number on the magic square. When you are finished, the sum of each row and column should equal 100.

1. $5\overline{)175}$ 2. $9\overline{)234}$ 3. $8\overline{)136}$ 4. $9\overline{)198}$

5. $10\overline{)90}$ 6. $7\overline{)70}$ 7. $4\overline{)200}$ 8. $5\overline{)155}$

9. $3\overline{)126}$ 10. $5\overline{)85}$ 11. $7\overline{)175}$ 12. $9\overline{)144}$

13. $4\overline{)56}$ 14. $6\overline{)282}$ 15. $10\overline{)80}$ 16. $6\overline{)186}$

1.	2.	3.	4.
5.	6.	7.	8.
9.	10.	11.	12.
13.	14.	15.	16.

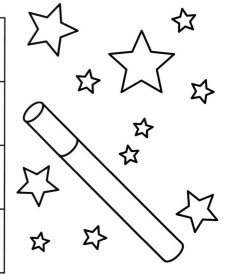

Bonus Box: What do you think is the sum of all 16 boxes on the magic square? On the back of this paper, add all 16 boxes and check your guess against the correct answer.

Money Matters

Do you want to avoid being shortchanged the next time you buy something? Well, you are going to need to know how to make change! Each sales tag below shows the total purchase amount by one person after shopping at The Toy Factory. Each person paid with a $50.00 bill. Write each person's name on the line in front of the amount of change that he or she received. Were any of The Toy Factory's customers shortchanged?

Change Received	**Amount Spent**

1. one five, four ones, two quarters, one dime, one nickel

2. one twenty, one five, two quarters, three dimes, two pennies

3. two twenties, two quarters, one dime, one nickel, three pennies

4. one twenty, one ten, four ones, one quarter, one penny

5. one twenty, one five, three ones, two quarters, two dimes

6. four ones, three quarters, two dimes

7. one ten, one five, one one, one quarter, one dime, one nickel

8. one ten, two quarters, two dimes, one penny

9. one twenty, one ten, one five, three ones, two quarters, one nickel

10. one twenty, one one, two quarters

11. two twenties, one five, three quarters

12. one ten, one five, one dime, four pennies

13. two ones, one nickel

14. one twenty, one five, four ones, one quarter

15. one ten, three ones, one quarter, one dime

Bob — $4.25

Rasheeda — $36.65

Dom — $40.35

Christina — $33.60

Steven — $34.86

Maurice — $20.75

C. J. — $21.30

Brandy — $24.18

Tyler — $11.45

Jerome — $15.74

Juan — $39.29

Laura — $28.50

Maria — $47.95

Elijah — $9.32

Leeza — $45.05

Bonus Box: Choose three of the sales tags above. Calculate the amount of change needed for each sales tag if a $100.00 bill was given to the clerk. Write the amount of change needed using the least number of bills and coins.

Make A Match!

Cut apart the seven individual pieces that make up the puzzle below. Starting with the fraction 2/5 on the large triangle, match the dot at each fraction on one edge of a puzzle piece to its equivalent fraction on the edge of another puzzle piece. (It may help to first reduce each fraction to its simplest form.) Keep doing this until you have matched each edge. When you are finished, you will have created an animal. What is it? _____

Bonus Box: If the value of one of the smallest triangles is $3.00, what is the total value of all seven puzzle pieces?

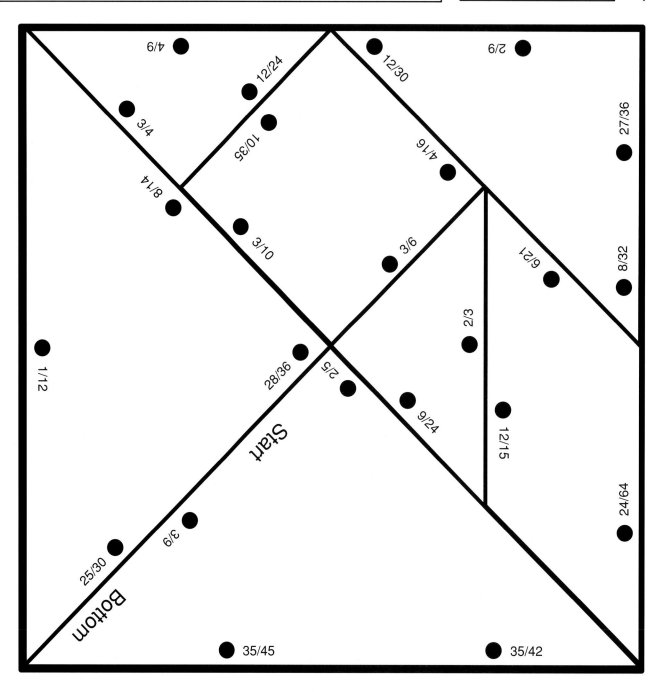

Track Meet Mix-Up

Oh no! The judges at the track meet mixed up all the prize ribbons. Use the clues and the roster below to write the name of the correct player on each ribbon. Then use the color key at the bottom of the page to color each ribbon correctly.

Roster

Harry Simpson 56.90 seconds	Robert Smith 57.19 seconds
Bailey Birch 57.00 seconds	Tim Schmut 57.46 seconds
Mark Gut 57.50 seconds	Bill Blatt 56.85 seconds
Mike Glark 57.09 seconds	

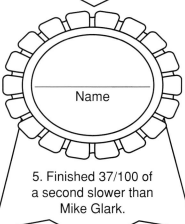

Name

2. Ran the race 1/10 of a second faster than Bailey Birch.

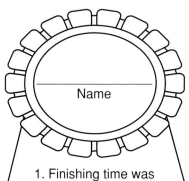

Name

1. Finishing time was between 57.16 and 57.25 seconds.

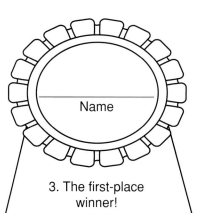

Name

3. The first-place winner!

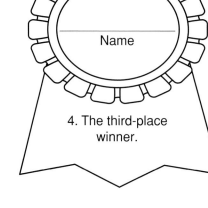

Name

4. The third-place winner.

Name

5. Finished 37/100 of a second slower than Mike Glark.

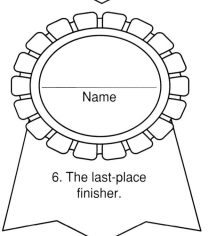

Name

6. The last-place finisher.

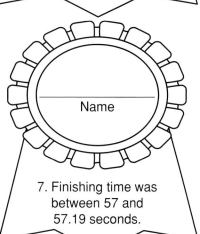

Name

7. Finishing time was between 57 and 57.19 seconds.

Color Key

1st = blue	5th = green
2nd = red	6th = brown
3rd = purple	7th = yellow
4th = orange	

Bonus Box: How much faster was the finishing time of the first-place runner than that of the seventh-place finisher? Write your answer on the back of this page.

Patterns in geometry

Fun With Patterns

Use a colored pencil or crayon to color one-half of the eight triangles in each of the squares in the first row. Be sure to color each square differently. Then follow the steps in the center of this page.

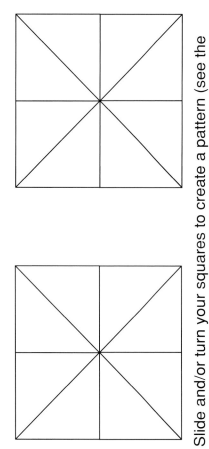

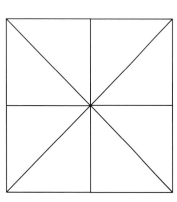

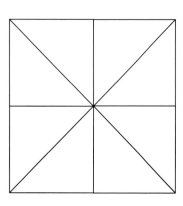

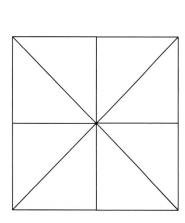

1. Choose your favorite design from the above squares and color the second row of squares with the same pattern.
2. Cut out the five identical squares (including the one in the first row).
3. Slide and/or turn your squares to create a pattern (see the examples below).
4. Paste your pattern onto a 9" x 12" sheet of construction paper and write the rule for your pattern underneath it.

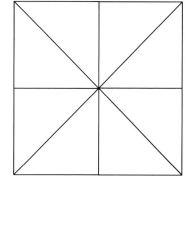

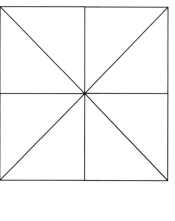

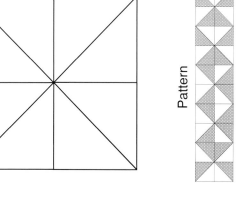

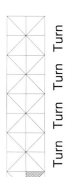

Pattern

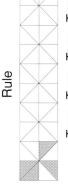

Rule

Turn Turn Turn Turn

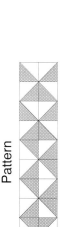

Pattern

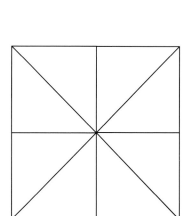

Rule

Turn Slide Turn Slide

©1997 The Education Center, Inc. • The Mailbox® Superbook • Grade 4 • TEC453

Who's Wearing Those Shoes?

Mr. Robner's class at East Lake Elementary is studying graphs. His students gathered data about the types of shoes that fourth graders wore to school. The three graphs below display some of the data that was collected. Now it is time to analyze each graph. Use the graphs to answer each question below.

Fourth Graders' Shoes On Monday

Sandals	🦶🦶🦶🦶
Boots	🦶
Athletic Shoes	🦶🦶🦶🦶🦶🦶
Other	🦶🦶🦶

🦶 = 10 fourth graders

1. What type of graph is this?
_____
2. What does each footprint represent?
_____
3. How many students wore athletic shoes? _____ sandals? _____ boots? _____ other? _____
4. Draw another symbol that you would use to represent the data in this graph.

5. What type of graph is this?
_____
6. Which class wore the most athletic shoes the week of November 8? _____
7. What was the average number of students wearing athletic shoes in Mrs. Barst's class?_____
8. What might be the reason for Mrs. Alkin's class averaging a low number of athletic shoes for that particular week?
_____

Students Wearing Athletic Shoes 11/8–11/12

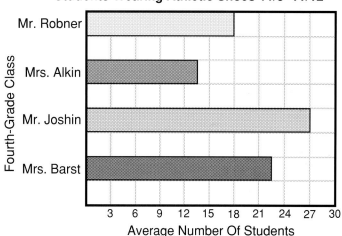

Fourth-Grade Class — Average Number Of Students

9. What type of graph is this?
_____
10. How many fourth graders wore athletic shoes on Tuesday? _____
11. Between which two days did the number of students wearing athletic shoes increase by 20?
_____
12. How many fourth graders wore athletic shoes on Thursday and Friday combined?
_____

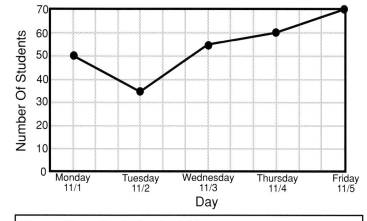

Fourth Graders Wearing Athletic Shoes

Bonus Box: On the back of this page, create a pictograph to show the types of shoes your classmates are wearing. Follow the example of the first graph on this page.

Sketching For Solutions

Sometimes it may be helpful to sketch or draw a picture or diagram when trying to solve a problem. The picture will help you understand the data in the problem. Solve each of the problems below by drawing a picture on the sketch pad; then write your solution on the line provided.

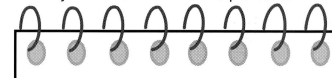

 1. Jake evenly spaced out a number of candles equal to his age around the perimeter of his square birthday cake. Each side had six candles. How old is Jake?

Solution: _____

 2. There are 16 baseball teams entered in the spring tournament. If each team plays until it loses, how many games must be played to determine a winner?

Solution: _____

 3. Calvin, Carl, Chris, and Cory are sitting on a log in front of a campfire with their scout leader, Camden. Calvin is sitting to the left of Carl. Carl is sitting directly to the left of Cory. Chris is sitting between Cory and Camden. In what order are they sitting?

Solution: _____

 4. If December 3 is a Tuesday, on what day would the following January 22 be?

Solution: _____

5. Marie got on an elevator. She went down 9 floors, up 11 floors, and then down 6 floors and got off the elevator. If she got off at the 15th floor, at what floor did she get on the elevator?

Solution: _____

Bonus Box: If December 3 were a Tuesday, on what day would your next birthday be?

SOCIAL STUDIES

MAP SKILLS

"Geog" Your Memory

Help students remember geographic features with a fun game of Geography Memory. Give each student a copy of the game reproducible on page 240, and the "Geography Glossary" on page 239 (if needed). Have the student follow the directions on his reproducible and play a round of the game. Then encourage him to find a partner, then combine and mix up their cards. Instruct the students to take turns turning over two cards. If a player's cards show a geographic feature and its definition, the student keeps the cards. If not, the cards are turned back over. After all cards are picked up, the student with the most cards wins.

mountain range

a group or chain of mountains

Make Mine A Map

From resource maps to road maps—maps come in different sizes and are used for different purposes. However, there are some features that *most* maps have in common. To help students identify the similarities and differences between maps, post several different kinds around the room. Then divide students into small groups and have each group go to a map. Direct the group to list everything it sees on the map. After about five minutes, have each group rotate clockwise and repeat the process.

When each group has recorded its information, instruct it to highlight the similarities and differences with different-colored markers. Conclude the activity by discussing students' findings, pointing out the basic parts and purposes of each map.

U.S. Map
1. title
2. compass rose
3. scale
4. grid

The Key Is The Key!

The key to using any map is its key, of course! Copy the symbols from a variety of maps each on a separate index card; then display the maps. Explain to students that a mapmaker uses special colors, marks, or symbols to make reading the map easier. A special box on the map called a *key,* or *legend,* explains the meaning of each symbol. Next give each student one of the index cards. Direct the student to use one of the displayed map keys to identify the meaning of the symbol, then find the symbol on the map.

Follow up the activity by giving each small group of students a state map. Give a copy of page 241 to each child; then have each group complete the reproducible activity.

10

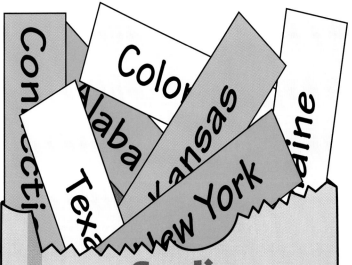

Scaling A Map

When it comes to using a map scale, practice makes perfect! Show students a scale from a wall map of the United States. Explain that a map scale is important because it is used to show the real distance between two points. Line up an index card under the scale; then put a mark on the card for each distance shown, starting with zero. Show students how to use the card to measure the distance between two points on the map. Next give each student a strip of paper. Instruct the student to write a different state name on the strip; then put the strips in a bag. Have a student pull two strips from the bag, go to the map, and find the distance between the capital cities of the two states. Continue with other students. Follow up the activity by having each student complete the reproducible on page 242.

Our State's Big Book Of Maps

Get your students into maps in a *big* way with this activity! Begin by brainstorming the many kinds of maps. (See the examples below.) Ask students which types of maps could be used to study your state. Next divide students into small groups. Give each group a three-foot sheet of bulletin-board paper, markers, scissors, and reference materials. Assign each group a map-related topic such as products or landforms. Direct the group to research the topic for information about your state. Then have the group trace an outline of your state onto its paper using an opaque or overhead projector. Finally instruct each group to use its information to create a state map that also includes a title, key, and compass rose. Compile the maps in a big book to display in your school's library.

Types Of Maps:

- landform map
- map of major colleges and universities
- Native American tribes map
- state parks map
- physical map
- points-of-interest map
- population map
- product and natural resource map
- rainfall map
- vegetation map
- wildlife map
- transportation map

Mapping Your Roots

Reinforce geography skills while encouraging students to research a bit of family history. Give each student a copy of the reproducible on page 244. After each student has completed the sheet, write the listed map-key topics on the chalkboard; then survey students about their finished maps and compile the information. Next divide students into ten groups. Give each group a different map-key topic, a large sheet of chart paper, and markers. Direct each group to use the class data for its assigned topic to create a large graph on the chart paper. Display the completed graphs around the room.

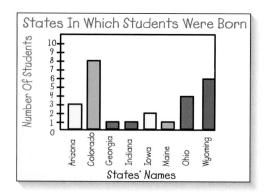

Mystery State

Students love a good mystery—so how about adding a little intrigue to your study of maps? Write a different sentence or group of sentences that gives directional clues for getting from your state to another state on each of ten index cards. (See the example.) Then duplicate one copy of a U.S. map for each student. After reviewing *cardinal* (north, south, east, and west) and *intermediate* (northeast, northwest, southeast, and southwest) directions, read each clue card aloud one at a time. Instruct each student to follow the directions and mark the mystery state on her map. After students have marked their maps, reread each card one at a time and have a volunteer show how she identified the mystery state on a wall map. Extend the activity by having each student write her own mystery-state directions for the class to follow.

Starting in Iowa, go south one state. (*Missouri*) Then, from the northeast corner of this state, go three states east; (*Ohio*) then go one state northwest. (*Michigan*)

A Map In A Month

Wrap up your map study with an activity that will keep students mad about maps the whole month long! Give each student a 12" x 18" sheet of construction paper, a copy of the calendar on page 243, the "Geography Glossary" on page 239, yarn or ribbon, a ruler, and crayons. Direct the student to construct a map of an imaginary or a futuristic country by following the day-by-day instructions on the calendar. Each day on the calendar highlights a different part of a map, so by the end of the month each student will have completed her very own map masterpiece!

Monumental Mail

Obtain several postcards that depict various monuments throughout your state. Share the postcards with students and discuss why landmarks or monuments are created. Then assign each student a Native American tribe from your state. Have the student investigate the history of the tribe and whether a state monument or landmark has been erected in its honor. Next give each student a copy of the reproducible pattern on page 245. Direct the student to draw and color a commemorative landmark (real or imagined) for its tribe on the bottom of the pattern. On the top of the pattern, have the student write a few sentences explaining where the landmark is located, its meaning, and why it was created. Then have him add an address, cut out the pattern, fold it on the dotted line, and glue the sides together. Finally put students' postcards in a large envelope and have a student deliver them to other grade-level classes.

Native Americans Flip Chart

Areas all across our nation have a historical link to Native Americans. Make Native Americans part of the study of your state with this activity:

1. Stack several sheets of chart paper—one for each Native American tribe from your state, plus an extra for a cover.

2. Cut an inch off the bottom sheet; then cut each consecutive sheet one inch shorter than the previous one until you can arrange the sheets according to the illustration.

3. Write the name of a tribe from your state on the bottom of each sheet (except for the shortest one).

4. Divide students into pairs or small groups. Give each group one of the sheets.

5. Have each group research its tribe for information about food, clothing, shelter, religion, education, arts and crafts, leisure, government, etc. Then have students fill their group's paper with an illustration and caption for each topic discussed.

6. Attach the chart paper together with two metal rings as shown, using the smallest sheet as a cover. As you flip the chart, have each group share its information.

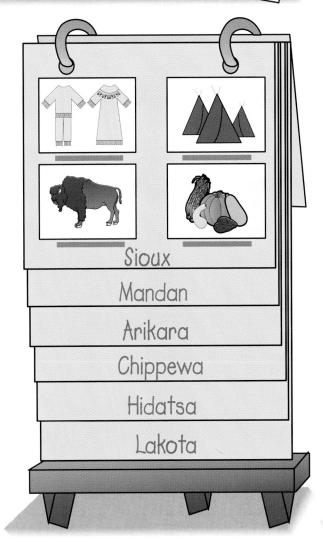

Sioux

Mandan

Arikara

Chippewa

Hidatsa

Lakota

STUDYING MY STATE

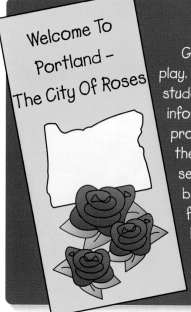

Welcome To Portland – The City Of Roses

State-Study Road Trip

Get your students on the road to studying your state with this attractive display. Post a road map of your state on a large bulletin board or wall area. Divide students into pairs and assign each pair a city within your state to research for information, such as area in square miles; population; climate; resources; products produced; and attractions such as state parks, landmarks, and museums. Then have the pair compile its information into an eye-catching visitor's guide with topic sections, descriptive sentences, and illustrations. (Share several sample travel brochures with students, if desired.) Also have the pair include specific directions from your school to the assigned city using the road map posted on the bulletin board. After each pair shares its visitor's guide, display the guide around the map near its city. Then have each pair connect the guide to its city with two pushpins and a length of yarn.

The Tourist Trap

Mention the word *tourists* to your students, and the word *souvenirs* will probably come to mind. So why not have students review your state by creating their own state-of-the-art state souvenir shop? Here's how:

Materials for each group: 8 1/2" x 11" sheet of white construction paper, markers or colored pencils, scissors, a stapler, four-inch piece of string or yarn, 3" x 5" index card, reference materials

Steps:

1 Brainstorm with students a list of specific souvenirs to sell in your shop, such as a framed picture of the state bird, a replica of the state flower, postcards of famous landmarks, or a T-shirt picturing a famous person from your state's history.

2 Divide students into groups of three. Have each group choose one of the souvenirs from the list.

3 Have each group research the state information it will display on its souvenir.

4 Direct the group to draw a picture of the souvenir on its construction paper, then color and cut it out.

5 Instruct the group to make a price tag that includes a description of the souvenir and its price on the index card, then staple it to the souvenir with the string.

6 After each group shares its souvenir, have the group mount the project on a bulletin board titled "State-Of-The-Art Souvenirs."

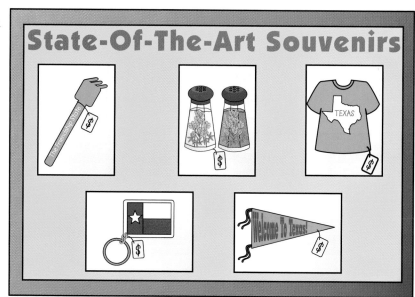

Imaginary Getaway

Your students' interest in the study of your state is just a postcard away with this idea!

1. Assign each pair of students a city from your state to research.
2. Direct each pair to choose an attraction—such as a famous landmark, historical site, national park, or resort area—for which its city is famous.
3. Give each pair a copy of the postcard pattern on page 245.
4. Direct each pair's members to imagine they have visited their city's attraction and are sending a postcard to their classmates. Have the pair draw and color a picture that illustrates the attraction on the bottom of the pattern. Then have the pair write a description of the attraction (without naming its city) and an address on the top.
5. Have the pair cut out the pattern, fold it on the dotted line, and then glue the sides together.
6. Post a map of your state on a bulletin board. For every postcard, place two pushpins and a length of yarn or string on the board.
7. In turn, have each pair share its postcard and use a pushpin to post it with the illustration facing outward near the map.
8. Finally have the class guess the name of each pair's getaway city. Let the student who guesses correctly attach the string from the postcard to the city on the map.

Our State From A To Z

Looking for a way to get students to be more descriptive about your state? It's as easy as A-B-C with this idea!

Materials for each pair of students:
2 sheets of poster-size paper, scissors, glue, markers or colored pencils, resources such as magazines and state travel brochures

Steps:

1. Assign each pair of students two letters of the alphabet. Make sure that each pair gets no more than one difficult letter such as Q, X, or Z.
2. Have each pair label the top of each sheet of paper with one of its letters.
3. Have each pair cut out pictures and words that begin with its letters *and* describe your state's features from the magazines and brochures, and glue them to the appropriate page. Features could include your state's bird, tree, or flower; famous people; landmarks; natural resources; and products produced.
4. If a pair cannot find a certain picture or word, have the students draw or write their own version.
5. After each pair completes the activity, compile the pages in alphabetical order and add a title page; then bind the pages together. Share the book one letter at a time, having each pair explain its findings.

5. I was born just south of Elizabethtown, Kentucky.

4. My formal schooling lasted only about one year.

3. I studied law and became a lawyer in 1836.

2. I was the first president to be assassinated.

1. I was president during the Civil War.

Who Am I? Abraham Lincoln

Who Am I?

Test your students' knowledge of your state's famous citizens using a game riddled with teamwork! Give each student an index card and the name of an important person in your state's history. Have the student research the person for five facts, then write a numbered sentence for each fact on his card. Instruct the student to list the facts in descending order, with the more difficult facts written first. (See the example.) After each student completes his card, collect and mix up the cards.

Next divide students into teams. In turn, read the clues on a card to a team. Starting with clue number five, read one clue at a time. After reading a clue, give the team time to guess the name of the person. If the team guesses correctly after you read the first clue, it earns five points. If the team guesses correctly after the second clue, it earns four points, and so on. If the team cannot guess the person's name, reveal the answer; then move on to the next team and read a different card. When all cards have been read, reward the team with the most points.

What's In A Name?

What's in a name? Have your students determine just what *is* behind the names of different cities in your state. Assign each student a different city; then provide each student with the address of her city's chamber of commerce. Direct each student to write a letter to the organization requesting background information about the city's name. After you mail students' letters, have each child write a hypothetical explanation about the city's naming. When each student's information arrives, have her share both the fictional and real reason to see if her classmates can determine which is the true version.

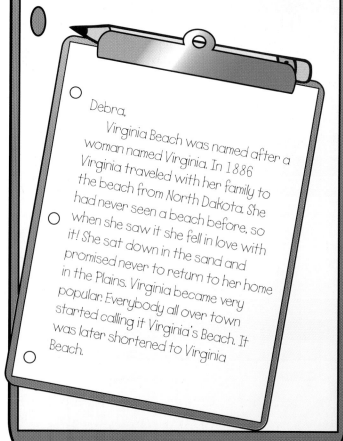

Debra,

Virginia Beach was named after a woman named Virginia. In 1886 Virginia traveled with her family to the beach from North Dakota. She had never seen a beach before, so when she saw it she fell in love with it! She sat down in the sand and promised never to return to her home in the Plains. Virginia became very popular. Everybody all over town started calling it Virginia's Beach. It was later shortened to Virginia Beach.

The Road Through Time

Have students gather important information about the history of your state with this creative display. Cover a long bulletin board with light-colored paper. Then staple several four-inch-wide sheets of black construction paper end-to-end on the board to create a road. Draw chalk lines on the sheets to represent road divider lines. Add road signs such as "Statehood Ahead" or "Patriot Crossing."

Next have each student design a car cutout on construction paper. Assign each child a date and corresponding event in your state's history to research. Have the student record the date and a description of the event on her car. Collect the cars and arrange them in chronological order on the display; then have each student share her information in the order of its occurrence.

State-Of-The-Art Stationery

What student wouldn't like to write an assignment on a decorative sheet of paper—especially one she designed herself? Give each student a copy of the reproducible on page 246. Direct the student to follow the directions on the sheet for completing the activity. After all the designs are complete, post them in the classroom. Then have each student vote for the design she likes best. Duplicate a copy of the winning design for each student to use during your state-study activities, such as writing a letter to a chamber of commerce, a state official, or a pen pal in another state.

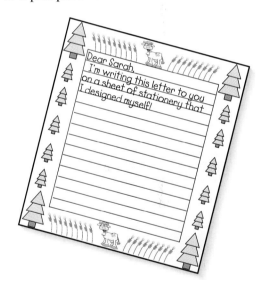

State Plates

Put class creativity in high gear with this fun activity! Begin by asking students to describe your state's current license plate. Discuss the significance of the plate's symbol(s) and motto, and how long the state has used the plate. Then ask students, "If a new plate were designed, what symbols could be used to represent the state (such as its flower, a special animal, or a natural resource)?" Give each student a 4" x 11" sheet of paper and challenge her to design a colorful new plate. After each student completes her plate, have her share it with the class and explain why it should be adopted as the official state plate.

Picturing Population

Help students get the picture about population with this fun pictographing activity!

The Population Of Vermont	
Montpelier	🧍
Burlington	🧍🧍🧍🧍
Rutland	🧍🧍
South Burlington	🧍
Bennington	🧍
Barre	🧍
Brattleboro	🧍
🧍 =10,000 people	

1. Draw a graph like the one shown on a large sheet of paper, filling in the names of several cities in your state (including its capital city). Post the graph on a wall or bulletin board.

2. Duplicate multiple copies of the pattern on page 247.

3. Find the population of your state's capital city. Determine the number of people each symbol on your pictograph will represent; then use one pattern to trace enough symbols to represent the capital city's population onto construction paper.

4. Cut out the symbols and tape them on the graph next to the capital city's name.

5. Explain to students that *pictographs* use symbols to represent numbers. Use the graph as an example, pointing out the symbol that represents your capital city's population.

6. Divide students into groups. Assign a city from the graph to each group and have the group research the city's population.

7. Give each group a pattern, several 8 1/2" x 11" sheets of construction paper, scissors, and masking tape. Direct the group to round its population figure to the nearest 5,000; then have it trace the appropriate number of symbols onto the construction paper, cut them out, and place them on the graph next to its city's name.

8. After the graph is complete, have each group share its findings.

State Plot Puzzle

Incorporate graphing skills with your state study using the following nifty idea:

1. Have each student label the horizontal and vertical axes on a sheet of graph paper as shown.

2. Show students how to find a point on the graph when a pair of numbers, or *coordinates,* are given. For example, give students the coordinates (2, 5). Direct them to start at the (0, 0) point, move to the right of the graph two places, and then up five places.

3. Have each student randomly plot points on his graph for each letter of the alphabet (see the illustration).

4. Give each student a list of terms related to your state. Direct the student to create a puzzle that gives a clue and a set of coordinates for each term.

5. After each student has completed his puzzle, have students trade papers and solve each other's puzzles.

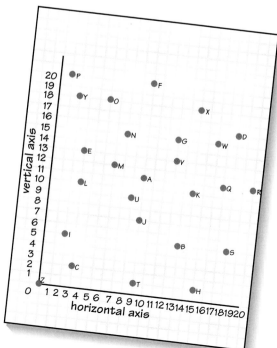

CURRENT EVENTS

Mapping Out The News

Help your students determine the different issues presented in news reports with this hands-on activity:

1. Label a large construction-paper circle "In The News"; then post it on a large wall or bulletin board.
2. Cut out a supply of smaller circles—about five to ten more than the number of students in your class.
3. Ask students to name the types of topics a news story may describe, such as the environment, the government, sports, or science and technology. As students respond, label each smaller circle with a topic.
4. Attach the smaller circles to the larger circle with yarn to create a web.
5. Direct each student to find a news article in a newspaper. Instruct her to read the article, determine its topic, and highlight the specific facts that support her answer.
6. After each student has shared her article, have her glue it to one of the extra circles as shown. Then have her connect her circle to the appropriate issue circle with yarn.

The Heart Of The Story

Give your students practice sorting through all of the technical jargon in news articles to arrive at the heart of a story. Have each student bring in a current news article related to a state or country you are studying. Have the student read the article and highlight *who* it is about, *what* happened, *when* it happened, *where* it happened, and *why* or *how* it happened. Direct the student to accordion-fold a 4" x 17 1/2" strip of red construction paper into five 3 1/2-inch sections. Have her draw the design of a heart on the front of the folded paper as shown, then cut out the heart. (Be sure the student doesn't completely cut the folded edge.) Finally direct the student to unfold her paper and label each heart with one of the five *W*s as shown. Then have the student write a sentence about each of her article's "*w* details" on a heart. Display the heart strips on a bulletin board titled "Getting To The Heart Of A Story."

STUDYING OTHER STATES

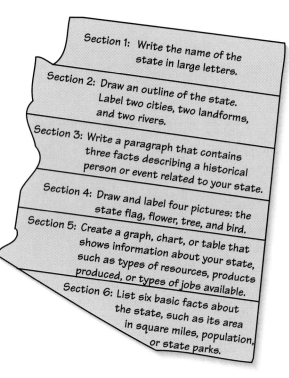

Section 1: Write the name of the state in large letters.

Section 2: Draw an outline of the state. Label two cities, two landforms, and two rivers.

Section 3: Write a paragraph that contains three facts describing a historical person or event related to your state.

Section 4: Draw and label four pictures: the state flag, flower, tree, and bird.

Section 5: Create a graph, chart, or table that shows information about your state, such as types of resources, products produced, or types of jobs available.

Section 6: List six basic facts about the state, such as its area in square miles, population, or state parks.

State On A Wall

Here's an idea for a creative project that will result in a stately wall display. Divide the class into teams of four. Assign each team a state and give it a large sheet of bulletin-board paper, markers, and reference materials related to its state. Instruct the team to draw a large outline of its state on its paper, dividing it into six numbered sections. Then direct the team to research its state and record its findings on its outline as shown. Have each team present its completed project; then display the projects on a wall in the classroom or hallway.

For more state activities see pages 248–250.

Make A State Cake

Here's a sweet idea to get your students' juices flowing during a study of the U.S. states! Pair each student; then assign each pair a state that the class has been studying. Supply each pair with six strips of light-colored construction paper that are graduated in length. Direct the pair to label each strip like the example shown, then draw a labeled illustration for each one. Direct each pair to layer its strips in a cakelike fashion, taping together the backs of the strips. Post the cakes on a large wall, taping a real candle at the top of each one. Finally have each pair share its state and enjoy the sweet rewards of a job well done!

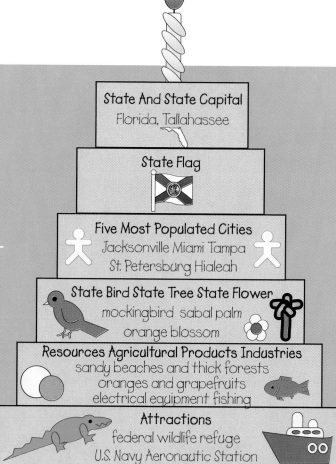

State And State Capital
Florida, Tallahassee

State Flag

Five Most Populated Cities
Jacksonville Miami Tampa
St. Petersburg Hialeah

State Bird State Tree State Flower
mockingbird sabal palm
orange blossom

Resources Agricultural Products Industries
sandy beaches and thick forests
oranges and grapefruits
electrical equipment fishing

Attractions
federal wildlife refuge
U.S. Navy Aeronautic Station

United States Map

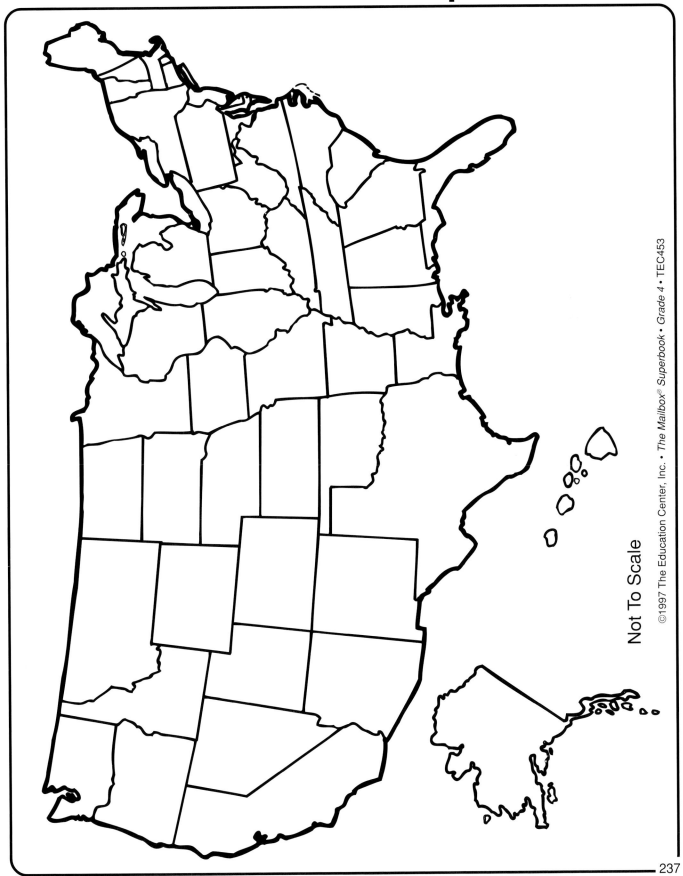

Not To Scale

World Map

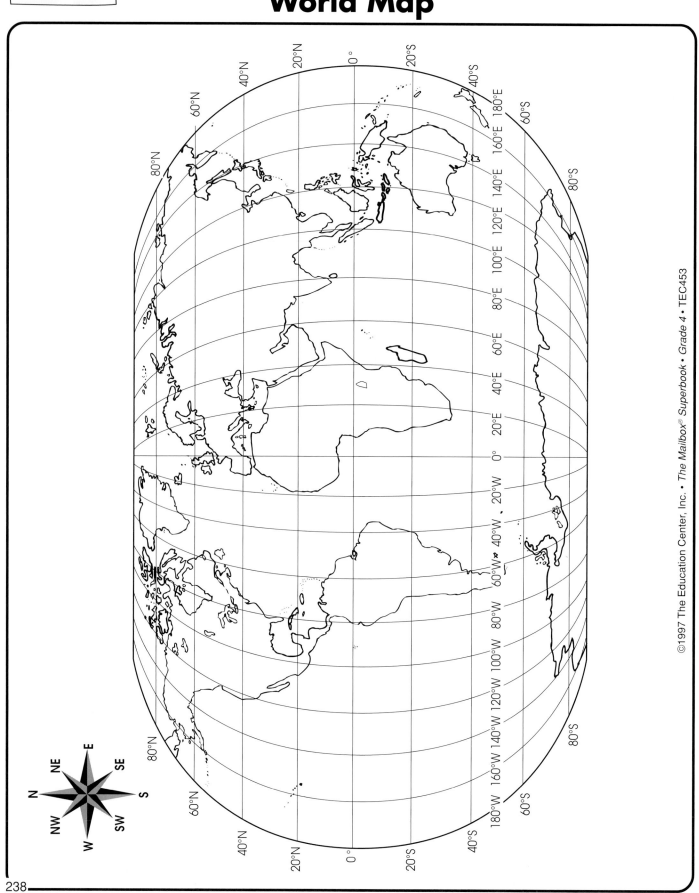

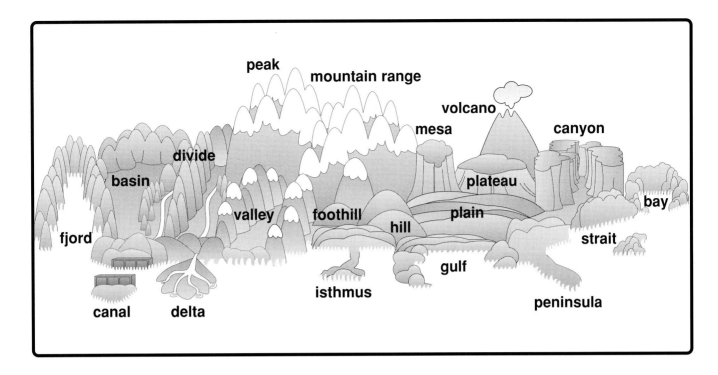

Geography Glossary

basin
a land area mostly surrounded by higher land

bay
a small area of ocean partly surrounded by land

canal
a waterway dug across land

canyon
a narrow valley with high, steep sides

delta
a soil deposit at a river's mouth, usually triangle-shaped

divide
a high ridge of land between areas with different river basins

fjord
a narrow inlet of sea between high, steep banks

foothill
a low hill at the base of a mountain

gulf
a large area of ocean partly surrounded by land

hill
a small, raised part of land lower than a mountain

isthmus
a narrow strip of land connecting two larger land areas

mesa
a flat-topped hill with steep sides

mountain range
a group or chain of mountains

peak
the pointed top of a mountain

peninsula
land surrounded by water on three sides

plain
a large area of flat or gently rolling land

plateau
an area of high, flat land

strait
a narrow water passage between two larger bodies of water

valley
low land between mountains or hills

volcano
a hill or mountain formed by molten rock forced through the earth's surface

Note To The Teacher: Use with " 'Geog' Your Memory" on page 226 and "A Map In A Month" on page 228.

Recognizing geographic features

"Geog" Your Memory

Too many geographic features to remember and too little time? Well, here's a game that will help you jog your memory—Geography Memory! Cut out each card below. Mix up the cards, then lay them facedown on your desk. Turn over two cards at a time. If the cards show a picture of a geographic feature and its definition, keep the matching pair. If not, turn the cards back over and try again. When you are ready, challenge a friend to a game of memory!

basin	a land area mostly surrounded by higher land	**bay**	a small area of ocean partly surrounded by land	**canal**
a waterway dug across land	**canyon**	a narrow valley with high, steep sides		
delta	a soil deposit at a river's mouth, usually triangle-shaped	**divide**	a high ridge of land between areas with different river basins	**fjord**
a narrow inlet of sea between high, steep banks	**foothill**	a low hill at the base of a mountain		
gulf	a large area of ocean partly surrounded by land	**hill**	a small, raised part of land lower than a mountain	**isthmus**
a narrow strip of land connecting two larger land areas	**mesa**	a flat-topped hill with steep sides		
mountain range	a group or chain of mountains	**peak**	the pointed top of a mountain	**peninsula**
land surrounded by water on three sides	**plain**	a large area of flat or gently rolling land		
plateau	an area of high, flat land	**strait**	a narrow water passage between two larger bodies of water	**valley**
low land between mountains or hills	**volcano**	a hill or mountain formed by molten rock forced through the earth's surface		

Note To The Teacher: Use with "'Geog' Your Memory" on page 226. Provide each student with a pair of scissors. Use the "Geography Glossary" on page 239 as an answer key.

🗝 That's The Key! 🗝

What's the key to using a map? The key is, of course! Mapmakers use special marks or symbols on a map to make reading the map easier. The symbols are written in a special box on the map called a *key,* or *legend*. This key helps explain the meaning of each symbol.

Use a map of your state to help you answer the following questions. Write your answers in the blanks.

_____ 1. Draw the symbol that represents your state's capital.

_____ 2. Name an interstate highway that runs through your state.

_____ 3. How many airports are in your state?

_____ 4. What state park is nearest to your hometown?

_____ 5. Name two counties that border each other.

_____ 6. Does your state have a military base?

_____ 7. Draw the symbol that represents a scenic route on your map.

_____ 8. What state highway would you take to get from the northeast section of your state to the southwest section?

_____ 9. In what section of your state can you find a wildlife refuge?

_____ 10. Name a major city that is close to your state's capital.

_____ 11. Starting at your hometown, in what direction would you travel to reach the nearest airport?

_____ 12. Find and name a point of interest in your state.

In the boxes below, draw and color the map-key symbol used for each item. (If no symbol is given, create your own.)

state park	airport	railroad	interstate highway

Indian reservation	mountain peak or range	shopping center	tourist attraction

Bonus Box: A *rebus story* uses symbols in place of some of the words in a story. On the back of this sheet, write a rebus story about an imaginary vacation. Use the symbols from the map in place of some of the words in your story.

©1997 The Education Center, Inc. • *The Mailbox® Superbook* • *Grade 4* • TEC453

Note To The Teacher: Use with "The Key Is The Key!" on page 226. Provide each student group with a map of your state.

Name _____   *Using a map key*

Scaling It Down To Size

A map *scale* shows you how far it is between two places. For example, the scale may show that one inch on the map equals 50 miles on earth. If two cities are three inches apart on the map, they are really 150 miles apart (50 miles x 3 inches).

Look at the city map below. Find the scale. Line up an index card or a slip of paper under the scale. Put a mark on the card for each distance shown on the scale starting with zero. Use the card and scale to answer the following questions. (Be sure to measure from point to point.) Write your answers in the blanks.

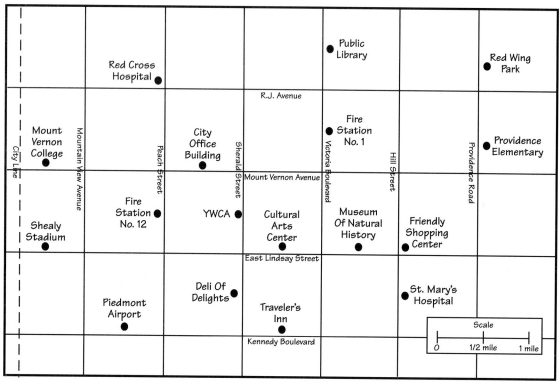

_____ 1. How many miles are represented by one inch on the map?

_____ 2. How many miles is it to the Piedmont Airport from the City Office Building?

_____ 3. Which fire station is nearest to Red Cross Hospital?

_____ 4. What is the distance between the two hospitals?

_____ 5. How far is it from Peach Street to the city line at Mount Vernon Avenue?

_____ 6. If you traveled from Providence Elementary School to Red Wing Park, what would be the distance?

_____ 7. Pick a street. If you traveled it from end-to-end, how far would you travel?

_____ 8. How far is it from Friendly Shopping Center to the intersection of Mountain View Avenue and East Lindsay Street?

_____ 9. What is the distance from Mount Vernon College to Shealy Stadium?

_____ 10. How many miles are between the Traveler's Inn and the Museum of Natural History?

_____ 11. How far is the YWCA from the Cultural Arts Center?

_____ 12. What is the distance from the Deli of Delights to the Public Library?

Bonus Box: Create a key that includes a symbol for each place shown on the map.

©1997 The Education Center, Inc. • *The Mailbox® Superbook* • Grade 4 • TEC453 • Key p. 318

Note To The Teacher: Use with "Scaling A Map" on page 227. Provide each student with an index card or a slip of paper to complete the activity.

Map In A Month

Make a map in a month, you say? No problem! Just follow the directions in the appropriate box each day. After you have added the information to your map, color in the box to show you are finished with that step.

Monday	Tuesday	Wednesday	Thursday	Friday
Read over the directions in each box. Make sure you understand the terms used and how to complete each part of your map. Use references and other maps if you need help.	What is your country going to be like? Is it a land of monsters or a land of the future? Think of a theme for your country. Keep this theme in mind when making your map.	On a 12" x 18" sheet of white construction paper, draw an outline of your imaginary country. Make the outline fill up about 3/4 of your paper.	Give your country a name. Write the name at the top of your paper. °Pegasarius°	On the back of this sheet, list 15 geographic features to add to your map. Include landforms and waterways. Use the "Geography Glossary" on page 239 for help. Add these features to your map. Beware of Quicksand!
Write a name for each landform and waterway on your map. Stick to your theme and be creative! For example, if your country is candy-coated, include a name such as "Caramel Canyon" or "Peppermint Prairie."	Add a compass rose to your map.	Add a scale of miles to your map. 1 inch=100 miles	Label five cities on your map. Create a symbol to indicate the capital city. •Satyron •Minotaurus	Any special attractions in your country, like a 300-foot waterfall or a pit of quicksand? Add at least three attractions to your map.
What kind of climate does your country have? Label your country's climate zones.	What kinds of plants and animals live in your country? Label your map with three of each.	Add a key to your map. Include symbols for geographic features, cities, attractions, plants, animals, etc. Also, if you didn't draw symbols for these features on your map before, do it now. Volcano	Use a ruler and a pencil to draw a grid on your map. Make sure your grid boxes are the same size.	Add an index to your map so visitors to your country can quickly find features and places. Index
A *motto* is a word, phrase, or sentence written on something to describe it. Write an original motto for your country below its name. To The Future!	Make your map colorful using crayons or colored pencils. Red Blue Orange Green Purple Yellow	Ask a partner to check your map. Did you include all of the required items? Did you label the map correctly?	A *cartographer* is a person who makes maps. Write your name somewhere on the map you have just made. Audrey Alphin	Share your map with the class. Roll up the map and tie it with a piece of yarn or ribbon.

©1997 The Education Center, Inc. • *The Mailbox® Superbook • Grade 4 • TEC453*

Note To The Teacher: Use with "A Map In A Month" on page 228. Provide each student with a pencil, a 12" x 18" sheet of white construction paper, a ruler, a piece of yarn or ribbon, crayons or colored pencils, and a copy of "Geography Glossary" on page 239. Reference materials may also be needed.

243

Mapping Your Roots

Have you ever wondered about where the members of your family were born or where they lived? Well, here's one way to get to the root of the question! With the help of a family member, research to find out the states in which you and your relatives have lived. Next draw a different symbol in each blank on the map key at the right; then use the symbols to mark the appropriate states on the map.

Map Key

_____ My state of birth

_____ Parents' state(s) of birth

_____ Grandparents' state(s) of birth

_____ States in which I've lived

_____ States in which my parents lived as children

_____ States in which my grandparents lived as children

_____ States in which other family members lived

_____ States I've visited

_____ One state I'd like to visit but haven't yet

_____ One state I'd like to "put down roots in" when I grow up

_____ Other

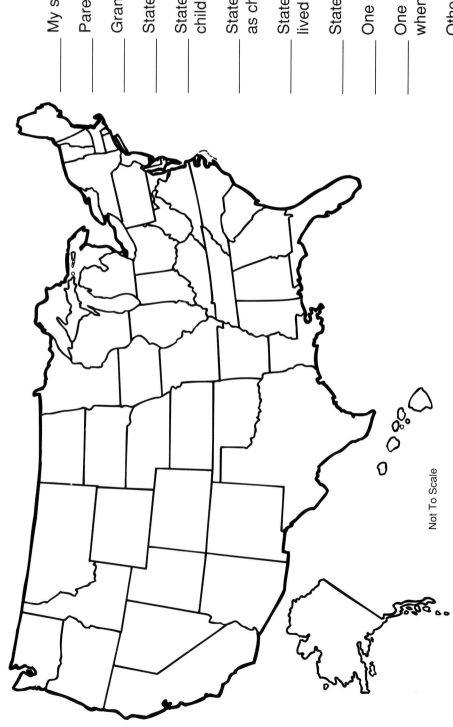

Not To Scale

Bonus Box: On the back of the sheet, write the names of the different states in which you and your family members have lived; then rewrite them in alphabetical order.

Note To The Teacher: Use with "Mapping Your Roots" on page 228.

Pattern

Use with "Monumental Mail" on page 229 and "Imaginary Getaway" on page 231.

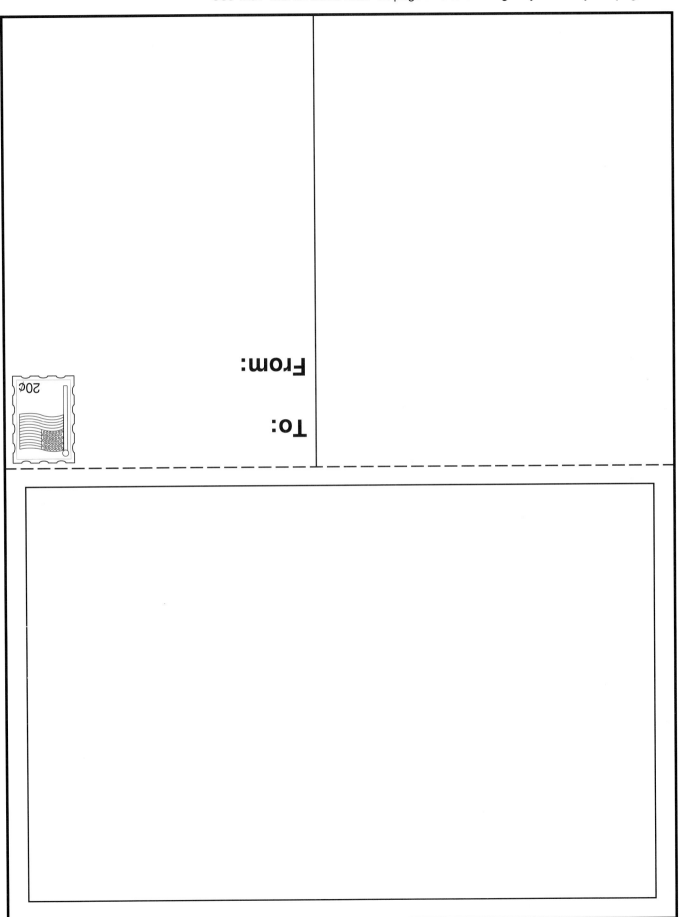

From:

To:

20¢

State-Of-The-Art Stationery

What makes your state special? Is it its magnificent mountains or beautiful beaches? Or is it its famous folks or the products it produces? Share what makes your state special by creating some state-of-the-art stationery. Decorate the border of the paper below with pictures of the things that make your state special. Then cut out the paper along its edges.

Note To The Teacher: Use this with "State-Of-The-Art Stationery" on page 233. Provide each student with a
246 pencil, colored pencils or crayons, scissors, and appropriate reference materials.

Old Flag, New Flag

A state's flag is very important. It may symbolize its land, people, government, and ideas or beliefs. What does your state flag look like? What is the meaning behind its words or symbols?

Research your state's flag; then decorate the smaller flag below so that it looks like this flag. On the lines below it, write a sentence that explains its meaning. Then on the larger flag, design a new state flag with pictures or symbols that are meaningful to your state. On the lines below the flag, write a sentence that explains its meaning.

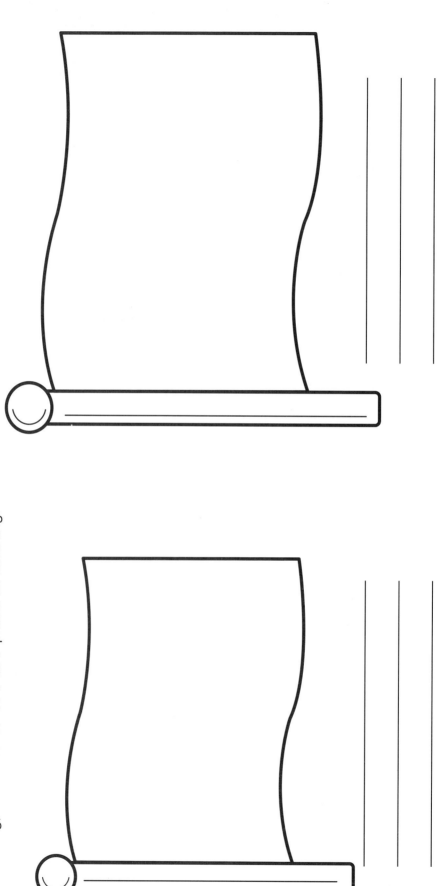

©1997 The Education Center, Inc. • *The Mailbox® Superbook* • *Grade 4* • TEC453

Bonus Box: On the back of this sheet, write a paragraph to the governor of your state. Tell why the state should adopt your new design.

Note To The Teacher: Provide each student with markers or colored pencils and appropriate reference materials.

Backpacking Across Your State

You're going on a journey—a state-study journey. With all of the things to see and do, where are you going to keep all of your souvenirs? How about in a backpack? Follow the directions listed below to construct your own state-study backpack. Then complete each project listed below. As you work, store each completed project inside your state-study backpack. Happy traveling!

State-Study Back Pack

Materials: one plain, brown paper grocery bag; two 2" x 24" strips of cloth; two brad fasteners; a stapler; one small piece of yarn; scissors; markers or colored pencils

Directions:

Step 1: Cut along three of the bottom-flap edges of the bag as shown below. This will be your flap.

Step 2: Add two brad fasteners: one at the bottom of the flap, and the other one about one inch below the flap. Then tie a piece of yarn to the top brad; then wrap it around the bottom brad to secure the flap.

Step 3: Close the opening of the bag, folding the edges over about one inch; then staple it shut.

Step 4: Staple each cloth strip to the back side of the bag as shown. Be careful not to staple the flap shut.

Step 5: Decorate your backpack.

Step 1

Step 2

Step 3

Step 4

Items to include in your state-study backpack:

1. an illustration of the state bird
2. an illustration of the state tree
3. an illustration of the state flower
4. an illustration of the state flag
5. a map and key that show the state's land regions, landforms and bodies of water, or natural resources
6. an illustration and description of an agricultural product and a manufactured product that the state produces
7. a chart showing the names of three famous people from the state's history, the dates they lived, and their achievements
8. a graph that compares the population of the five largest cities in the state
9. a timeline showing five important dates and events in the state's history
10. a travel brochure that illustrates and describes four major tourist attractions in the state

©1997 The Education Center, Inc. • *The Mailbox® Superbook • Grade 4* • TEC453

Note To The Teacher: Provide each student with the materials listed on this sheet and any necessary reference materials.

State Minibook

Complete the sentence listed on each page below. Then draw and color an illustration to go with each sentence on each page. When you have completed all the pages, cut them out along the bold lines. Finally bind the pages together using a hole puncher and yarn or brads to form a minibook of your state.

My State Minibook _____ (name of state) Written by: _____	One thing I already knew about my state was… 1
One of the most interesting things I learned about my state was… 2	One thing I learned my state is most known for is… 3
One thing I want to go see in my state is… 4	One thing I would change about my state is… 5

Bonus Box: On the back of this sheet, write as many words as you can that describe your state—such as *huge, populated,* and *forested.* Use a thesaurus if you need help.

Note To The Teacher: Assign each student a state that the class has recently studied. Then provide each student with one copy of this page, scissors, markers or colored pencils, a hole puncher, brads or yarn, and reference materials. Instruct each student to follow the directions on the sheet for completing the activity; then have each student share her completed minibook with her classmates.

SCIENCE & HEALTH

Scientific Method

How Does Your Boat Float?

Sail into the scientific method with this fun flotation experiment. Give each student a copy of the lab report on page 263; then divide your class into groups.

Materials for each group: clay, 10 metal washers, a clear bowl filled with water, paper towels

Procedure:
1. Write this assignment on your lab sheet: "Determine the boat shape that will float in water and stay afloat when more weight is added to it." Record your group's hypothesis on your sheet.
2. Shape the clay into a rounded ball. Place it in the water to see if it will float. Record the results.
3. Form the clay into other shapes until you find one that floats well. Record your results.
4. After you find the boat shape that works best, add one metal washer at a time into the boat.
5. Continue adding one washer at a time until the boat begins to sink. Record your results and conclusions at the bottom of your lab sheet.

Explanation: The rounded ball of clay will sink in the water. When the clay is molded into a shape with a broad bottom and steep sides, it will float. The clay still weighs the same, but the new shape allows it to displace more water and stay afloat.

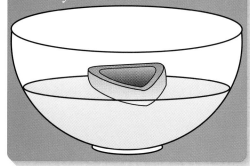

Blast Off!

You can bet your boosters students will have a blast with this experiment on rocket propulsion! Give each child a copy of page 263; then divide your class into groups.

Materials for each group: 1 Fuji® film canister with a lid; 1 Alka-Seltzer® tablet; water; scissors; 1 copy of the rocket pattern on page 264, duplicated on tagboard; markers or crayons; tape

Procedure:
1. Write this assignment on your lab sheet: "Find out how rockets work." Record your group's hypothesis on your sheet.
2. Cut out the rocket pattern. Make the rocket following the instructions on the sheet.
3. Fill the film canister one-third full of water. Place the Alka-Seltzer® tablet in the canister.
4. Very quickly snap the canister lid in place. Turn the rocket right side up, place it on a flat surface, and stand back for the launch.
5. Record the results and your conclusions on your lab sheet.

Explanation: When the tablet was placed in the water, a gas began to form. As the pressure inside the canister increased, it caused the lid to come off and the rocket to shoot upward. When rocket propulsion occurs, gas builds up or expands inside the rocket. This gas presses against the rocket in all directions. The gas pushing on one side of the rocket is balanced by the gas pushing against the opposite side. The gas flowing to the rocket's rear escapes and is not balanced by gas pressure in the front of the rocket. This uneven distribution of gas pressure propels the rocket forward.

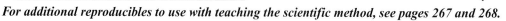

For additional reproducibles to use with teaching the scientific method, see pages 267 and 268.

Worm Your Way In

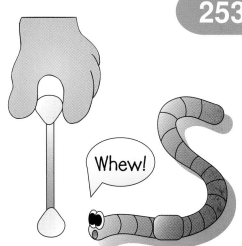

Looking for a science activity that students are sure to dig? Give each child a copy of page 266; then conduct this activity in small groups or as a demonstration. After the experiment, point out to students that even though an earthworm does not have eyes or ears, it does have a brain and a nervous system that responds to external stimuli such as light, touch, and heat. Explain to students that, in the activity, they used the scientific method to make observations about earthworms. Then discuss the difference in the worm's reaction to the water and the vinegar. Conclude by having students release the worms outside in a damp area of soil.

Whew!

Something's Fishy Around Here!

Hook students on animals with this fishy lesson! Give each student a copy of page 263; then conduct this demonstration:

Materials: aquarium or fishbowl with goldfish or other small fish, large-mouthed jar (such as a pickle jar), small fishnet, thermometer, water, large bowl, ice, stopwatch or watch with second hand

Procedure:

1. Have each student write this assignment on his lab sheet: "Determine what happens to the respiration of a fish when water temperature becomes colder."

2. Have each child write his hypothesis on his lab sheet.

3. Fill the jar with water from the aquarium.

4. Use the fishnet to transfer a fish from the aquarium to the jar. Allow the fish 30 minutes to adapt to its new environment.

5. Find the temperature of the water in the jar. Have each student record the temperature on his sheet. Count and record the number of times the fish opens and closes its mouth and gills in one minute.

6. Place the jar inside a large, empty bowl. Gradually fill the bowl half-full of ice; then add enough water to fill the bowl. (**Important:** Do **not** add anything to the jar containing the fish. **Gradually** add the ice to the bowl. Too sudden a temperature change may harm the fish.)

7. Place the thermometer in the jar and check the temperature every minute. When the temperature has dropped 8 degrees Celsius, remove the thermometer. Count and record the number of times the fish opens and closes its mouth and gills in one minute. Then remove the jar containing the fish from the bowl of ice water.

8. Have each student write his conclusions at the bottom of his sheet.

Explanation: Cold-blooded animals such as fish cannot regulate their body temperature, which changes with the temperature of their surroundings. When the temperature warms up, cold-blooded animals become more active; when it cools down, they become less active.

For a research activity on vertebrates, see page 265.

Space

Exploring Our Solar System

Help students grasp the vast size of our solar system with this activity. Give each student a copy of page 269. Explain that astronomers measure the distance between objects in the solar system using the *astronomical unit,* or AU. Have students refer to page 269 to find the distance between the Sun and the Earth *(1 AU, or 93,000,000 miles/149,600,000 kilometers).* Explain that the distance between the Sun and the Earth represents 1 AU. Next review the distances between the Sun and other planets, pointing out that the astronomical units grow larger the farther the planet is from the Sun.

Next make ten circle cutouts to represent the Sun and the nine planets in our solar system. Label each circle; then head outdoors to a large area. Using 40 meters of string and a meterstick or yardstick, have students mark off the distance between the Sun and each of the paper planets using the following data:

Planet		Distance From Sun
Mercury	38 centimeters	15 inches
Venus	72 centimeters	29 inches
Earth	1 meter	1 yard 3 inches
Mars	1 meter 52 centimeters	1 yard 24 inches
Jupiter	5 meters 20 centimeters	5 yards 23 inches
Saturn	9 meters 52 centimeters	10 yards 13 inches
Uranus	19 meters 20 centimeters	20 yards 29 inches
Neptune	30 meters	32 yards 18 inches
Pluto	39 meters 40 centimeters	42 yards 25 inches

LIGHT

Reflecting On Mirrors

Get students reflecting on the difference between convex and concave mirrors with this activity. Collect a shiny, metal spoon from your school cafeteria for each student pair. Direct each pair to look at the back of its spoon, noting the direction in which it curves. Explain that the spoon back is an example of a *convex mirror*—a mirror with a reflecting surface that curves outward. Have each pair describe the reflection it sees in the spoon back. Then explain that the reflection from a convex mirror is smaller than the object being reflected. Next direct each pair to turn its spoon over and note the direction in which the spoon front curves. Explain that the spoon front is an example of a *concave mirror*—a mirror with a reflecting surface that curves inward. Have each pair describe the reflection that appears in its spoon; then point out that the reflection from a concave mirror is magnified. Use the examples listed below to guide students in brainstorming a list of uses for convex and concave mirrors.

Convex Mirrors (cause light rays to spread apart, giving a wider view of objects): car rear-view mirrors, store monitoring mirrors

Concave Mirrors (gather and focus light, giving a magnified view of objects): shaving mirrors, make-up mirrors, reflecting telescopes, flashlights, car headlights

Puzzled By Pencils

Get right to the point with this lesson on light refraction! Divide your class into small groups; then give each student a copy of the experiment on page 270 to complete. Students should note that the pencil did not change when viewed through the empty jar. When viewed in water, the pencil appeared broken or twisted. Why? Students saw the top of the pencil just through the air and the glass, and the bottom part through water. Light travels more slowly through water than through glass and air; therefore, the light's direction changes a little, causing students to see the two parts of the pencil in different places. When viewed in oil, the pencil appeared even more broken. The denser the liquid, the more it refracts light and the more displaced the pencil appears.

Matter

What's The Matter?

Your students will know exactly what's the matter after playing this game! Provide students with the following definitions:

solids—*have form and possess hardness and rigidity; have the ability to resist changes in shape*

liquids—*have no shape of their own; have the ability to flow; take the shape of any container in which they are placed*

gases—*have no shape of their own; have low densities compared to solids and liquids; exert pressure in all directions; are compressible*

Solid	Liquids	Gas
wood	water	oxygen
stone	gasoline	helium
cloth	shampoo	carbon
plastic	juice	dioxide

Next divide students into groups. Have each group divide a paper into three columns, labeling one column for each state of matter. Give each group five minutes to brainstorm and list examples of the three states of matter. Tell students that a group will earn a point for each item it names that has been classified correctly and does not appear on another group's list. Explain that the more creative an answer is, the less likely it is that another group will have the same answer. After five minutes, review each of the categories one at a time and identify the winning team.

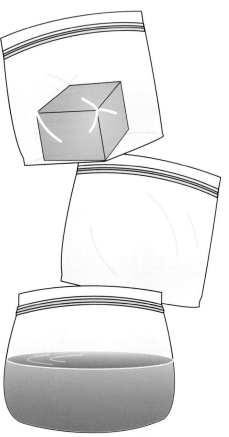

Bag It!

Investigate the three states of matter—solid, liquid, and gas—with the following demonstration.

Materials: three 1-quart resealable plastic bags, a solid object such as a block of wood, 1 cup of water

Procedure:

1. Place the solid object in one bag. Pour the water into another bag. Seal both bags tightly.

2. Blow into the third bag and quickly seal the bag.

3. Explain to students that each bag represents one of the three types of matter: solid, liquid, gas. Have students identify the type of matter represented by each bag.

4. Direct students to observe and record the characteristics of the three types of matter. Have students answer questions about each form of matter, such as:
   • Is it visible?
   • Can it change shape easily?
   • Does it allow a solid object to be moved through it?

5. Challenge students to find examples of the three states of matter in your classroom.

Explanation: Solids and most liquids are visible, but most gases are not. Solids do not change shape easily and do not allow a solid object to be passed through them easily. Liquids and gases do change shape easily and allow solid objects to be passed through them.

Weather

Wherever The Wind Takes Us

Blow students away with this fun, windy, weather-wise lesson! In 1805 British Rear Admiral Sir Francis Beaufort devised a scale to measure the effects of wind strength on sailing vessels. This system became known as the Beaufort wind scale. Explain to students that using the Beaufort wind scale is a good way to estimate wind speeds. Then give each student a copy of page 271 and a file folder. Have the student glue the wind scale and the data collection chart inside the folder. For the next 12 days, have each student fill in his chart by observing specific weather conditions, including wind speed and direction. Challenge each student to record his own forecast for the following day's weather in the correct space on the chart; then have him check the official forecast and record it on his chart. After each student completes his chart, have him average the Beaufort numbers to find the average wind speed for the days listed on the chart.

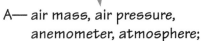

Weather Words Border

Let the clouds roll in with this fun weather-vocabulary activity! Draw a cloud outline on a sheet of unlined paper. Then make one copy for each student. Assign each student a weather word to research from the list below. Have the student define the word on his cloud pattern, and then draw an illustration. Post the cut-out clouds in alphabetical order as a border around your classroom walls. As you come across one of the weather words in your study, refer to the cloud that features it. Then have each student record the definition for the word in his science notebook.

anemometer: an instrument that measures wind speed.

A— air mass, air pressure, anemometer, atmosphere;
B— barometer, Beaufort wind scale;
C— Celsius, climate, cloud, condensation;
D— dew;
E— evaporation;
F— Fahrenheit, fog, forecast, front;
G—global warming;
H—humidity, hurricane, hygrometer;
I— isobar;
J— jet stream;
K— knot;
L— lightning;
M—meteorologist;
N— National Weather Service;
O— observation station;
P— precipitation, prediction;
R— radar, rainbow, rain gauge;
S— satellite, storm;
T— temperature, thermometer, thunderstorm, tornado;
U— updraft;
V— vapor, visibility;
W—warning, watch, weather, wind, weather vane;
Z— zone

SOUND

How Does Sound Travel?

Use the hands-on reproducible activities on page 272 to teach students how sound travels. Have pairs of students complete the activities.

- **Activity 1:** Students will observe that the paper strip moves when the tube is tapped. Ask why this occurs; then explain that the tap makes the air in the tube vibrate, causing a sound wave to travel down the tube through the hole. As it passes over the paper strip, the wave causes the air to move the strip.

- **Activity 2:** Students will observe that the marbles bump into one another until the last one rolls away from the line. The marbles represent molecules of air bumping into one another as a result of sound traveling through them. The energy is transferred from one marble to the next until it reaches the last marble, which rolls away when it receives the energy. The air molecules through which sound waves travel—like the marbles—ultimately bump into one another until they reach our eardrums.

- **Activity 3:** Have students describe the pattern of the rope's movement. Explain that this wave action is similar to the wavelike path along which sound travels. Have each student draw the pattern he saw in the rope on the back of page 272.

Sound Conduction

Use this simple activity to demonstrate that sound travels better through solid objects than through air. Give each pair of students two metal spoons and one three-foot length of yarn. Direct the pair to tie one of the spoons in the middle of the string. Instruct one partner to wrap the ends of the string around his index fingers as shown. Have the other student strike his partner's spoon with the other spoon, observing the sound generated. Then have the first student carefully stick his index fingers into his ears. Have his partner strike the hanging spoon again. Have the student holding the string explain how this sounded (*it sounded louder*). Have partners switch jobs and repeat the activity. Ask students why they think they could hear the sound better through the string than through the air. (*The first time the spoon was tapped, the vibrations traveled through the air in all directions; only a few of the sound waves reached the student's ears. The second time the spoon was struck, the vibrations traveled up the string directly to the ear. The sound was much louder because sound travels better through solids than through air.*)

ENVIRONMENT

To Be Biodegradable Or Not To Be?

So what's the big deal about trash anyway? Show students the danger of tons of trash with this activity. First share the definition of *biodegradable* (able to be decomposed, especially by bacterial action). Then give each student a copy of the experiment on the bottom half of page 273. Have students work in groups to conduct the experiment. Explain that the water and shaking simulate the elements breaking down material over a period of time. Guide students in determining that food and nonglossy paper are biodegradable, but plastic wrap and aluminum foil are not. When exposed to enough bacteria, air, water, wind, and sunlight, the food and nonglossy paper will be broken down, but the plastic wrap and aluminum foil will not change. When nonbiodegradable items are placed in landfills, they do not break down.

Extend this activity by sharing the following facts with your class:

> Daily, Americans throw away about 38,000 tons of glass along with enough aluminum cans to make about 30 jet planes.

> Americans throw out 150,000 tons of wrappers, bags, and boxes each day.

> 70% of the garbage thrown out each day ends up in landfills.

> There are about 5,500 operational landfills in the United States today. It is estimated that about three-fourths of these landfills will be full by the year 2020.

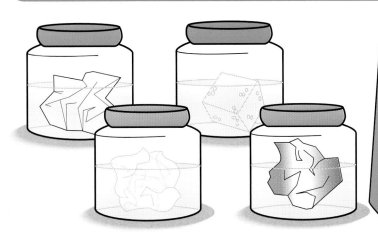

Plastic Reuse Contest

Turn recycling into a fun, creative contest with this earth-friendly idea! Announce that you will be holding a contest to find the most creative idea for reusing a plastic bottle or jar. To demonstrate one way, have each student fill a large plastic jar (such as a peanut-butter jar) half-full of potting soil and plant a few bean seeds in it. Direct the student to water the seeds until the soil is damp, then place the jar lid on tightly. Set the jars in a window and wait for the seeds to sprout. Explain that plants like those in the terrariums keep our environment healthier by giving us oxygen—a by-product of *photosynthesis*—to breathe. Also, reusing plastic containers makes less waste to go into landfills.

Next challenge each student to invent a new way to reuse a plastic jar or bottle. Give students one week to work on their projects; then set up a display area to showcase the contest entries. Provide each student with a copy of the entry form at the top of page 273 on which to briefly describe her entry and its environmental benefits. Have your principal or another teacher judge the entries. Offer a small prize to the winner, such as a reused jar filled with sugarless candy. Conclude by inviting other classes to your room to view the display.

Nutrition

Food Guide Pyramid

Tempt students' taste buds with this mouthwatering game on the Food Guide Pyramid!

1 Have each student cut out several pictures of food from magazines and grocery store ads—selecting pictures of healthful foods in addition to favorite snacks.

2 Divide students into small groups. Evenly divide the pictures among the groups. Give one copy of the Food Guide Pyramid on page 274 to each student to use as a bingo card.

3 Have each group remove all but three junk-food pictures from its picture collection and put the remaining pictures in a small paper bag.

4 Have members of each group take turns pulling a picture out of the bag and determining into which food group it belongs. The student who draws the food item uses a penny or another marker to cover the corresponding section on her Food Guide Pyramid.

5 If a student selects a food represented by more than one food group, she must identify the groups into which the item falls and then select one group to cover on her gameboard. If a student draws a junk-food item, she must clear her card and start over.

6 A player calls, "Bingo!" when she has a marker on each food group.

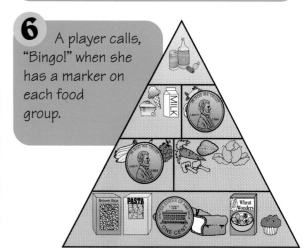

Food-Label Investigations

Teach students some real-world skills with this lesson on reading food labels. Ask each student to bring in two food labels from home; then give each child a copy of page 275. Review the two labels featured on the sheet. Pair students and have them answer the questions at the bottom of the sheet. When each pair has finished, discuss which of the two foods is more healthful and why. Point out that fat and processed sugar are at the top of the Food Guide Pyramid (see page 274) and should be used sparingly. Discuss the difference between processed or refined sugar and natural sugars. *(In processed sugar all the vitamins and other nutrients are removed during the refining process; this type of sugar acts only as a source of energy and does not provide any essential nutrients. Some sugars are found naturally in foods such as apples, peaches, and milk.)* Ask students to which food group each food belongs. Then have each child compare the two labels he brought from home and answer the same questions. Also pose the following questions:

➤ How many total milligrams (mg) of sodium are there in this package? *(Multiply the number of servings in the package by the amount of sodium per serving.)*

➤ How many total grams (g) of fat are there in this package? *(Multiply the number of servings in the package by the amount of total fat per serving.)*

➤ Approximately how many servings of this food would total 2,000 calories—an average daily intake? *(Divide 2,000 by the number of calories in one serving of the food.)*

The Human Body

Bone Builders, Incorporated

Here's one activity that's guaranteed to be a "bone-fide" success! Give each group of students a ball of clay, a small cup, a textbook, and 50 plastic drinking straws. Have groups follow these steps:

1. Divide the clay into two lumps. Press each lump into a circle slightly larger than the rim of the cup.

2. Gently press the rim of the cup into each circle to form a slight impression.

3. Stick 25 of the drinking straws into one circle along the impression. Lean the straws in different directions

4. Stick the remaining straws into the second circle so they stand up straight.

5. Predict what will happen when you carefully place the book on top of each circle of straws. Then test your predictions and record your observations. (The book should cause the first circle of straws to collapse. If balanced carefully, the book should rest on the second circle of straws because the straws' arrangement is stronger. The second arrangement is similar to the structure of materials in bone. Because of this arrangement, human bones are—pound for pound—stronger than wood, concrete, or steel!)

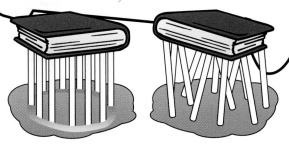

Joint Jargon

Help students bone up on the human body's joints with this demonstration:

1. Explain that the place where two or more bones meet is called a *joint*. The human body has several different types of joints.

2. Open and close a door. Ask: "Which of your joints resembles a door hinge?" *(elbows, knees)* Explain that these types of joints are called *hinge joints*.

3. Rotate a doorknob. Ask: "Which of your joints move in the same way?" *(wrists, ankles)* Explain that these types of joints are called *pivot joints*.

4. Demonstrate a mortar and pestle. Ask: "Which of your joints move in the same way?" *(shoulders, hips)* Explain that joints like these are called *ball-and-socket joints*.

5. Have students listen to the sound the mortar and pestle makes. Ask: "Do your shoulders and hips make a similar sound when you walk?" *(no)* Tape a cotton ball to the end of the pestle; then rotate it in the mortar. Have students compare the new sound to the one created by the uncovered pestle *(it should be quieter because the cotton pads the pestle)*. Explain that the ends of bones are covered with a smooth substance called *cartilage* that reduces friction between the bones where they meet at a joint.

6. Add a tablespoon of cooking oil to the mortar, and rotate the pestle. Ask: "How does the pestle sound now?" *(It should be quieter because the oil lubricates the pestle.)* Explain that the human body makes a special fluid that lubricates the joints, preventing injuries and helping joints work smoothly with little effort or wear.

Seeing The Pulse

Take a close-up look at the hardest-working machine in your body with this experiment. Show students how to use the fingertips to find a pulse at the wrist; then have each child find his pulse. Next give each student a small amount of modeling clay and a drinking straw. Have the student place the clay on his wrist over the place where he felt his pulse the strongest. Then have him carefully stick the straw into the clay so that it stands straight up from the wrist. Instruct the student to rest his arm on his desk; then ask him to describe what is happening. *(The straw should twitch slightly with each surge of blood made by each heartbeat.)* Have the student count the twitches he sees for one minute. Explain that this is his resting heart rate. Next have him remove his pulse meter and do jumping jacks for three to five minutes. Have the student quickly replace his pulse meter and check his heart rate again. Discuss why the heart rate is higher after exercise. *(The heart pumps more quickly during exercise. The heart must pump blood more rapidly to the lungs so they can replenish the oxygen in the blood cells more quickly.)*

I beat 35 times in 30 seconds!

Let's see—that's 70 beats per minute!

Heart-Rate Math

Combine a little math with your study of the heart. A person's heart rate is measured in how many times per minute her heart beats. Explain to students that there are several ways to calculate the heart's rate. One way is by counting the number of beats in 30 seconds and multiplying that number by two. Use a sample count, such as 35 beats, and demonstrate the math on the chalkboard. Then have students count their heartbeats for 15 seconds. Ask: "How many 15-second periods are in one minute?" Guide students to determine that if heartbeats are counted for 15 seconds, the resulting number must be multiplied by four to find the heart rate. Continue with other lengths of time, such as 5, 10, and 20 seconds. Use the reproducible on page 276 to give students more practice computing heart rates.

Name(s) _____

Date _____

Science Lab Report

Assignment/Purpose: _____

Hypothesis: _____

_____

Materials needed: _____

_____

Procedure: _____

_____

_____

_____

_____

_____

_____

Results: _____

_____

_____

_____

_____

_____

Conclusions: _____

_____

_____

_____

_____

Note To The Teacher: Use with "How Does Your Boat Float?" and "Blast Off!" on page 252, and with "Something's Fishy Around Here!" on page 253. Also use with any other science experiments completed by your students.

Directions For Rocket Construction:

1. Cut out the three rocket parts shown.
2. Color the body of the rocket with markers or crayons.
3. Tape the body of the rocket around the film canister as shown. Make sure that the canister lid is sticking out from the bottom of the rocket about two to three centimeters so that the lid can be easily removed. Secure the rocket body with additional tape. Do <u>not</u> tape the rocket body to the canister.
4. Cut along the solid lines on each of the four fins. On each fin, fold the flaps along the dashed lines in opposite directions. Then tape each fin to the base of the rocket body as shown. Be sure to space the four fins equal distances from each other.
5. Shape the half-circle into a cone and secure it with tape as shown. Attach the cone to the rocket top.

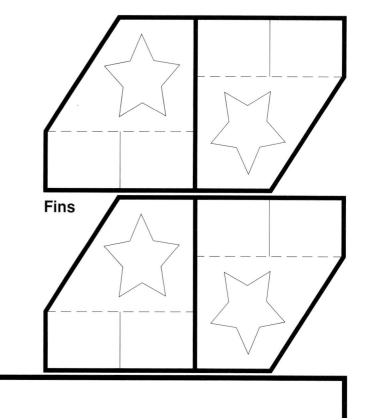

Fins

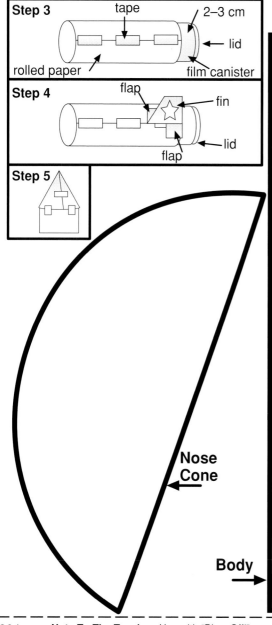

Step 3 tape 2–3 cm lid rolled paper film canister

Step 4 flap fin lid flap

Step 5

Nose Cone ←

Body →

Note To The Teacher: Use with "Blast Off!" on page 252.

Completing a chart, research

Those Amazing Vertebrates

A *vertebrate* is an animal with a backbone and a *cranium* (braincase). There are about 40,000 species of vertebrates. Scientists divide these species into eight classes, six of which are listed below.

Directions: Research each class and fill in the chart. Then study the animals pictured at the bottom of the page. Cut out each animal and glue it in the appropriate illustration column.

Class	Cold-Blooded Or Warm-Blooded	Type Of Body Covering	Method Of Breathing	Other Attributes	Examples	Illustration
Chondrichthyes (sharks and other fish with skeletons of cartilage)		some covered with scales, others scaleless				
Osteichthyes (bony fish)	cold-blooded					
Amphibia (amphibians)			most breathe with lungs, some have gills, some have lungs and gills			
Reptilia (reptiles)		dry, scaly skin				
Aves (birds)				all birds have wings, do not have teeth, have a hard bill (or beak)		
Mammalia (mammals)					cats, dogs, cattle, goats, people, apes, hogs	

Cut along the dotted lines.

frog

tuna

shark

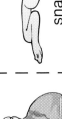

cat

snake

duck

Worm Your Way In

Earthworms are often called *night crawlers*. They are found around the world in moist, warm soil. Each segment of an earthworm's body (except the first and last) has four pairs of *setae*, or bristles, to help it move. An earthworm does not have eyes or ears, but it does have a mouth and is sensitive to heat, touch, and light. Earthworms range in length from 1/25 inch to 11 feet!

Parts Of An Earthworm:

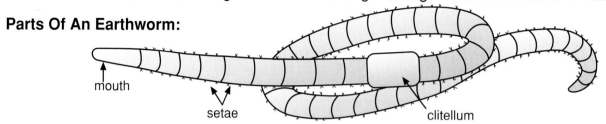

mouth

setae

clitellum

Directions: Follow the instructions below to worm your way into this fun lesson about earthworms.

Hypothesis: How will an earthworm react to a strong scent (since it does not have a sense of smell)?_____

Materials: one earthworm, damp paper towels, two cotton swabs, vinegar, water

Procedure:

1. Place an earthworm on a damp paper towel.
2. Identify the worm's *clitellum*—the large band on the worm.
3. Identify the worm's head by looking for the end of the worm's body closest to the clitellum.
4. Moisten a cotton swab with water.
5. Hold the moistened cotton swab near, but not against, the worm's head. Record the worm's reaction to the water swab in the chart below.
6. Hold the water swab near the tail end of the worm. Observe and record the worm's reaction.
7. Moisten a second cotton swab with vinegar.
8. Hold the vinegar swab near, but not against, the worm's head. Record the worm's reaction to the swab.
9. Hold the vinegar swab near the tail end of the worm. Observe and record the worm's reaction.
10. Record your conclusions at the bottom of this sheet.
11. Take the worm outside and release it in a moist area of soil.

Results: _____

	Head	Tail
Water Swab		
Vinegar Swab		

Conclusions: _____

Note To The Teacher: Use with "Worm Your Way In" on page 253.

Science Safety

Play it safe as you conduct scientific investigations by following these rules:

1. ALWAYS get your teacher's permission before beginning an investigation.

2. Tie back long hair and roll up baggy sleeves.

3. NEVER point the end of a test tube toward yourself or others.

4. NEVER put your eyes or face up close to a chemical mixture.

5. NEVER taste, touch, or eat a substance unless you are told to do so by an adult.

6. When you are finished with an investigation, wash your hands and all utensils thoroughly.

7. Always clean up your work area completely.

8. Report any accident or injury, no matter how small, to your teacher.

Safety Contract

I, _____, have read and understand the safety rules listed above. I recognize my responsibility and promise to observe all science safety rules in my classroom at all times.

_____	_____
Student Signature	Date
_____	_____
Parent Signature	Date

Note To The Teacher: Duplicate one copy of this form for each student. As a class, review the rules. Have each student sign the contract; then have her take it home to have a parent sign.

Name _____

ADMIT ONE **ADMIT ONE** # Your Ticket Out **ADMIT ONE** **ADMIT ONE**

Before you leave our classroom, talk with your group about what you learned during today's science activity. Then have one group member record the answers to the questions below.

Today our group learned:

1. _____
2. _____
3. _____

We have questions about:

1. _____
2. _____
3. _____

Group members' signatures:

_____   _____

_____   _____

_____   _____

Name _____

Science Lab Evaluation

Activity: _____   Date: _____

Scientists Names	**Jobs**
_____	_____
_____	_____
_____	_____
_____	_____
_____	_____

Rate your group using the following scale: 4 = excellent, 3 = good, 2 = fair, 1 = poor

1. We finished our activity on time.   4   3   2   1
2. We cooperated with each other.   4   3   2   1
3. We followed directions.   4   3   2   1

Complete the following sentences:

4. The one thing we did well was _____

_____.

5. We need to work on _____

_____.

Note To The Teacher: Use these two forms when you want student groups to evaluate their work on science activities.

Solar System Fact Sheet

Planet	Named for	Diameter	Length of day	Length of year	Surface temperature	Distance from the Sun Note: 1 AU = 93,000,000 miles
Mercury	the Roman god of travel who was a messenger for the other gods	3,026 miles	59 Earth days	88 Earth days	−292°F to 806°F	0.40 AU
Venus	the Roman goddess of love and beauty	7,504 miles	243 Earth days	about 225 Earth days	869°F	0.72 AU
Earth		7,909 miles	24 hours	about 365 days	average of 59°F	1 AU
Mars	the Roman god of war	4,208 miles	about 25 Earth hours	about 2 Earth years	−184°F to 77°F	1.5 AU
Jupiter	the Roman king of the gods	88,536 miles	10 Earth hours	about 12 Earth years	−238°F at the cloud tops	5.2 AU
Saturn	the Roman god of agriculture	74,400 miles	11 Earth hours	about 29.5 Earth years	−238°F at the cloud tops	9.5 AU
Uranus	the earliest supreme god of the Greeks	32,116 miles	17 Earth hours	about 84 Earth years	−355°F	19.2 AU
Neptune	the Roman god of the sea	30,690 miles	16 Earth hours	about 165 Earth years	−355°F	30 AU
Pluto	the Roman god of the dead	1,860 miles	6 Earth days	about 248 Earth years	−369°F to −342°F	ranges from 29.5 to 49.2 AU

©1997 The Education Center, Inc. • *The Mailbox® Superbook* • *Grade 4* • TEC453

Note To The Teacher: Use with "Exploring Our Solar System" on page 254.

Puzzled By Pencils

Use this experiment to find how substances—such as oil, water, and air—affect light travel.

Materials for each group: 1 clear glass, water, vegetable oil, 1 pencil, paper towels

Procedure:

1. Predict what will happen when a pencil is viewed through the side of a glass filled with each substance listed in the table below. Write your predictions in the data chart.
2. Place the pencil in the empty glass; then look through the side of the glass at the pencil. Draw what you see in the data chart.
3. Fill the glass half-full with water. Look through the glass's side at the pencil. Then draw what you see in the data chart.
4. Empty the water from the glass. Then fill it one-third full with vegetable oil.
5. Place the pencil in the oil and look at it through the side of the glass. Draw what you see in the chart below.

Results: _____

_____

Data Chart

Item	Prediction	Actual Results
air		
water		
vegetable oil		

Conclusions:

How did the appearance of the pencil change when viewed through different substances?

_____

_____

Why do you think this happened? _____

_____

Note To The Teacher: Use with "Puzzled By Pencils" on page 255.

BEAUFORT WIND SCALE

Beaufort Number	Name	Miles Per Hour	Effect on Land
0	Calm	less than 1	Calm; smoke rises straight up in the air
1	Light air	1–3	Weather vanes don't move; smoke drifts
2	Light breeze	4–7	Weather vanes move; wind felt on face; leaves rustle
3	Gentle breeze	8–12	Leaves and small twigs rustle; flags extend
4	Moderate breeze	13–18	Small branches sway; dust and paper blow about
5	Fresh breeze	19–24	Small trees sway; waves break on inland waters
6	Strong breeze	25–31	Large branches sway; hard to use umbrellas
7	Moderate gale	32–38	Whole trees sway; hard to walk against wind
8	Fresh gale	39–46	Twigs break off trees; walking against wind even harder
9	Strong gale	47–54	Slight damage to buildings; shingles blow off roof
10	Whole gale	55–63	Trees uprooted; major damage to buildings
11	Storm	64–73	Widespread damage; very rare occurrence
12–17	Hurricane	74 and above	violent destruction

Weather Log

Meteorologist: _____

Date and Time	Wind Speed (Beaufort number)	Wind Direction	Temperature	Precipitation	My Forecast For Tomorrow	Official Weather Forecast For Tomorrow	Was My Forecast Accurate?

©1997 The Education Center, Inc. • The Mailbox® Superbook • Grade 4 • TEC453

Note To The Teacher: Use with "Wherever The Wind Takes Us" on page 257.

How Does Sound Travel?

Directions: Complete the following activities to find out how sound travels.

Activity 1: Sound Tube

Hypothesis: How does sound travel? _____
_____

Materials: toilet-paper tube, piece of cardboard, rubber band, plastic wrap, scissors, 4" strip of paper, tape, pencil

Procedure:
1. Trace one end of the toilet-paper tube on the cardboard.
2. Cut out the traced circle.
3. Punch a hole in the center of the circle with the pencil.
4. Tape the circle securely to one end of the tube.
5. Cover the other end of the tube with the plastic wrap. Secure the wrap with the rubber band.
6. Fold the paper strip in half. Tape one end to the top of your desk, leaving the other end sticking up as shown.
7. Line up the hole in the cardboard so that it is directly above the paper strip. Tap the plastic end of the tube sharply.

Results And Conclusions: _____
_____
_____

Activity 2: Losing Your Marbles

Hypothesis: How does sound travel?
_____
_____
_____

Materials: 5 same-size marbles, ruler

Procedure:
1. Place four marbles in a straight line on your desk.

2. From about four inches (10 cm), flick the fifth marble directly into the line of marbles.

Results And Conclusions:
_____
_____
_____
_____

Activity 3: Making Waves

Hypothesis: What pattern does sound travel in? _____
_____
_____

Materials: 1 jump rope

Procedure:
1. Have a partner firmly hold one end of the jump rope while you do the same with the other end.

2. Stand close enough so that the rope touches the ground.

3. Shake your end of the rope while your partner holds the other end still.

Results And Conclusions:
_____
_____
_____

Note To The Teacher: Use with "How Does Sound Travel?" on page 258.

Reduce, Reuse, And Recycle!
Plastic Reuse Contest

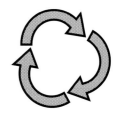

Contestant Name: _____

Entry Title: _____

Entry Description: _____

_____

_____

_____

_____

Name_____ *Recycling experiment*

Breaking It Down

Find out more about biodegradable items with this experiment.

Materials: 4 baby-food jars (or other jars with lids); 4 types of garbage: a piece of nonglossy paper, a piece of aluminum foil, a piece of plastic wrap, a piece of bread; water

Procedure:
1. Fill each jar half-full with water.
2. Place one piece of garbage in each jar. Close the jar tightly.
3. Shake each jar vigorously. Record the results on the chart below.

Results: _____

Item	Results
Nonglossy Paper	
Aluminum Foil	
Plastic Wrap	
Bread	

Conclusions: _____

_____

Note To The Teacher: Use the top portion of this page with "Plastic Reuse Contest" on page 259. Use the bottom portion with "To Be Biodegradable Or Not To Be?" on page 259.

The Food Guide Pyramid

The U.S. Department of Agriculture (USDA) and the Department of Health and Human Services (DHHS) have developed a set of guidelines for people to follow to help promote good health. These guidelines are outlined in the Food Guide Pyramid.

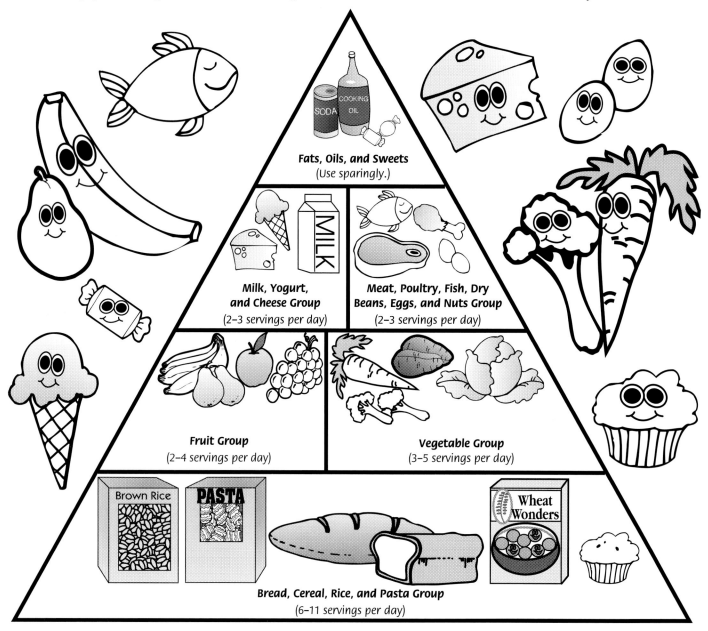

Fats, Oils, and Sweets
(Use sparingly.)

Milk, Yogurt, and Cheese Group
(2–3 servings per day)

Meat, Poultry, Fish, Dry Beans, Eggs, and Nuts Group
(2–3 servings per day)

Fruit Group
(2–4 servings per day)

Vegetable Group
(3–5 servings per day)

Bread, Cereal, Rice, and Pasta Group
(6–11 servings per day)

Dietary Guidelines For Improved Nutrition
- Eat a balanced diet.
- Limit your consumption of cholesterol and saturated fats.
- Limit your consumption of sugar and sodium.
- Avoid alcohol.
- Avoid overeating.
- Include fiber in your diet.
- Cook and store foods properly.
- Be aware of common food myths and misinformation.

Note To The Teacher: Use with "Food Guide Pyramid Bingo" and "Food-Label Investigations" on page 260.

Lookin' At Labels

Directions: Use the information on each food label to answer the questions below.

Unsweetened Pineapple

Nutrition Facts

Serving Size 1/2 cup

Servings Per Container 4

Amount Per Serving

Calories 70   Calories from Fat 0

	% Daily Value*
Total Fat 0g	0%
Saturated Fat 0g	0%
Cholesterol 0mg	0%
Sodium (salt) 10mg	0%
Total Carbohydrate 17g	6%
Dietary Fiber 1g	4%
Sugars 15g	
Protein 0g	
Vitamin A	0%
Vitamin C	20 %
Calcium	0%
Iron	2%

*Based on a 2,000 calorie diet

Snack Mix

Nutrition Facts

Serving Size 1/2 cup

Servings Per Container 9

Amount Per Serving

Calories 180 Calories from Fat 90

	% Daily Value*
Total Fat 10g	15%
Saturated Fat 1.5g	8%
Cholesterol 0mg	0%
Sodium (salt) 380mg	16%
Total Carbohydrate 18g	6%
Dietary Fiber 1g	4%
Sugars 1g	
Protein 0g	
Vitamin A	0%
Vitamin C	0%
Calcium	0%
Iron	6%

*Based on a 2,000 calorie diet

1. Which food is higher in Vitamin C? _____

2. Which food is higher in iron? _____

3. Which food is higher in sodium (salt)? _____

4. Which food is higher in total fat? _____

5. Which food is higher in total sugars? _____

6. Do you think the sugar in the pineapple is natural or processed? _____

   Why? _____

7. Which food is more healthful? _____

   Why? _____

Bonus Box: Use the information on serving size and servings per container to figure out how many cups are in each container of food. Show your work and answers on the back of this page.

Note To The Teacher: Use with "Food-Label Investigations" on page 260.

Don't Miss A Beat!

Help Dr. Cora Nary figure out the heart rates per minute of her patients using the information provided. Show your work on the back of this page. The first one has been done for you.

1. Mrs. Ventricle's pulse is 40 beats in 30 seconds. What is her heart rate per minute?

    60 ÷ 30 seconds = 2

    2 x 40 = 80 beats per minute

2. Sara Cardiac's pulse is 25 beats in 15 seconds. What is her heart rate per minute?

3. Mr. Heart's pulse is 15 beats in 10 seconds. What is his heart rate per minute?

4. Mr. Atrium's pulse is 11 beats in 6 seconds. What is his heart rate per minute?

5. Ms. Mitral's pulse is 17 beats in 20 seconds. What is her heart rate per minute?

6. Mrs. Valve's pulse is 49 beats in 30 seconds. What is her heart rate per minute?

7. Arthur Artery's pulse is 13 beats in 12 seconds. What is his heart rate per minute?

8. Victoria Vein's pulse is 37 beats in 30 seconds. What is her heart rate per minute?

9. Vince Vessel's pulse is 28 beats in 15 seconds. What is his heart rate per minute?

10. Mr. Oxygen's pulse is 52 beats in 20 seconds. What is his heart rate per minute?

Bonus Box: Because his/her heart rate per minute is so low, who do you think must have been asleep during Dr. Cora Nary's examination? _____ Because his/her heart rate per minute is so high, who do you think had to run the hardest to the appointment? _____

TECHNOLOGY

TECHNOLOGY

LESSON-PLAN TEMPLATES

Take advantage of today's technology for hassle-free lesson planning! To plan a week in advance, create a lesson-plan template on your computer for each day of the week. Include general headings on each day's template, such as a daily classroom schedule, time with specialists (art, music, etc.), student resource times (speech, reading lab, etc.), and special events or programs. Save the templates on the hard drive or on a disk. Then, when planning for the week ahead, just open up the file and add your information. Be sure to save each lesson plan as a separate file so that your template is ready to use the next week. Having the templates already in place cuts your lesson-writing time in

DAILY SCHEDULE MONDAY

8:30–9:10	Homeroom/Morning Work
9:10–10:10	Lanuage Arts
9:40–10:10	Reading Lab (Kenny, Margaret, Jason)
10:10–10:20	Bathroom Break
10:20–11:20	Math
11:20–12:15	Lunch, Bathroom Break
12:15–12:55	Art
12:55–1:40	Social Studies
1:40–2:10	P.E.
2:10–2:45	Computer/Silent Reading/Journal Writing
2:45–3:00	Prepare To Go Home
Today's Special Events:	

SCHEDULING MADE SIMPLE

One of the most difficult aspects of managing a classroom computer is finding time for everyone to use it. Hold a short journal-writing session first thing in the morning and a silent-reading period right after lunch. Then schedule two students during each of these periods to work at the computer (see the sample schedule below). Have students first work on basic computer operating techniques, then progress to more difficult programs and tasks. For example, a simple desktop publishing activity is great for acquainting students with the computer early in the year. Have each student choose a favorite piece of work from his writing portfolio. Direct him to type, edit, and revise his piece. If desired, have him experiment with adding clip art and graphics to his page. Afterward print each student's page. Bind the pages in a class portfolio titled "Author Picks."

	M	T	W	T	F
Journal Writing	Mary Bob	Katie Ian	Joel Erin	Robert Terry	Chris Allen
Journal Writing	Jane Joe	Judy Mike	Jeff Amy	Leslie Jim	Alexis Joshua

Seating Chart Rx

How many times have you designed a classroom seating chart only to have to redesign it? Help alleviate this headache by using the timesaving features of a drawing software program! First use the program to draw a box to represent a student's desk. Copy and paste a box for each desk in your classroom. Next arrange the boxes and type a student's name in each one. Then print the chart and post it for student, substitute, and visitor reference. Be sure to save the chart on the hard drive or on a disk. Then, anytime you need to change the arrangement, simply copy each student's name and paste it in a different box or drag each box to a new area.

Super Student Secretaries

As you teach your class how to use the computer and various computer programs, get some valuable help by assigning a student to be your secretary. Direct the secretary to take notes on the instructions you present to the class. After the lesson, check his notes, editing what's written and adding any missing information. Next have the secretary use the computer to type the notes and decorate the page with clip art and other graphics. Print the page, laminate it, and display it by the computer. Each time you introduce a new program, designate a new secretary to help you. Students will benefit from the written instructions and love being your helpers.

OUR COMPUTER RULES:

1. No food or drinks allowed near the computer.

2. Be gentle with equipment.

3. Only two students allowed at the computer, unless otherwise directed.

Cups On Computers

Cut down on interruptions during technology instruction with this simple solution! Place a brightly colored plastic cup beside each computer in your classroom or school computer lab. If a student needs help, have her signal you by placing the cup on top of her computer, then continue working. When there is a logical break in instruction, answer the student's question. Both you and your students will appreciate this hassle-free signal for help!

ASK THREE BEFORE ME

Throughout your technology instruction, your students are sure to have questions and need guidance. So before beginning, share a special rule—"Ask three before me." Explain that if a student has a question while using the computer, he must ask three of his classmates for help before turning to you. You may wish to assign three different children to be computer tutors each week, or just let your students determine who can help them. (Kids usually know which classmates are the computer experts!) When a student asks you a technology-related question, be sure to ask, "Did you ask three before me?" With this easy tip, you'll see fewer computer-related interruptions and more student cooperation.

Color-Coded Keyboards

Practicing keyboarding skills has never been easier with this hands-on idea! Obtain a copy of a computer keyboard. Make a transparency of the keyboard; also duplicate a copy on white construction paper for each student. Use wipe-off markers to color the home-row keys and outline the remaining keys on the transparency as shown. Review with the class how to correctly place hands and fingers on the keyboard; then have each student use the markers and transparency example to color her own keyboard. Instruct the student to cut out her keyboard; then laminate each keyboard for durability. Mount each student's keyboard on top of her desk with masking tape. Then, when students have free time, they can practice keyboarding without leaving their seats!

CD-ROM Scavenger Hunt

Overwhelmed by the wealth of information available on the Internet? Here's an easy way to ease students (and yourself!) into what may be an intimidating task. Before accessing the Net, give students practice searching for information using an electronic encyclopedia. Enlist the aid of your school's media specialist in obtaining a CD-ROM-based encyclopedia. Provide students with an overview of how to use the software; then prepare a schedule for its use. Divide students into pairs and give each pair a copy of page 283. Instruct each pair to complete the activity as directed on the reproducible. Afterward discuss students' findings as a class; then get ready to connect students to the Net using the idea to the right, "Surf The Net With Bookmarks."

I'm a gold mine of information!

Universal Encyclopedia

SURF THE NET WITH BOOK-MARKS

The Internet is a great tool for finding current information on just about any topic. Point students in the right direction—and prevent them from accessing inappropriate Internet information—by creating *bookmarks,* or place markers, for specific web sites. To set a bookmark, simply go to the site you want your students to access and choose "Add Bookmark" from the Bookmark pull-down menu. Mark the sites desired, and they will be added to the list in the order that you enter them. Next pair students. Give each pair a copy of page 284 and prepare a schedule for using the computer. Have students follow the directions on the sheet for completing the activity.

After pairs have completed the activity, discuss their findings as a class. By taking a little time to bookmark certain sites, you'll promote use of the Internet while making students' surfing much more educational.

CLASS NEWSLETTER

Give parents the inside scoop on classroom happenings with a student-made, computer-generated newsletter. Each report-card period, have students brainstorm a list of lessons, activities, and special programs in which they participated. Then pair students and have each pair draw a number. Direct the pair who drew number 1 to select a topic from the list. Then have the pair with number 2 select a topic, and so on. Instruct each pair to write the first draft of its article on paper, edit and revise the article, and then enter the final copy on a designated computer. Direct pairs to include catchy headlines and graphics. After all articles are entered into a file on the designated computer, select a team of students to create a layout and banner for the newsletter. If desired, add a special "Looking Ahead" section to let parents know about upcoming lessons and events. Print the newsletter; then make a copy to send home with each student.

ENGROSSING GRAPHICS

What student doesn't love jazzing up his writing assignments using the fonts and formats of desktop publishing programs? But sometimes students get so engrossed in creating graphics that they neglect their writing. Prevent this from happening by having students write, edit, revise, and show their work to you *before* adding any clip art or graphics. Students will get a kick out of personalizing their work, and you'll rest easy knowing they spent high-quality time on their writing.

Super Stacks

Get students involved in creating a multimedia presentation using a *hypertext authoring program*, such as HyperCard®, HyperStudio™, or SuperCard®. These programs show information in the form of *stacks*. Stacks are collections of cards that are linked together; readers click on buttons to travel from one card to another. Select a hypertext authoring program to use in your classroom. Carefully read the directions and create several practice stacks yourself. Then demonstrate the key processes to students: creating cards, adding text and simple graphics, making buttons, and creating links.

Next divide students into pairs and assign each pair a project. Have each pair use index cards to write a rough draft in the order the pair will use when creating the hypertext cards. Prepare a schedule; then have each pair create its presentation. Tell each student pair that then it can add new information, rearrange sections of text, and add graphics and sound clips to the cards. Finally have each pair share its presentation with the class. Or assign small groups to choose stacks to view.

LET THE SHOWS BEGIN!

Lights, camera, action! Transform students into future Steven Spielbergs with the help of a video camera and videocassette recorder. First choose the type of presentation that your students will make (see the examples shown below). Divide students into groups; then assign each group a specific topic on which to base its video. Next outline for students the steps involved in creating a video—conceptualization, storyboards, scripts, rehearsals, sound, and editing. Also introduce students to the camera's zooming, panning, and fading capabilities. Schedule a time for each group to practice using the camera. (This will also give students a chance to be silly and make mistakes before actually shooting their videos.) Finally have each group film its video. Then serve up some popcorn, turn out the lights, and let the shows begin!

TYPES OF PRESENTATIONS:

- classroom news reports
- classroom rules and procedures
- historical reenactments
- special projects
- book reports
- biographical interviews
- subject-related lessons
- presenting stories or skits for other classes

Math Word Problems Via E-Mail

Using *E-mail* (electronic mail) is a great way to get students excited about almost any assignment—even the often-dreaded math word problems! Pair students and assign each pair a different problem-solving strategy, such as making an organized list, guess-and-check, and finding a pattern. Next direct the pair to create and edit a word problem off-line (without an Internet connection), using any word-processing program. Instruct the pair to save its problem as *text*, so the problem can be read regardless of the type of computer being used. Afterward compile the files and E-mail them to another class to solve.

You Have Mail

Great Graphing!

Enhance any graphing assignment by having students record their results using a drawing software program. First have students brainstorm survey topics such as favorite songs, best brands of sneakers, and weirdest movies. Record their responses on the chalkboard. Then divide students into groups of three or four, and have each group choose a topic. Instruct the group to survey their classmates and record the information collected on a sheet of paper. Then have each group use the drawing program to create a bar graph, pie graph, or pictograph detailing the data collected. Have each group print its graph and share its data with the class.

Favorite Snacks

CD-ROM Scavenger Hunt

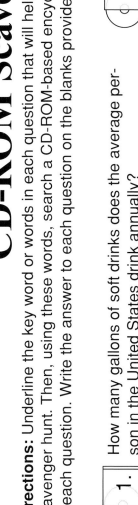

CDs aren't just about cool tunes! A **CD-ROM encyclopedia** gives you access to all kinds of neat information!

Directions: Underline the key word or words in each question that will help you start your CD-ROM scavenger hunt. Then, using these words, search a CD-ROM-based encyclopedia to find the answer to each question. Write the answer to each question on the blanks provided.

1. How many gallons of soft drinks does the average person in the United States drink annually? _____

2. On what continent is the country of Zimbabwe located? _____

3. Name three things that insects eat. _____

4. Does a tree ever stop growing? _____

5. When and where were ice-cream cones first served? _____

6. What kind of animal is a *narwhal?* What special feature does the male of this species have? _____

7. What university did Thomas Jefferson found? _____

8. When did the cartoon character Mickey Mouse first appear? _____

9. How deep is the Grand Canyon? _____

10. Why do people perspire? _____

11. How many pounds does the average adult boar weigh? _____

12. In what country did the Olympic Games begin? _____

13. From what kind of metal are license plates made? _____

14. Where is money made in the United States? _____

15. Why did the ancient Egyptians *mummify,* or preserve, a person's body after he died? _____

16. What is the wind speed at the center of a tornado? _____

©1997 The Education Center, Inc. • *The Mailbox*® *Superbook* • *Grade 4* • TEC453 • Key p. 319

Note To The Teacher: Use with "CD-ROM Scavenger Hunt" on page 280. Provide each student with a copy of this sheet and access to a multimedia encyclopedia. If desired, have the student cut and paste the answer to each question on your computer's notepad, then print the answers to turn in to you.

Name(s) _____

Surf The Net!

Hey, dude, welcome to the Internet—home of the *WWW,* or the World Wide Web! The web is the place where oceans of information are made available to you. To help you as you surf your way through the Net, follow the directions beside each number below. Then answer each question on the blanks. Happy surfin', dude!

1. A *browser* is a computer program used to search the Internet. What's the name of the browser you are using? _____

2. How do you open the browser? _____
   _____

3. After opening the browser, describe two buttons you see on the bar at the top of the screen.
   _____

4. Click on one of the buttons. Describe what happens. _____
   _____

5. Next choose a web site listed in the Bookmark menu. Click on the site. List three *links* (pictures or words that lead to other sites) you see on the screen. _____
   _____

6. Select one of the links by clicking on the picture or word. As your browser is searching for that site, what do you see happening on the screen? _____
   _____

7. Look at the buttons at the top of the screen. Which button do you click to return to the previous page? Which button moves you forward a page? _____
   _____

8. Click on the search button. In the dialog box, type in the name of an animal you'd like to learn more about. Press *search* and describe what you see. _____
   _____

9. How do you quit the browser? _____
   _____

Note To The Teacher: Use with "Surf The Net With Bookmarks" on page 280. The answers to the questions will vary depending on the browser you are using in your classroom.

Name(s) _____

"Computerrific!"

Complete the activity listed on each computer below. After you finish each activity, print it and store your work in a folder. Then color the computer screen to show that you are finished with that activity.

Signature: _____

Date Due: _____

Use a word-processing program to type a descriptive paragraph from a favorite book.

Type the paragraph using single space. Next cut and paste the paragraph; then change it to double space.

Use a draw/paint program to create a sign advertising an imaginary event at your school, such as a carnival, dance, or ball game.

Use a desktop publishing program to type the names of all the students in your class. Type the names of the girls, then the boys. Next put the list into two columns—one for girls and one for boys.

Use a draw/paint program to design a sheet of personalized stationery. Use a special font, style, border, or graphic on your stationery. Then write a friendly letter to a classmate using your stationery.

Use eight of this week's spelling words in a different sentence. Then highlight the spelling words, using different styles of text, such as **bold**, *italic*, underline, outline, and shadow.

Use a draw/paint program to create a special invitation for a birthday party. Include your name and the date, time, and location of the party. Add three different graphics to your invitation.

Type your name using five different fonts and letter sizes.

Use a draw/paint program to design a decorated nametag for your desk. Use a special font, style, border, or graphic on your tag.

Note To The Teacher: Ask your school's media specialist or computer specialist for help in obtaining a basic word-processing, desktop publishing, and draw/paint program. If you do not have access to a printer, have each student save the activities on a floppy disk.

Three Cheers To

_____!
(student name)

For your "computerrific" efforts at the computer!

_____   _____
(teacher signature   (date)

Name: _____

Date: _____

Punch a hole after each activity you complete; then turn in your card for a special treat!

1. _____ ○
2. _____ ○
3. _____ ○
4. _____ ○
5. _____ ○
6. _____ ○

Note To The Teacher: After completing the desired number of activities in this unit, duplicate a copy of the award at the top on construction paper for each student. Program the punch card at the bottom with six computer activities that you want students to complete. Then duplicate a copy for each student. As the student completes an activity, have him punch a hole in the circle next to the activity. Reward each student who has a completely punched card with a special treat.

HOLIDAY & SEASONAL

Halloween Hangman

Want to scare up a fun way to practice spelling during the bewitching month of October? A game of Halloween Hangman will do the trick! Duplicate page 295 for each pair of students. Provide students with the materials listed at the top of the page; then let them prepare and play the game as instructed in the directions. Use this fun game to practice vocabulary terms by requiring that a student who correctly guesses a word also give the term's definition.

Ghostly Giggles

Make it a ho-ho-Halloween with this reading motivation/art activity! Ask your media specialist to gather a collection of Halloween (or scary) riddle books. Place these books in your classroom library. After students have had a chance to read the books, have each child bend, pull, and shape a clothes hanger into a ghost form as shown. Help each student cover his hanger with plastic wrap. Then spray-paint each ghost with white paint. When the ghosts are dry, have students add large wiggle eyes to them.

Next have each child copy his favorite riddle on an index card and its answer on another card. Then direct the student to glue his riddle card to the front of his ghost. Hang each ghost from a pushpin on a bulletin board. Behind his ghost, have the student staple his answer card. Encourage students to read each other's riddles, checking the answers by lifting the ghosts. Is that a ghostly giggle or a haunted "ho-ho-ho" I hear?

The Scary-Go-Round

What is the mummy's favorite ride at the fair?

This Turkey Needs Dressing!

Encourage responsibility and teamwork with this gobblin' great challenge! Post a simple turkey body on a bulletin board as shown. Cut out ten large feather shapes for each of your student groups, assigning a specific color to each group. Place each group's feathers in a separate file folder. Starting early in November, challenge each group to earn feathers for "dressing" the turkey. Post a list of ways groups can earn a feather, such as turning in all assignments for the day or working cooperatively during a group activity. When a group earns a feather, let one of its members staple the feather to the turkey. On the day before Thanksgiving, award small prizes to the team with the most feathers on the board.

"Tree-riffic" Display

Create a holiday display that's nothing short of "tree-riffic"! Give each student a 4 1/2" x 6" piece of green construction paper. Have him tear brightly colored pieces of gift wrap or tissue paper; then have him glue the pieces onto the paper to make a holiday ornament. Arrange these projects in a tree shape as shown on your classroom door, a wall space, or a bulletin board.

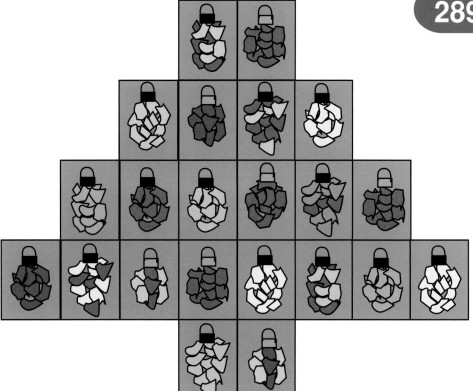

Gift-Box Centers

Give students the gift of learning with easy-to-make boxed centers. Number 10 to 15 holiday gift tags; then label each with a math problem. Tape the tags on a lidded holiday gift box. Mount an answer key on the inside of the box's lid. Place several of these boxes at your math center. During free time, have a student take a box to his desk and solve the problems on his paper. Direct the student to check his work by lifting the lid from the box and using the key. After he has checked his work, have the student correct any problems he missed, then turn in his paper by placing it in the box. Check the boxes at the end of the day to remove any completed work. Make other boxes labeled with review questions, words to alphabetize, writing topics, or any other skill of your choice.

1. 58 x 12

10. 72 x 46

Deck The Halls With Descriptive Words

Shine the holiday spotlight on descriptive writing and adjectives with this fun activity. On a large index card, have each student draw or glue a picture of a special gift she is either giving or wants to receive. On the back of the card, have her list ten carefully chosen adjectives describing the gift. Place all of the cards in a holiday gift bag. When you have a few extra minutes, draw a card from the bag and read the adjectives. Challenge students (other than the child who listed the adjectives) to try to guess the identity of the gift based on the adjectives. Help students conclude that the more specific the adjectives, the easier the identification.

1. sleek
2. fast
3. speedy
4. two-wheeled
5. expensive
6. quick
7. purple
8. flashy
9. silver
10. lightweight

Hanukkah Word Challenge

Celebrate the holiday of Hanukkah with this fun word challenge. Give each student a file folder. Then have him follow the directions below to create a holiday puzzle folder. Place the finished folders at a center for lots of free-time fun.

Festival Of Lights

1. What is fifty percent?
2. What do you call a large meal?
3. What does a bride wear?
4. What is a synonym for strike?
5. What is the opposite of love?
6. What do you hope your clothes do?
7. What animal besides a dog can bark?
8. What is an animal doctor?
9. What is a synonym for work?
10. What do you cook on?

Key
1. half
2. feast
3. veil
4. hit
5. hate
6. fit
7. seal
8. vet
9. toil
10. stove

STEPS:

1. Write "Festival Of Lights" at the top of a sheet of paper.
2. List at least ten words made from the letters in "Festival Of Lights."
3. Write a question beside each of your words. For example, if you list *half,* your question might be "What is fifty percent?"
4. Use markers, crayons, or colored pencils to decorate the front of your folder.
5. Open the folder and write "Festival Of Lights" on the left side. List ten of your questions on the right side. Be sure to number the questions.
6. Write an answer key to your questions on the back of the folder.

Kwanzaa Banners

Reinforce the basic principles of Kwanzaa with this group project. First discuss the holiday with students, using books gathered by your media specialist. Review with students the *Nguzo Saba*—the seven principles on which the holiday is based—as outlined on page 303. Then divide your students into groups. Have each group work together to collaboratively write a short paragraph for each principle. In each paragraph have students explain what they think the principle means and how they can apply it in their lives.

Once the paragraphs have been edited, give each group a copy of page 303 duplicated on sturdy paper and the supplies listed on that page. Then have each group follow the steps on page 303 to create an eye-catching banner.

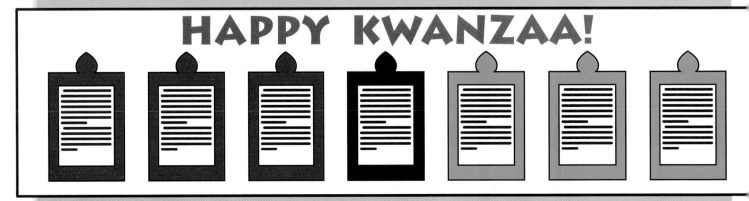

New Year Calendars

Ring in the new year with a gift-giving project! Ask your school's media specialist to gather resources that list the special days of the year (such as holidays, births/deaths of famous people, anniversaries of historical events, etc.). Introduce the books to students; then divide your class into groups. Have each group choose one staff member they would like to honor; then give each group one of the reference books, along with the materials and instructions below. For fun let students wear party hats and use noisemakers to make the presentation of the calendars to their honorees especially memorable.

Materials for each group:
12 sheets of 12" x 18" construction paper
12 copies of a blank calendar grid
12 sheets of white duplicating paper
copy of a calendar for the new year (duplicate the small one in your checkbook)

markers, crayons, or colored pencils
glue
hole puncher
two large brads

Steps:

1. Use the copy of the calendar to help you fill out the 12 blank grids for the new year.
2. Use the reference books to list one special event or holiday for each month.
3. Research each event if necessary; then illustrate it on a piece of white paper. Be sure to mark that special event on the appropriate calendar page.
4. Glue each illustration at the top of a large sheet of construction paper as shown. Glue the matching calendar grid below it.
5. Stack the calendar sheets in order. Punch two holes at the top and bind the pages together with brads.
6. Present your calendar to your group's honoree.

Keeping The Dream Alive

Join hands for peace with a student-made display that keeps the dream of Dr. Martin Luther King, Jr., alive. Have each student trace his hands on red, white, and blue paper. After each student has cut out his three tracings, mount them on a bulletin board as shown. Surround the message with star cutouts that students have labeled with ways they can promote peace in their homes, schools, and neighborhoods.

Valentine Verses

Tip your hat to Cupid and the season of love with a poetry activity that's truly a treat! For each student, fill a small Ziploc® bag with ten candy conversation hearts. Challenge each student to use the words and phrases on her hearts in a Valentine's Day poem. When students have finished their poems, have each child copy her verse on a heart shape cut from red or pink construction paper. While you staple these heartfelt verses on a bulletin board, let your enthusiastic poets eat their candy inspirations.

Will you be mine?
I think you're fine!
My heart beats for you.
Don't make me blue!

Black History Updates

Celebrate Black History Month this February with a research activity that results in a great display. Assign one of the famous African-Americans listed below to each child. Have the student research his person and prepare a short talk on his or her life and accomplishments. Also have the student prepare some type of visual—such as a poster, cutout, or timeline—to accompany his talk. Beginning in February set aside time early each day for two students to give a "morning update" on their famous African-Americans. After the morning's updates, mount those students' visuals on a bulletin board or wall space. As your display grows, so will students' knowledge and appreciation of our country's rich African-American heritage.

Famous African-Americans

Ronald McNair	Charles Richard Drew	Booker T. Washington
Rosa Lee Parks	Louis Armstrong	Benjamin Banneker
Jesse Owens	Sidney Poitier	Daniel Hale Williams
Marian Anderson	Matthew Henson	Charlie Parker
Langston Hughes	Fannie Lou Hamer	Oprah Winfrey
Phillis Wheatley	Jackie Robinson	Thurgood Marshall
Shirley Chisholm	Leontyne Price	Arthur Ashe
Mary McLeod Bethune	Gwendolyn Brooks	W. E. B. Du Bois
Ernest Everett Just	Ralph Bunche	Garrett Morgan

Are You Rich?

Leprechauns are usually associated with pots of gold, but does that make them rich? As a critical-thinking St. Patrick's Day activity, ask students what criteria they would use to classify a person as rich. Point out that many people consider themselves rich if they possess such nonmaterial things as good health or peace of mind. List some of your students' suggestions on the board. Then have each child list ten items she thinks would make her rich. After the list is finished, have the student go back over it and rank the items in order of importance. Finally have each child copy her list on a large circle cut from yellow construction paper. Post the circles on a bulletin board decorated with a leprechaun and a black pot.

Katie
1. the love of my family
2. the good health of everyone I love
3. the ability to walk
4. the ability to see
5. a good home to live in
6. a bedroom of my own
7. my dog, Dodger
8. my best friend, Samantha
9. my new bicycle
10. my trip to summer camp each year

Jelly-Bean Graphs

Boost graphing skills this Easter season with the help of a bag of jelly beans. Divide students into small groups. Give each group a small brown lunch bag filled with several handfuls of colorful jelly beans. Be sure groups do NOT open their bags. List the different jelly-bean colors on the chalkboard; then have each group predict how many of each color is in its bag, listing its predictions on a piece of paper. Next give each group a set of markers and a set of colored pencils. Have the group use the markers to make a bar graph to illustrate its predictions.

Next have each group open its bag and sort the jelly beans by color. Direct the group to show the actual numbers of jelly-bean colors in its bag by drawing a second set of bars on the graph with the colored pencils. Post the resulting double-bar graphs in your classroom so students can compare their data.

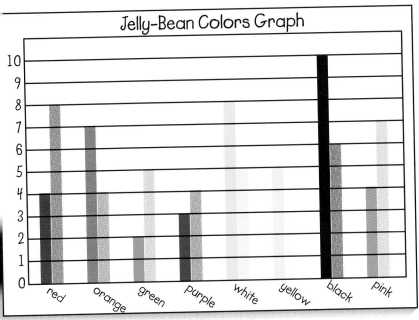

Jelly-Bean Colors Graph

Use It Again!

To celebrate Earth Day, how about challenging students to do a little mental recycling? List the following items on the board:

♻ an outdated world map

♻ an old telephone book

♻ a leaky umbrella

♻ an empty milk jug

♻ a dried-up ballpoint pen

♻ an old record album

♻ one snow ski

♻ an empty cereal box

♻ an outdated dictionary

♻ a plastic six-pack holder

Challenge each student to list one or two new uses for each of the items. Provide time for students to share their responses.

Year-End Book Reviews

Looking for a way to end your reading program with a bang? Several weeks before the last week of school, brainstorm with students a list of all the books the class has read during the year (including any read-alouds you shared with students). Divide the class into several groups; then assign each group several of the book titles from the list. Provide copies of the books so groups can spend time reviewing them together. Next have each group write a brief review of each of its assigned books, including a summary of the plot and the group's opinion of the novel. After all reviews have been written and edited, bind them between two decorated covers. Title the volume "Our Favorite Books Of The Year." Add this student-made book to your classroom library. Not only will this project remind students of how much they accomplished over the past year, but it will also be a great book to share with your new class next year.

Leftover Lifesaver

Put restless students and leftover supplies to work for you! Mount white background paper on a bulletin board. Place half-used markers, pens, stickers, and other leftover materials in a box. When students finish their work, let them use the supplies to decorate the board. You'll finish the year with a creative bulletin board and fewer leftovers to pack away.

It Was A Banner Year!

Celebrate the end of a banner school year with this fun art project. Begin by having students brainstorm a list of favorite memories of the past year. On a piece of newsprint, have each child sketch a design for a banner that commemorates some of those memories. Once the designs are complete, give each student a 12" x 16" felt or paper rectangle (felt makes a more durable banner that will become a real keepsake). Provide students with glue, scissors, rulers, felt and fabric scraps, glitter, paint pens, and other art supplies to use for decorating their banners. Be sure each child leaves the top two inches of her banner undecorated. Help the student fold the top two inches of her banner over a coat hanger as shown; then use a hot glue gun to glue down the edge. It's an unforgettable keepsake for an unforgettable year!

HALLOWEEN HANGMAN

A Game For Two Players

Materials for each pair of students: crayons or markers, scissors, sheet of paper, pencil, spelling list

Directions:
1. Color the scarecrow parts below. Then cut them out and spread them out on the playing surface.
2. Decide who will be Player 1 and who will be Player 2.
3. Player 1 secretly chooses a spelling word from the list. Then he or she draws blanks on the paper—one for each letter in the word.
4. Player 2 guesses a letter in the secret word. If the guess is correct, Player 1 writes that letter in the correct blank or blanks. Player 2 can either try to guess the word or can guess another letter.
5. If Player 2 incorrectly guesses the word or guesses a letter that isn't in the word, Player 1 chooses a scarecrow part.
6. If Player 2 correctly guesses the word before Player 1 completely builds the scarecrow, Player 2 gets to choose the next secret word. If Player 1 completely builds the scarecrow before Player 2 guesses the word, Player 1 chooses the next secret word.

Note To The Teacher: Use with "Halloween Hangman" on page 288. Provide each pair of students with the materials listed above.

Peter And His Pumpkins

Peter, the great pumpkin eater, has gone overboard growing pumpkins this year. First he planted extra seeds in his patch. Then he treated them with a super-duper fertilizer. So now Peter has more pumpkins than ever before. And they're LARGER than any he has ever seen!

Now that it's Halloween, Peter is hoping to get rid of his pumpkins. Can you give him some suggestions? Just answer the following questions. Use the back of this page if you need more room. Make sure your answers are in complete sentences.

1. How should Peter advertise his pumpkins for use as jack-o'-lanterns? _____
_____

   How should he price these pumpkins?_____
_____

2. Peter's next idea? Using hollowed-out pumpkins as flowerpots! What problems might result from this idea? _____
_____

3. Next Peter decides that there must be a new food that can be made with pumpkins. What could it be? What other ingredients would this new food include?_____
_____

4. Not only does Peter have a lot of pumpkins, but he also has huge leaves and long vines. What possible use could they have? _____
_____

5. Peter decides that he won't grow pumpkins next year. What other crop could he plant next fall that would earn money? What uses could this crop have?_____
_____

Bonus Box: On another sheet of paper, design a billboard for Peter's roadside pumpkin stand.

Simple as Pie?

Chef Boyarturkey is marketing his own new brand of frozen pumpkin pie this Thanksgiving. A pie box is shown below. For some reason, the pies aren't selling. Can you guess why?

Study the box carefully. Find all of the mistakes the chef made. List them in the blanks below the box. Hint: You should find 13 mistakes.

Chef Boyarturkey's
Pumkin Pie
Frozen for you're convenience
Store at room temperature
Yummy!
Nothing tastes better then are pie!

Net Weight 1 lb. (15 oz.)

Ingredients: enriched flower, shortening, spices, milk, eggs, and preservatives

Use by Nov. 31, 1998

Baking instructions:
Preheat oven to 400°C.
Bake for 45 minutes.

Microwave instructions:
Place on metal sheet.
Heat on high for 55 minutes.

Container Made With Recycled Pumpkin

_____   _____

_____   _____

_____   _____

_____   _____

_____   _____

_____

Bonus Box: Some of the mistakes on the box are wrong homonyms. On the back of this sheet, list six sets of homonyms of three words each (such as *to, too,* and *two*). Here are three suggestions to help you get started: *he'll, rein,* and *rite.*

Turkey Trail

Play this game with a friend to see who can catch Thanksgiving dinner first!

Directions:

1. Place game markers on START.
2. Decide who will start.
3. Player 1 rolls a die and moves that many spaces.
4. Player 1 follows the directions on the space where he lands. Player 2 checks Player 1's answer using the key.

5. If correct, Player 1 remains on that space.
6. If incorrect, Player 1 returns to his or her last space.
7. Player 2 then takes a turn.
8. The first player to reach the turkey wins!

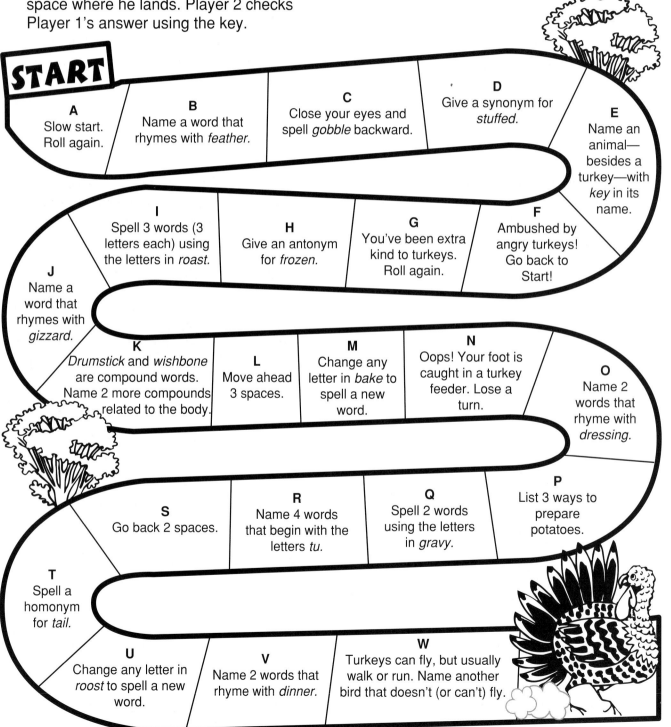

START

A Slow start. Roll again.

B Name a word that rhymes with *feather.*

C Close your eyes and spell *gobble* backward.

D Give a synonym for *stuffed.*

E Name an animal—besides a turkey—with *key* in its name.

F Ambushed by angry turkeys! Go back to Start!

G You've been extra kind to turkeys. Roll again.

H Give an antonym for *frozen.*

I Spell 3 words (3 letters each) using the letters in *roast.*

J Name a word that rhymes with *gizzard.*

K *Drumstick* and *wishbone* are compound words. Name 2 more compounds related to the body.

L Move ahead 3 spaces.

M Change any letter in *bake* to spell a new word.

N Oops! Your foot is caught in a turkey feeder. Lose a turn.

O Name 2 words that rhyme with *dressing.*

P List 3 ways to prepare potatoes.

Q Spell 2 words using the letters in *gravy.*

R Name 4 words that begin with the letters *tu.*

S Go back 2 spaces.

T Spell a homonym for *tail.*

U Change any letter in *roost* to spell a new word.

V Name 2 words that rhyme with *dinner.*

W Turkeys can fly, but usually walk or run. Name another bird that doesn't (or can't) fly.

Note To The Teacher: Duplicate this gameboard for each pair of students. Provide each pair with a die, a copy of the answer key on page 319, and two game markers, such as two different-colored kernels of corn.

Hanukkah Lights

Hanukkah is the Jewish holiday of the festival of **lights.** *Hanukkah* means "dedication." It begins on the eve of the 25th day of the Jewish month of Kislev. Hanukkah lasts for eight days.

About 2,000 **years** ago, the Jews were ruled by a Syrian king, Antiochus IV. He forced them to worship Greek gods. He **placed** Greek idols in their temple. Any Jewish person who refused to worship the Greek gods was killed.

An old Jewish priest, Mattathias, refused to obey the king. He **led** his five sons and many followers against the king's army. Although they were outnumbered, the Jewish people won battle after battle. In 165 B.C., they recaptured Jerusalem.

While cleaning the temple, the Jewish people looked for oil. They wanted to use the oil to light the special **holder** of eight candles **called** a menorah. Only a small jar of oil could be **found.** Surprisingly, it lasted for eight days! Hanukkah is celebrated each year in honor of this miracle and the Jewish victory.

The menorah has nine branches, with eight candles and one **higher** candle in the center. The *shamus,* or center candle, is the "servant candle." It is **used** to light a candle each of the eight nights of Hanukkah.

Directions: Three of the words on each candle below are made from the same base word as one of the bold words in the story. Write each **bold** word on its matching candle. Then cross out the word in the group that does not belong with the other four. The first one is done for you.

1. *called*
recall
~~locally~~
caller
uncalled-for

2. ____
holdup
holdout
shoulder
holding

3. ____
yearn
yearly
yearlong
yearling

4. ____
finding
newfound
foundation
fined

5. ____
displace
palace
placement
replace

6. ____
height
highness
hijack
highest

7. ____
leader
leadership
mislead
plead

8. ____
lightning
slight
relight
lighting

9. ____
useful
reuse
refuse
usefulness

Bonus Box: Circle two words in the story that have both a prefix and a suffix. Underline the base word in each one.

CRAZY ABOUT CARDS

Everyone loves to send cards to friends and family at Christmas. Greeting-card companies print cards for special people. There are cards to send to your neighbor, your uncle, your teacher—even your pet!

Listed below are some card ideas. Choose three that interest you. Then, on another sheet of paper, write a poem (six to eight lines) that's just perfect for the inside of each card. Include at least one rhyming poem.

Write the poem for a card:

1 from Santa to his elves

2 to your mail carrier

3 to one of your grand-parents

4 to your favorite cartoon character

5 to a TV personality

6 from a Christmas tree to its family

7 from a department store owner to her employees

8 from one twin sister to another

9 from a partridge to a pear tree

10 to your principal

11 to a cousin you've never met before

12 from Rudolph to Santa

13 from a puppy to his family

14 to a millionaire who just gave you a truckload of gifts

15 from a little boy or girl to a snowman

16 to your congressperson

17 to your best friend

18 from a football coach to his team

19 to someone who lives in a foreign country

20 from Santa to you

Bonus Box: Place a 9" x 12" sheet of white construction paper on your desk horizontally. Fold its left edge over to the right edge to create a greeting card. Of the three poems you wrote, choose your favorite one and copy it inside the greeting card. Then decorate the front and inside of your card.

Mileage By Mail

Aunt Lola lives in Los Angeles, California. Each year she sends gifts to friends all over the United States. First she mails the gifts going the longest distances. Then she mails the closer ones. The last gift she mails is the one that travels the shortest distance. Help Aunt Lola plan this year's mailings:

1. Find each city listed below on the map. Label each city in the first blank beside its circle.
2. Use a centimeter ruler and the map scale to find the approximate distance from Los Angeles to each city.
3. Write the distance in the second blank beside the circle.
4. Number the circles 1–12. 1 = city *farthest* from Aunt Lola; 12 = city *nearest* Aunt Lola

Cities:

Denver, Colorado
New York City, New York
Seattle, Washington
Boston, Massachusetts
Detroit, Michigan
Nashville, Tennessee
Albuquerque, New Mexico
Miami, Florida
Dallas, Texas
Kansas City, Missouri
New Orleans, Louisiana
San Francisco, California

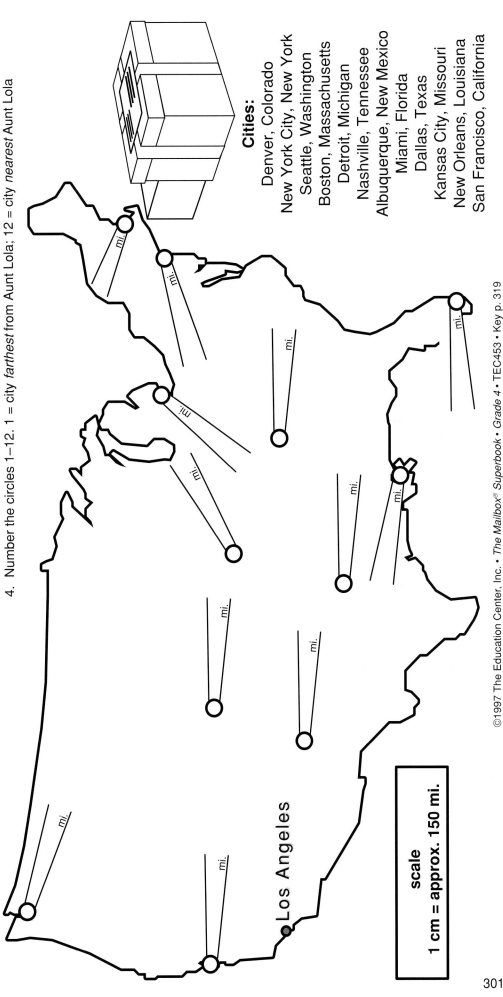

Los Angeles

**scale
1 cm = approx. 150 mi.**

Gilda's Gifts

Gilda has wrapped her gifts, but she's forgotten whom they're for! Help her by matching each gift shown to one of her friends: Merri, Holly, Carole, Nick, Rudolph, or Noel. Gilda has given you some clues, including a few you don't need! Read each clue carefully. Cross out the ones that don't help. Then write the name of each friend below his or her gift.

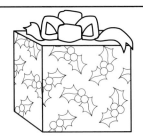

Clues:

1. No two gifts have the same wrapping paper.
2. Only the girls' gifts have words on the gift wrap.
3. Rudolph and Holly love stars.
4. No one has candy canes on his or her gift wrap.
5. Five gifts have wrapping paper that matches their gift tags.
6. Carole's gift wrap message has the most letters.
7. Nick and Noel are cousins.
8. Nick's gift wrap has either a bell or a stocking on it.

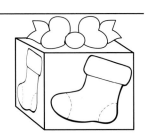

And The Stockings Were Hung...

An *attribute* is a fact that describes a person or thing. For example, a number can be *even* or *odd*. A line can be *straight* or *curved*. A friend may always wear *jeans*.
Look at the stockings in each row, column, and diagonal in the box below. See if you can name an attribute for each group of three stockings.
Letters name the rows, columns, and diagonals. You should list eight different attributes. The first one—ABC—is done for you.

ABC   names begin with *M* and end with *a*

DEF   _____

GHI   _____

ADG   _____

BEH   _____

CFI   _____

AEI   _____

GEC   _____

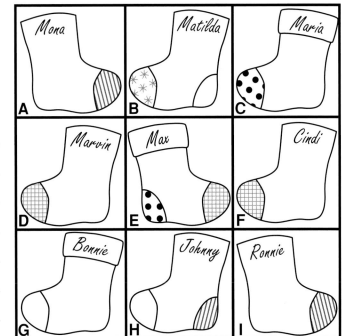

Making A Kwanzaa Banner

Materials:

candle pattern, cut out

pencil

scissors

three sheets of red construction paper

three sheets of green construction paper

one sheet of black construction paper

seven 4" x 5" pieces of white paper

tape

3 1/2-yard length of white bulletin-board paper

Steps:

1. Use the pattern to trace three green and three red candles. Also trace one black candle. Cut out the tracings.

2. Copy each of your paragraphs on a piece of white paper. Tape each paragraph on a candle:
   Umoja—black candle
   Kujichagulia, Ujamaa, Kuumba—red candles
   Ujima, Nia, Imani—green candles

3. Glue the candles in a row on the white bulletin-board paper. Be sure to glue them in this order from left to right:
   Kuumba—Ujamaa—Kujichagulia—Umoja—Ujima—Nia—Imani

4. Display your banner on a classroom or hallway wall.

Pattern

Nguzo Saba
(en-GOO-zoh SAH-bah)
The Seven Principles Of Kwanzaa

Day 1: Umoja (oo-MOH-jah)
Unity—*Helping one another in the family and community.*

Day 2: Kujichagulia (koo-jee-chah-goo-LEE-ah)
Self-Determination—*Making our own decisions.*

Day 3: Ujima (oo-JEE-mah)
Collective Work And Responsibility—*Working together to make life better for one another.*

Day 4: Ujamaa (oo-jah-MAH-ah)
Cooperative Economics—*Building and supporting our own businesses.*

Day 5: Nia (NEE-ah)
Purpose—*Being aware that our lives have meaning and purpose.*

Day 6: Kuumba (koo-OOM-bah)
Creativity—*Using our imagination and hands to create.*

Day 7: Imani (ee-MAH-nee)
Faith—*Believing in ourselves, our ancestors, and our future.*

Calendar facts; adding & subtracting

INTRODUCING THE NEW YEAR!

January 31 days

It's New Year's Day—the first day of a brand-new year! Let's take a closer look at the upcoming year.

Directions: Write the number of days in each month on its calendar page. January is done for you. (For this activity, it is *not* a leap year.)

July ____days

1. January has 31 days, so February 1 is the 32nd day of the year. What is the date of the:
   a. 60th day? _____   b. 90th day? _____   c. 100th day? _____

February ____days

2. If a date is late in the year, it's easier to start at 365 (December 31) and go backward. What is the date of the:
   a. 360th day? _____   b. 350th day? _____   c. 330th day? _____

August ____days

3. If January 1 is a Monday, then January 8, 15, 22, and 29 are also Mondays. Why?

   _____
   _____

March ____days

4. January 1 is a Tuesday. On what day of the week will the following dates fall? (Make a quick sketch of a calendar month if you need help.)
   a. January 10? _____
   b. January 15? _____
   c. January 20? _____
   d. February 1? _____

September ____days

April ____days

5. February 1 is a Wednesday. How many Wednesdays will February have? _____

6. March 1 is a Wednesday. How many Wednesdays will March have? _____

October ____days

7. You're going on a 25-day cruise that begins on Friday, January 5.
   a. On what *date* will the cruise end?

   _____

   b. On what *day of the week* will the cruise end?

   _____

May ____days

November ____days

June ____days

8. Day 183 is the middle day of the year. What is its date?

   _____

December ____days

Bonus Box: What is your *birthdate?* _____ On what *day of this year* will your birthday fall? (for example: the 80th, the 112th, etc.) _____
On what *day of the week* will your birthday fall? _____

Ice-Cube Creations

Winter is a great time for building snowpeople, snow forts, and ice sculptures. Each shape below was built with ice cubes. Can you tell how many cubes were used for each one? Write the number in the blank near each picture.

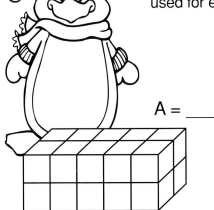

A = _____

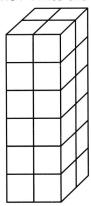

B = _____

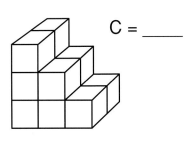

C = _____

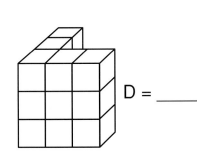

D = _____

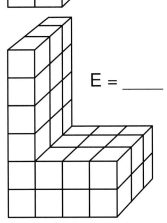

E = _____

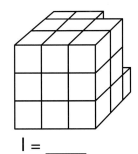

F = _____

Ice cubes are missing from each of the following sculptures. How many cubes were used to build each one?

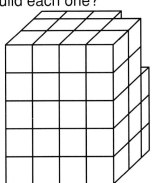

G = _____

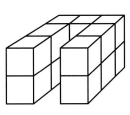

H = _____

I = _____

Bonus Box: Each picture below is a bird's-eye view of one of the sculptures A–F above. It shows what the sculpture would look like if you were up in the sky looking down at its top. Can you match each sculpture A–F with its top? Write a letter in each blank.

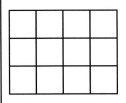

_____

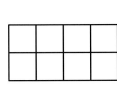

_____

_____

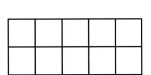

_____

_____

_____

What Would You Do For Peace?

Dr. Martin Luther King, Jr., won the Nobel Peace Prize in 1964. This award is given each year to the person who has done the most to promote peace on Earth. The money awarded to Dr. King totaled $54,600. He gave most of the money to groups that were working for justice in a peaceful way. Today the prize money for this award is about $1,000,000.

If you won the Nobel Peace Prize, how would you use the $1,000,000 in prize money to promote world peace? Explain your answer on the lines below.

Bonus Box: On another sheet of paper, design a symbol for peace.

Note To The Teacher: Have each student color the border around his writing with crayons, markers, or colored pencils. Then have him cut out his answer around the border. Display students' writings on a bulletin board titled "What We Would Do For Peace."

They Made History!

Black History Month is celebrated in the United States each year during the month of February. The names of some famous African-Americans are hidden in the grid below. To discover their names, write the letter of each ordered pair of numbers on the lines below each description. The first one is started for you.

1. The most famous leader of the Underground Railroad

   H
   (6,6) (7,1) (1,2) (8,3) (2,1) (4,8)   (4,8) (3,6) (8,8) (9,5) (7,1) (4,2)

2. The first African-American to serve as a justice on the United States Supreme Court

   (4,8) (6,6) (3,6) (1,2) (6,3) (9,1) (9,1) (1,7)   (9,5) (7,1) (1,2) (2,4) (6,6) (7,1) (3,3) (3,3)

3. She refused to give up her bus seat to a white passenger.

   (1,2) (9,1) (2,4) (7,1)   (4,0) (7,1) (7,1) (1,2) (7,9) (2,4)

4. The first black person to play modern major-league baseball

   (1,9) (7,1) (0,5) (7,9) (8,3) (2,1)   (1,2) (9,1) (8,8) (8,3) (4,2) (2,4) (9,1) (4,2)

5. The first African-American to serve as chairman of the Joint Chiefs of Staff

   (0,5) (9,1) (3,3) (8,3) (4,2)   (4,0) (9,1) (4,5) (2,1) (3,3) (3,3)

Grid (points):
- J (1,9)
- K (7,9)
- B (8,9)
- M (9,9)
- T (4,8)
- D (2,8)
- H (6,8)
- U (3,6)
- W (5,6)
- H (6,6)
- G (6,3)
- I (8,3)
- N (5,2)
- L (3,2)
- S (2,4)
- C (1,5)
- R (2,1)
- E (2,1)
- P (4,1)
- A (7,2)
- O (9,2)

(grid axis: 0–10 horizontal, 0–10 vertical)

6. Use the grid to find the points to spell the name of the famous African-American who gave the "I Have A Dream" speech. Write each ordered pair above its letter. The first one is done for you.

   (1,7)
   D   R.   M   A   R   T   I   N   L   U   T   H   E   R   K   I   N   G,   J   R.

©1997 The Education Center, Inc. • *The Mailbox® Superbook • Grade 4* • TEC453 • Key p. 320

Bonus Box: Use the grid to write the ordered pairs of numbers for your name. (You may need to add some of the letters in your name to the grid.)

"HEART-Y" PHRASES

Celebrate Valentine's Day with this "heart-y" challenge! Each sentence below contains an *idiom*—a phrase whose meaning can't be understood from the individual words used in it. The hearts are labeled with the definitions of the idioms. Use the context clues found in each sentence to match each idiom with its definition. Write the letter of the heart containing the definition on the line.

to stop being mean; to be kind, generous, or sympathetic
A

to be very disappointed
B

with great feeling; sincerely
C

a kind, generous, or forgiving nature
D

to feel very sorry for
E

to be seriously affected by; to feel deeply
F

by exact memorizing; so well that you remember it
G

a change in the way one feels or thinks about an idea
J

to show your feelings openly; to show everyone how you feel
I

to be startled or excited from surprise, joy, or fright
H

_____ 1. When Charleton saw the shiny new bicycle, his <u>heart skipped a beat</u>.

_____ 2. After Mrs. Smith volunteered to help the elderly, we knew she must have a <u>heart of gold</u>.

_____ 3. Ellen had a <u>change of heart</u> and canceled her trip.

_____ 4. Even though we were only kidding, Fiona <u>took</u> our teasing <u>to heart</u>.

_____ 5. It's easy to tell if Burke is happy or sad, because he <u>wears his heart on his sleeve</u>.

_____ 6. Phyllis's <u>heart sank</u> when she heard that the field trip was canceled.

_____ 7. Shana thanked her fans <u>from the bottom of her heart</u>.

_____ 8. <u>Have a heart</u>, Wendy, and let me wear your new shirt to the dance.

_____ 9. Brad knew the new spelling words <u>by heart</u>.

_____ 10. Olivia's <u>heart goes out to</u> the poor children of the community.

Bonus Box: What do you think it means to put your *heart and soul* into something? For example: *Joe put his heart and soul into fixing up the club house.* Write your answer on the back of this page.

RETURN TO SENDER

Valentine's Day is celebrated on February 14. It is a day to exchange gifts and cards with caring or funny messages. This Valentine's Day is not very funny for Valerie. All of the cards that she sent in the mail were returned to her because she did not write the zip codes on the envelopes. Help her figure out the correct zip code for each envelope by solving the math problem below it. Write the solution on the envelope's blank line. Then these Valentine's Day cards will be ready to go!

1.

Charlie Cocoa
14 Ounce Lane
Hershey, PA _____

```
  23,622
−  6,589
```

2.
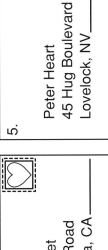

Susie Sweetheart
4 Ever Street
Valentine, NE _____

```
  23,067
×      3
```

3.
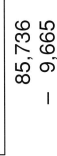

Elizabeth Bow
Cupid's Arrow Road
Lovell, WY _____

```
  9,159
×     9
```

4.

Flora Basket
12 Dozen Road
Santa Rosa, CA _____

```
  85,736
−  9,665
```

5.

Peter Heart
45 Hug Boulevard
Lovelock, NV _____

```
  91,029
−  1,610
```

6.

Cherry Blossom
R.D. # 5
Red Lodge, MT _____

```
  14,767
×      4
```

7.

Daniel Candy
790 Sweet Lane
Dalhart, TX _____

```
  39,511
×      2
```

8.

Elijah Hart
321 Red Avenue
Loveland, CO _____

```
  28,203
+ 52,334
```

9.

Goldie Ring
24 Carat Way
Goldendale, WA _____

```
  19,724
×      5
```

10.

Rose Scent
2 Thorny Way
Hartman, KY _____

```
  96,882
− 56,492
```

Bonus Box: Each address above names streets and cities that are perfect for Valentine's Day. Draw an envelope on the back of this paper. Then write an address on the envelope like the ones above. Design a Valentine's Day stamp for the envelope.

©1997 The Education Center, Inc. • *The Mailbox® Superbook • Grade 4 • TEC453 •* Key p. 320

Leapin' Leprechauns!

In honor of St. Patrick's Day, each definition below tells the meaning of a word that starts with the letters *gr,* just like in *green*. Fill in the blanks to spell the word that matches each definition. Use a dictionary if you need help. May the luck of the Irish be with you!

1. an event at which one receives a diploma   g r _ _ _ _ _ _ _ _ _

2. to hold tightly   g r _ _ _

3. sand; loose pieces of rock   g r _ _ _ _

4. green carpet-like plant that covers most baseball fields   g r _ _ _ _

5. a person who complains   g r _ _ _ _ _

6. to increase in size; to develop   g r _ _

7. a berry that grows on a vine and can be eaten dried or fresh   g r _ _ _

8. a breed of dog used for racing   g r _ _ _ _ _ _ _ _

9. a bride's partner   g r _ _ _

10. the force that holds you on the surface of the earth   g r _ _ _ _ _

11. drawings or slogans painted on public buildings   g r _ _ _ _ _ _

12. a building enclosed with glass in which plants are grown   g r _ _ _ _ _ _ _ _ _

13. two or more people   g r _ _ _

14. a device used for cooking outdoors   g r _ _ _

15. what a dog does when it's angry   g r _ _ _ _

Bonus Box: On the back of this paper, list as many green things as you can. Compare your list with a partner's list. Then cross out any words that appear on both papers. Next count the number of words that aren't crossed out on each paper. Who listed more green words?

Pollution Solutions

To celebrate Earth Day this year, take some time to think about how cars affect the environment. Read each statement below. Write whether you think each statement is *true* or *false.*

_____ 1. When cars are running, they burn gasoline. This releases toxic gases and other waste products into the air.

_____ 2. Drilling, processing, and transporting the oil used to make gasoline creates air, water, and land pollution.

_____ 3. Just one quart of automobile oil can pollute thousands of gallons of water.

_____ 4. Americans throw away enough cars every 20 minutes to form a stack as high as the Empire State Building.

_____ 5. Batteries, air conditioners, and other parts of junked cars can leak and pollute water or air.

_____ 6. Driving a car fast burns more gasoline than driving at the speed limit.

Each of the statements above is TRUE! So what can be done to cut down on the problems cars cause? One solution is to make a car that runs on something other than gasoline.

In the space below, draw your car for the future. Label any important parts. Then on the back of this paper, tell what you will use as fuel for your car. Also explain how your car will work.

Bonus Box: Below the explanation of how your car works, tell why your car won't end up in a junkyard polluting the air, land, and water.

A Tint Of Spring

Spring has sprung and with it comes beautiful colors. Use the colors of springtime to inspire a little poetry. Read the poem titled "Green" below. Then choose a color from one of the flower petals. Follow the form shown to write your own color poem. Check a box of 64 Crayola® crayons for help with the unusual color names. Or pick a color from your box of crayons, markers, or colored pencils.

Green is the taste of mint ice cream on a warm night,
      fresh salad in a chilled bowl,
      a baseball field in spring,
      the fragrance of sweet pickles.

Green is a hint of good luck on a bad day,
      the priceless treasures of the rain forest,
      a frog that sings in the evening,
      the scent of freshly cut grass.

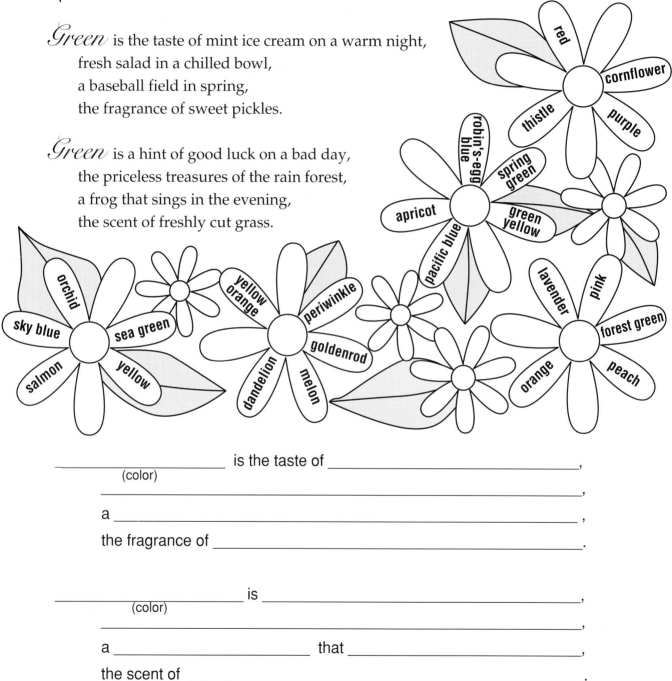

_____ is the taste of _____,
    (color)

_____,

a _____ ,

the fragrance of _____.

_____ is _____,
    (color)

_____,

a _____ that _____ ,

the scent of _____.

Bonus Box: Neatly copy your poem on a piece of drawing paper. Then add illustrations using the color that you wrote about in your poem.

Note To The Teacher: If you do not have a box of 64 Crayola® crayons on hand, have students look up some of the unusual color names in a dictionary; then have them choose the color in their crayons, markers, or colored pencils that is closest in hue.

Name _____

Synonym Sweets

Hop on over to the bookshelf and get a dictionary to use for this synonym challenge! Each word below has a matching *synonym*—a word with the same meaning—that can be found on a jelly bean in the jar. Write the correct synonym on the line. Then color the matching jelly bean. When all the synonyms have been found, there should be two uncolored jelly beans that are antonyms in your jar.

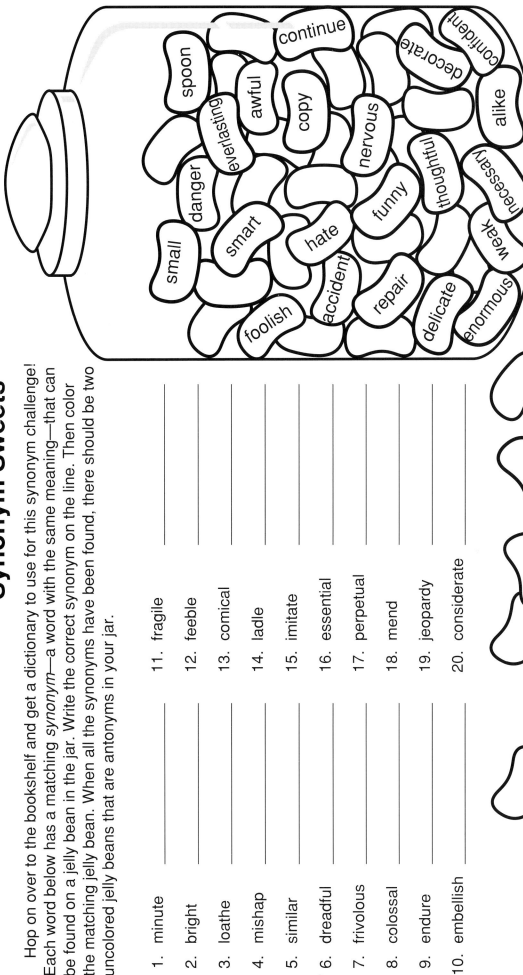

1. minute _____

2. bright _____

3. loathe _____

4. mishap _____

5. similar _____

6. dreadful _____

7. frivolous _____

8. colossal _____

9. endure _____

10. embellish _____

11. fragile _____

12. feeble _____

13. comical _____

14. ladle _____

15. imitate _____

16. essential _____

17. perpetual _____

18. mend _____

19. jeopardy _____

20. considerate _____

Bonus Box: Choose any five of the words listed above and write an antonym for each one. Remember that an *antonym* is a word with an opposite meaning.

Let The Reading Begin!

The school year is ending and summer reading is about to begin! Use colored pencils or markers to design two bookmarks. Design one bookmark for summer reading and the other to welcome a new student into your teacher's class next year. Include a brief message on each bookmark.

Bonus Box: On another sheet of paper, write the title of a great book you would recommend for summer reading. Then, without telling the outcome of the book, write a brief review of the book.

Note To The Teacher: Laminate and cut out each bookmark. Distribute one summer-reading bookmark to each student in your class. Give the other bookmarks to your new students on the first day of school in the fall. Post the book reviews from the Bonus Box activity so students can read them before summer vacation.

The End?

Is it the end of the school year, or the start of an interesting adventure? You make the call! Each paragraph below is the beginning of a story. Choose one and finish the story by writing both a middle and an ending on a sheet of notebook paper. Use what you learned this year about writing to make this a creative and suspenseful story to share with your class. Remember to proofread your story and make any corrections.

The last day of school was finally here. I looked at the classroom clock. It seemed to be ticking in slow motion. In 30 long minutes, I would be out of school and entering the world of summer fun. Suddenly the lights began to flicker. A strange light began to creep into the room between the cracks of the blinds on the back window. Then I heard…

My friends and I were picking captains for our basketball game as my class was lining up to go outside. When we walked closer to the door, I could hear screaming coming from the playground. It wasn't a bad kind of screaming. It was like the screaming that you hear when someone meets her favorite rock star. I walked out the door and saw…

California, here I come! I thought as I left school. I knew that once my parents saw my report card, I could start packing. I got all A's, and they were my ticket to a summer in California with my cousin. As I walked closer to my house, I could see that something was going on in front of the driveway. Boy, was I surprised to see…

I couldn't believe what a horrible day I was having! It was only 7:00 A.M. and already I had stained my favorite shirt, lost my homework to my hungry puppy, and misplaced my shoes. If I missed the bus, my mom would kill me! I found my shoes just in time to see the bus pulling up in front of the house. I zipped up my coat on the way out the door. When I looked up at the bus, I noticed something very strange—so strange that I should have never gotten on that bus. But I did, and…

Bonus Box: On another sheet of paper, write the beginning of a story for someone else to complete. Then give it to your teacher.

Note To The Teacher: Collect the story beginnings from the Bonus Box activity. Place them in your writing center for next year's class to finish.

Answer Keys

Page 109

Answers will vary.
1. 2; 1; 2
2. about 5
3. about 1 1/4 inch; about 1 3/4 inch; about 1/2 inch
4. 5 paper clips; 3 large paper clips
5. 18 1/2 inches; 47 centimeters
6. 10 paper clips; 4 paper clips
7. 8 inches
8. 9 inches; 36 inches; 81 square inches

Page 145

1.–4. Answers will vary.
5. Lake Huron, Lake Ontario, Lake Michigan, Lake Erie, Lake Superior
6. CIA *or* C.I.A.
7. Answers will vary.
8. Revolutionary War (or American Revolution)
9. Christmas
10. Sunday, Monday, Tuesday, Wednesday, Thursday, Friday, Saturday
11. Bill Clinton (until 2000)
12. Wednesday
13. Answers will vary.
14. Washington
15. Answers will vary.
16. Richmond
17. July
18. Answers will vary.
19. Answers will vary.
20. E. B. White
21. Answers will vary.
22. Civil War
23. Mercury
24. Answers should include two of the following: Atlantic Ocean, Pacific Ocean, Indian Ocean, Arctic Ocean.

Bonus Box: Answers will vary.

Page 146

Answers will vary. Possible answers include:

North America
United States of America—Americans
Canada—Canadians
Mexico—Mexicans

Europe
Spain—Spaniards
Italy—Italians
France—French
Germany—Germans

Asia
China—Chinese
Cambodia—Cambodians
Mongolia—Mongolians
Japan—Japanese

South America
Paraguay—Paraguayans
Peru—Peruvians
Venezuela—Venezuelans
Chile—Chileans

Africa
South Africa—South Africans
Ethiopia—Ethiopians
Libya—Libyans
Egypt—Egyptians

Australia
Australia—Australians

Bonus Box: Antarctica is virtually uninhabited with the exception of several scientific research stations. There are no people indigenous to the continent.

Page 149
1. Andrew was nervous.
2. Jennifer forgot her sunscreen.
3. There was a fly floating in Ray's lemonade.
4. The girls are in the Girl Scouts or another similar club.
5. Carrie's phone was off the hook.
6. Martin thought school would be canceled because of the snow.

Bonus Box: Answers will vary.

Page 214 ("Club Confusion!")

26 squares colored for the Cheerleaders
12 squares colored for the Band
11 squares colored for the Drama Club
14 squares colored for the Student Council
16 squares colored for the Tutoring Club
18 squares colored for the Yearbook Committee

Three percent of the gymnasium is left.

Bonus Box: Cheerleaders $32.50; Band $15.00; Drama Club $13.75; Student Council $17.50; Tutoring Club $20.00; Yearbook Committee $22.50

Page 215
1. 12 oranges, 1/2 honeydew melon, 1/2 cup cherries, 6 cups strawberries, 18 apples
2. 8 oranges, 1/3 honeydew melon, 1/3 cup cherries, 4 cups strawberries, 12 apples
3. 4 oranges, 1/6 honeydew melon, 1/6 cup cherries, 2 cups strawberries, 6 apples
4. 6 oranges, 1/4 honeydew melon, 1/4 cup cherries, 3 cups strawberries, 9 apples

Bonus Box: 60 oranges, 2 1/2 honeydew melons, 2 1/2 cups cherries, 30 cups strawberries, 90 apples

Answer Keys

Page 216

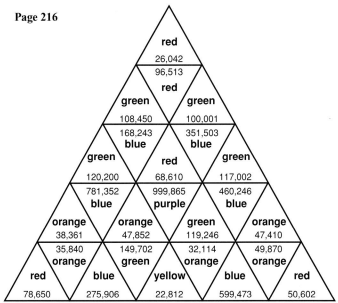

Bonus Box: Answers will vary.

Page 217

1. 42,288
2. 179,838
3. 68,658
4. 131,326
5. 104,940
6. 86,614
7. 155,582
8. 119,892
9. 105,648

Bonus Box: Answers will vary.

Page 218

1. **35**	2. **26**	3. **17**	4. **22**
5. **9**	6. **10**	7. **50**	8. **31**
9. **42**	10. **17**	11. **25**	12. **16**
13. **14**	14. **47**	15. **8**	16. **31**

Bonus Box: 400

Page 219

1. Dom
2. Brandy
3. Elijah
4. Jerome
5. C. J.
6. Leeza
7. Christina
8. Juan
9. Tyler
10. Laura
11. Bob
12. Steven
13. Maria
14. Maurice
15. Rasheeda

No one was shortchanged.

Bonus Box: Answers will vary.

Page 220

The animal is a swan.

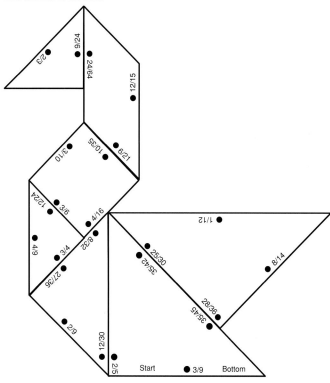

Bonus Box: There are 16 small triangles; therefore the value would be $48.00.

Page 221

1. Robert Smith—green
2. Harry Simpson—red
3. Bill Blatt—blue
4. Bailey Birch—purple
5. Tim Schmut—brown
6. Mark Gut—yellow
7. Mike Glark—orange

Bonus Box: The first-place finisher's time was 0.65 seconds faster than that of the last-place finisher.

Page 223

1. pictograph
2. 10 fourth graders
3. 50 students; 35 students; 10 students; 25 students
4. Answers will vary.
5. bar graph
6. Mr. Joshin's class
7. 23 students
8. Answers will vary.
9. line graph
10. 35 students
11. Tuesday and Wednesday
12. 130 students

Bonus Box: Answers will vary.

Answer Keys

Page 224

1. Jake is 20.

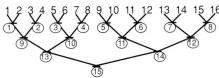

2. Fifteen games must be played to determine a winner.

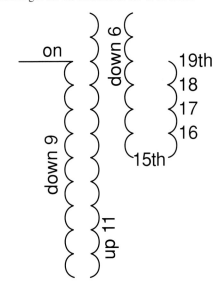

3. Calvin, Carl, Cory, Chris, Camden

4. January 22 would be a Wednesday.

| DECEMBER | | | | | | | | JANUARY | | | | | |
S	M	T	W	T	F	S	S	M	T	W	T	F	S
1	2	3	4	5	6	7				1	2	3	4
8	9	10	11	12	13	14	5	6	7	8	9	10	11
15	16	17	18	19	20	21	12	13	14	15	16	17	18
22	23	24	25	26	27	28	19	20	21	(22)	23	24	25
29	30	31					26	27	28	29	30	31	

5. Marie got on the elevator at the 19th floor.

Bonus Box: Answers will vary.

Page 242

All answers are approximate. Accept reasonable responses.

1. 1 mile
2. 2 miles
3. Fire Station No. 12
4. 3 1/2 miles
5. 1 1/2 miles
6. 3/4 mile
7. north to south: 3 3/4 miles; east to west: 6 miles
8. 3 1/2 miles
9. 1 mile
10. 1 1/4 miles
11. 1/2 mile
12. 2 3/4 miles

Bonus Box: Answers will vary.

Page 265

Answers will vary.

Chondrichthyes
(sharks and other fish with skeletons of cartilage)
• cold-blooded
• some covered with scales, others scaleless
• gills
• have skeletons made of cartilage, do not have an air bladder, about 790 species
• sharks, rays, chimaeras
• shark

Osteichthyes
(bony fish)
• cold-blooded
• scales
• gills
• bony skeletons, live almost anywhere there is water, almost all have fins
• bass, catfish, cod, herring, minnows, perch, trout, tuna
• tuna

Amphibia
(amphibians)
• cold-blooded
• scaleless, moist skin
• most breathe with lungs, some have gills, some have lungs and gills
• live part of their lives in water and part on land, live in moist habitats, most eat insects
• frogs, toads, salamanders
• frog

Reptilia
(reptiles)
• cold-blooded
• dry, scaly skin
• lungs
• vary greatly in size, long life spans, most have good vision
• lizards, snakes, turtles, crocodiles, terrapins, tortoises
• snake

Aves
(birds)
• warm-blooded
• all birds have feathers
• lungs
• all birds have wings, do not have teeth, have a hard bill (or beak)
• flamingo, duck, hawk, turkey, pigeon, bluebird, cuckoo, toucan
• duck

Mammalia
(mammals)
• warm-blooded
• hair
• lungs
• nurse their babies, live almost everywhere, protect their young, have well-developed brains
• cats, dogs, cattle, goats, apes, hogs
• cat

Page 275

1. unsweetened pineapple
2. snack mix
3. snack mix
4. snack mix
5. unsweetened pineapple
6. natural; The pineapple is unsweetened.
7. unsweetened pineapple; It is higher in Vitamin C, and lower in fat and sodium. It also has fewer calories than the snack mix.

Bonux Box: unsweetened pineapple = 2 cups (1/2 cup x 4 servings); snack mix = 4 1/2 cups (1/2 cup x 9 servings)

Page 276

1. 80
2. 100
3. 90
4. 110
5. 51
6. 98
7. 65
8. 74
9. 112
10. 156

Bonus Box: Ms. Mitral, Mr. Oxygen

Answer Keys

Page 283

1. <u>soft drinks</u>; 43 gallons
2. <u>Zimbabwe</u>; Africa
3. <u>insects</u>; plant life and almost anything else—fabric, cork, tobacco, paste, pepper, etc.
4. <u>tree</u>; grows as long as it lives
5. <u>ice cream</u>; 1904 World's Fair in St. Louis, Missouri
6. <u>narwhal</u>; whale, spiral ivory tusk (its only tooth) growing out of its jaw
7. <u>university</u>, <u>Thomas Jefferson</u>; University Of Virginia
8. <u>Mickey Mouse</u>; 1928
9. <u>Grand Canyon</u>; about 1 mile
10. <u>perspire</u>; to release heat from the body
11. <u>boar</u>; 350 to 500 pounds
12. <u>Olympic Games</u>; Greece
13. <u>license plates</u>; aluminum
14. <u>money</u>; U.S. Mint makes coins, Bureau Of Engraving And Printing makes paper money
15. <u>ancient Egyptians</u>, <u>mummify</u>; believed bodies had to be preserved to live on in the next world
16. <u>tornado</u>; more than 200 mph

Page 297

1. November has only 30 days, not *31*. (Use by Nov. 31, 1998)
2. Container made with recycled paper, not *pumpkin*. (Container Made With Recycled Pumpkin)
3. *your*, not *you're* (Frozen for you're convenience)
4. *Pumpkin*, not *Pumkin* (Chef Boyarturkey's Pumkin Pie)
5. *than*, not *then* (Yummy! Nothing tastes better then are pie!)
6. *our*, not *are* (Yummy! Nothing tastes better then are pie!)
7. The pie should be kept frozen. (Store at room temperature)
8. One pound equals 16 oz. (Net Weight 1 lb. [15 oz.])
9. Pumpkin was omitted from the ingredients list. (Ingredients: enriched flower, shortening, spices, milk, eggs, and preservatives)
10. *flour*, not *flower* (Ingredients: enriched flower, shortening, spices, milk, eggs, and preservatives)
11. Oven temperature should be 400°F. (Baking instructions: Preheat oven to 400°C.)
12. The pie should not be placed on a metal sheet for microwave cooking. (Place on metal sheet.)
13. The cooking time for a microwave oven should be less than the time for a regular oven. (Microwave: heat on high for 55 minutes. Regular oven: bake for 45 minutes.)

Bonus Box: he'll, heal, and heel; rein, rain, and reign; rite, write, and right

Other homonym triples include:

I'll, isle, aisle	flew, flu, flue	road, rode, rowed
buy, by, bye	gnu, new, knew	sew, sow, so
carat, caret, carrot	oar, or, ore	their, there, they're
cent, sent, scent	pair, pare, pear	vain, vein, vane
cite, site, sight	raise, rays, raze	ware, where, wear

Page 298

Answers will vary. Suggested answers include:

A

B heather, leather, tether, weather, whether

C e-l-b-b-o-g

D crowded, full, bursting, loaded, packed, jam-packed, jammed

E monkey, donkey

F

G

H thawed, unfrozen, melted

I rat, rot, oat, oar, art, sat, tar

J lizard, wizard, blizzard

K kneecap, fingernail, eyeball, eyelash, eyebrow, eyelid, jawbone, eardrum

L

M cake, fake, lake, make, rake, sake, take, wake, bike, babe, bade, bale, bane, bare, base

N

O blessing, guessing, messing, pressing, stressing

P potato salad, baked potatoes, french fries, scalloped potatoes, hash browns, mashed potatoes

Q gray, gay, gar, ray, rag, vary

R tuba, tusk, tub, tubby, tuna, tune, tuck, tug, turn, Tuesday, tugboat, tulip, tummy, tuxedo, turtle

S

T tale

U boost, roast, roust

V winner, thinner, sinner, spinner, inner, grinner, skinner, pinner

W emu, penguin, kiwi, ostrich, rhea

Page 299

	bold word	word that doesn't belong
1.	**called**	locally
2.	**holder**	shoulder
3.	**years**	yearn
4.	**found**	fined
5.	**placed**	palace
6.	**higher**	hijack
7.	**led**	plead
8.	**lights**	slight
9.	**used**	refuse

Bonus Box: *out<u>number</u>ed* and *re<u>captur</u>ed*

Page 301

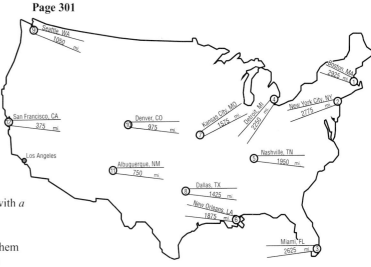

Page 302 ("Gilda's Gifts")

top-left gift: Carole
middle-left gift: Noel
bottom-left gift: Holly
top-right gift: Rudolph
middle-right gift: Merri
bottom-right gift: Nick

clues not needed: 1, 4, 5, and 7

Page 302 ("And The Stockings Were Hung…")

Accept all reasonable answers.
ABC: names begin with *M* and end with *a*
DEF: toes have checkered pattern
GHI: all three names rhyme
ADG: all names have the letter *n* in them
BEH: socks have both heels and toes
CFI: all names have the letter *i* in them
AEI: socks are facing right
GEC: socks have cuffed tops

Answer Keys

Page 304

January: 31 days
February: 28 days
March: 31 days
April: 30 days
May: 31 days
June: 30 days
July: 31 days
August: 31 days
September: 30 days
October: 31 days
November: 30 days
December: 31 days

1. a. March 1   b. March 31   c. April 10
2. a. December 26   b. December 16   c. November 26
3. Since there are seven days in a week, adding seven to any date results in the same day as that date.
4. a. Thursday   b. Tuesday   c. Sunday   d. Friday
5. 4
6. 5
7. a. January 29   b. Monday
8. July 2

Bonus Box: Answers will vary.

Page 305

A = 20 cubes
B = 24 cubes
C = 12 cubes
D = 15 cubes
E = 36 cubes
F = 24 cubes
G = 58 cubes
H = 14 cubes
I = 25 cubes

Bonus Box:
from left to right: E–F–D–A–B–C

Page 307

1. Harriet Tubman
2. Thurgood Marshall
3. Rosa Parks
4. Jackie Robinson
5. Colin Powell
6. (1,7) (1,2)   (9,5) (7,1) (1,2) (4,8) (8,3) (4,2)   (3,3) (3,6) (4,8) (6,6) (2,1) (1,2) (7,9) (8,3) (4,2) (6,3)   (1,9) (1,2)

Bonus Box: Answers will vary.

Page 308

1. H
2. D
3. J
4. F
5. I
6. B
7. C
8. A
9. G
10. E

Bonus Box: To put your *heart* and *soul* into a job means to do it enthusiastically and with strong feeling.

Page 309

1. 17033
2. 69201
3. 82431
4. 76071
5. 89419
6. 59068
7. 79022
8. 80537
9. 98620
10. 40390

Bonus Box: Answers will vary.

Page 310

1. graduation
2. grip
3. gravel
4. grass
5. grouch (or griper)
6. grow
7. grape
8. greyhound
9. groom
10. gravity
11. graffiti
12. greenhouse
13. group
14. grill
15. growls

Bonus Box: Answers will vary.

Page 313

1. small
2. smart
3. hate
4. accident
5. alike
6. awful
7. foolish
8. enormous
9. continue
10. decorate
11. delicate
12. weak
13. funny
14. spoon
15. copy
16. necessary
17. everlasting
18. repair
19. danger
20. thoughtful

Antonyms left in the jar: *nervous* and *confident*

Bonus Box: Answers will vary.